CONSTRUCTING IMPERIAL BERLIN

CONSTRUCTING IMPERIAL BERLIN

Photography and the Metropolis

Miriam Paeslack

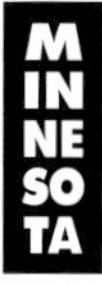

UNIVERSITY OF MINNESOTA PRESS
MINNEAPOLIS • LONDON

This book is supported by a grant from the Graham Foundation for Advanced Studies in the Fine Arts.

The author gratefully acknowledges financial assistance provided by the Julian Park Fund, College of Arts and Sciences, University at Buffalo, the State University of New York.

A portion of chapter 3 was previously published as "High-Speed Ruins: Rubble Photography in Berlin, 1871–1914," in "Photography and Preservation," ed. Jorge Otero-Pailos and Iñaki Bergera, special issue, *Future Anterior* 10, no. 2 (Winter 2013): 32–47; reprinted with permission of the University of Minnesota Press. A portion of chapter 3 was published in a different version as "'A Mind-Journey to One's Own History': The Photographic Documentation of the National Monument for Wilhelm I and of Berlin's City Palace's Façade in Photogrammetric Imagery," in *A New View: Architectural Photography from the National Museums in Berlin*, ed. Ludger Derenthal and Christine Kühn, exhibition catalog, Museum für Fotografie, Berlin (Berlin: Wasmuth, 2010), 41–44, 373–75; reprinted with permission of Kunstbibliothek, Stiftung Preussischer Kulturbesitz, Berlin.

Published by the University of Minnesota Press
111 Third Avenue South, Suite 290
Minneapolis, MN 55401-2520
http://www.upress.umn.edu

Printed in the United States of America on acid-free paper

The University of Minnesota is an equal-opportunity educator and employer.

24 23 22 21 20 19 10 9 8 7 6 5 4 3 2 1

Library of Congress Cataloging-in-Publication Data
Names: Paeslack, Miriam, author.
Title: Constructing Imperial Berlin : photography and the metropolis / Miriam Paeslack.
Description: Minneapolis : University of Minnesota Press, 2019. | Includes index.
Identifiers: LCCN 2018016694 (print) | ISBN 978-1-5179-0294-0 (hc) | ISBN 978-1-5179-0295-7 (pb)
Subjects: LCSH: Photography—Germany—Berlin—History. | Berlin (Germany)—Pictorial works. | Germany—Capital and capitol—Pictorial works.
Classification: LCC TR74.B47 P34 2019 (print) | DDC 770.943/155—dc23
LC record available at https://lccn.loc.gov/2018016694

For

Volkmar and Jordan

two Berliners,
one by birth, one by conviction

CONTENTS

INTRODUCTION

A Photographic City Portrait in the Making

> The entire complex of urban life can be thought of as a person rather than as a distinctive place, and the city may be endowed with a personality—or, to use common parlance—a character of its own. Like a person, the city then acquires a biography and a reputation.
>
> —ANSELM L. STRAUSS, *Images of the American City*

> Every city is an individual. One thinks back on each one of them as personality; each has its particular mood, its atmosphere, a particular physiognomy and character, which is unforgettably imprinted into one's memory.
>
> —KARL SCHEFFLER, *Berlin ein Stadtschicksal*

The image of imperial Berlin is closely linked to the culture of the Prussian state that shaped it. This state was the product of conflicting cultures and worldviews. The dominance of the military since the seventeenth century, paired with Protestant discipline and ethics, defined social and cultural hierarchies. Religious and cultural tolerance, artistic avant-gardism, and important scientific and industrial innovations created a platform for Berlin's emergence as a major European capital and metropolis by the end of the nineteenth century. But while this book focuses on a particular historical and geographical state of the city's imagery and its historic conditionality, it also understands its nineteenth-and early twentieth-century subject as part of a global system of urban and industrial cultures.

This book looks back on that era's photographic means and languages, while this foundational era in the city's history has been overwritten, questioned, combated, reappropriated, and nostalgically reenvisioned during the past twenty-five years. *Constructing Imperial Berlin: Photography and the Metropolis* tells a counternarrative to reductionist and essentializing readings of imperial Berlin by tapping into its images both as visual testimonies to that era and as generators of new narratives of the city. Such narratives are part of what Saskia Sassen defines as a "multilayered yet incomplete system,"[1] a system that is an ongoing process, a living thing.

When Mark Twain visited Berlin in 1891 and 1892, he made no secret of his frustration with the sharp experiential rift between his expectations and his experiences with the city. He had expected Berlin to share the picturesque beauty and historic gravity that he had found in other cities. Instead, the writer and critic (who had come to Berlin to report for the *Chicago Daily Tribune*) found himself having to describe and explain an unexpectedly "new" city that seemed to have been voided of all its history. Berlin, he recognized, was more like the growing industrializing cities in his home country than supposed peer cities such as Paris, London, and Vienna. He writes: "I feel lost in Berlin. It has no resemblance to the city I had supposed it was. . . . It seems to have disappeared totally, and left no sign. . . . It is a new city; the newest I have ever seen. Chicago would seem venerable beside it; for there are many old-looking districts in Chicago, but not many in Berlin."[2]

Twain's broadly generalized assumptions about Berlin and its image serve as an example of what art historian Michael Baxandall meant when he talked about the necessarily interpretive nature of descriptions.[3] Twain's polarizing, and deliberately exaggerated, report revealed the temptation to simplify and potentially dramatize Berlin's image for his readership back home. However, a comparative look across the Atlantic places Berlin into a framework and context that helps to develop a multifaceted argument about Berlin's imagery at the turn of the past century, especially when considering contemporaneous photographs of the city. This book addresses these photographs and traces Berlin's particular character—the "reputation" and "personality" mentioned by Anselm Strauss in the epigraph that began this introduction.

The city's biography, which has been determined by a breathtaking succession of destruction, reconstruction, division, and reunification in the nineteenth and twentieth centuries, lends itself to narratives of progress and defeat, demolition and construction, and reflections of the historic and evolving city. Such characteristics situate Berlin squarely in familiar debates of a city's place in the history of modernity, and this project aims to contribute to that debate. Berlin has been an easy candidate for such subsumption; by 1910, the city had already been characterized as being "condemned forever to becoming and never to being."[4] This text will explore how such claims of urban flux were configured by urban photography.

Cultural critic Max Osborn's reflections about Berlin, which he published in a daily newspaper in 1910, reveal some of the contradictions and antagonisms in Berlin's reputation that were debated within and outside Germany at the time:

> It is clear now that in front of our eyes a true metropolis emerges, out of a far too fast growing community, which is sweaty of "parvenu-ism" and the eagerness to show off. From this chaos, we realize now, rises modern life of character, from cluelessness unfolds a coherent organism. . . . Today already, we get the encouraging sense that the city is once again becoming a cohesive unit, forms again a face and a soul. And now, all of a sudden, we manage to bridge our relationships with the old and the new. Our modern identity, which has finally found solid ground in which it can be anchored, is joined by romantic sentiment. This is how Old and New Paris has always been regarded; their side-by-side was never considered a contrast but rather always two tightly connected parts of a large, logical, organic whole. We finally hope that sometime this is the future of Berlin.[5]

In this passage, Osborn raises some of the core issues discussed in this book. He both laments and celebrates the accelerated growth of the city after 1871, when it became the German capital; the friction between history and progress that was intensified by this development; the fragile balance between an open display of urban growth and wealth and attempts at anchoring the city in its historical roots; and, indirectly, the ideological tensions that amateur photography, and the profession of photography more generally, faced in imperial Berlin. Comparing the city to an organism, Osborn attempts to grasp and define the increasingly complex city, to reestablish what he considered a preexisting coherence and order that he found had vanished.

Osborn, unsurprisingly, invokes Paris, the capital of Germany's political and cultural archrival, which possessed a long-established, well-recognized, and cohesive cultural tradition and urban narrative that Berlin appeared to lack. Many other European metropoles and nations had also developed much earlier than Berlin and Germany.[6] Germany had never had a capital prior to 1871, and in the aftermath of Germany's unification, Berlin, which had grown at a moderate pace during the late eighteenth and early nineteenth centuries, faced the need and expectation to quickly become a metropolis. The resulting speed of its development elicited a double-edged response to the city as both "full of potential yet also as dangerously rootless and disordered."[7]

Berlin, the very late starter, caught up with its European rivals in respect to size and status in a very short time. Questions about the substance of national identity and its shared traditions lingered as the country processed its late, long, and complicated unification process. Cultural institutions and administrations sought to invent traditions by highlighting and interpreting historical districts and sites in cities and the countryside. In its rapid growth and fractured identity, Berlin made for a fascinating embodiment and metaphor for the entire country's identification struggles. Critics expressed preexisting and steadily more complicated and highly ambivalent perceptions of Berlin and of other growing cities, ranging between respect, admiration, ambivalence, and even condescension.[8] Some labeled it a "parvenu" or newcomer to the esteemed class of ancient cities in Europe and called it "American" or colonial, which owed both to its lack of history and to its unprecedented growth.

This comparison also suggested that Berlin as a "new" city stood for qualities of modernity that some contemporary thinkers embraced. Perhaps more than any other European metropolis, Berlin evolved into a prototypically modern city and came to signify boldness, entrepreneurship, cultural stimulation, consumption, and spectacle. It was no coincidence that starting in the 1890s, Berlin was the site of a number of ventures that projected the future of the city and nation, such as the 1896 trade exposition in Treptow Park, the 1908–9 urban planning competition, and the 1910 exhibition for Greater Berlin.[9] These events and the images they created of the city were profoundly shaped by contradictory visions, assumptions, and topoi that were linked to the metropolis either as a quintessentially modern and progressive place or as the locus of estrangement and alienation.[10]

Images of architecture and urban sites played a key role in establishing the terms under which contemporaries made sense of the rise of modern Berlin society. During the late nineteenth and early twentieth centuries, Berlin emerged as a city fraught with the questions that cities such as Paris, London, and Vienna had addressed decades earlier: How was progress to be absorbed by the city? What roles would its history have? How did it identify as a new capital? However, questions asked by the growing urban communities across the Atlantic, to which Berlin appeared to be strangely more related, were quite different. Here, an ambitious citizenry wondered how to become more efficient and prosperous, in what style and technology to most meaningfully and safely build its public and commercial buildings, and how to compete with other prospering urban centers in the region. In Berlin, more ambivalent questions evolved around how to negotiate the city's and country's history with its unprecedented growth. These issues materialized in images and pictorial narratives. Reproductive imagery communicated the new capital's transformation and fast-paced growth, its coming of age as a city among older European metropolises, and its engagement with modern-age consumption, technology, spectacle, and tourism. The resemblance of parts of such narratives with colonial ones and those of industrial and commercial achievement prevalent outside of Europe most likely never occurred to Berlin's city officials. Even if that had been the case, they would most likely have been reluctant to embrace it as it would have challenged Berlin's familiar, Eurocentric representational framework.

Berlin visuals shaped an urban image and expressed an urban imagination, an "urban imaginary" that was constituted by various image constellations, mental and material, individually and in sets. The urban imaginary that resulted from Berlin's rise and its photographic documentation is an accumulation and synchronous chronicling of experiences, impressions, and memories in and of a city. It is determined by a wide spectrum of perspectives and subject positions and is formed by various kinds of spatial practices, which include "architecture and planning, administration and business, labor and leisure, politics, culture, and everyday life."[11] The judgment of Berlin, and the image that emerged from it, was in part the result of the artificiality of Germany as a nation and a resulting lack of a coherent, unified, collective identity of Germans. Osborn hoped that the city would sort out its collective consciousness and develop an understanding of its capital, its head, its mind, and its symbolic center by the early decades of the twentieth century. However, coherence in both Berlin's image and the way it was perceived would never come to pass. Instead, the recognition of its contradictions and complexity ultimately formed the city, its image, and global perceptions of it, both in Osborn's time and into the twenty-first century.

In the context of this book, the notion of *urban image* includes the representational and transformative roles of visual media for the city as well as its role in the evolving complexity of ephemeral urban interactions. Such interactions, which I have called urban ineffabilities elsewhere, engage the shifting nature of urban processes.[12] The urban image also requires a conceptual extension to be understood not only literally as one single image, but also as a kind of performing, active assemblage of urban imaginaries. This space is produced and reproduced through human intentions and is to be understood based on Henri Lefebvre's concept of urban space production as "an interlinkage of geographic form, built environment, symbolic meanings, and routines of life."[13] *Production* in this context implies an analogy between space and other economic goods, where the unique role of photography joins forces with the space of the city. This book deals with surveys, sequences, and images that reveal the concept of the urban image. Every image and set of images here relate to one another through a certain narrative, while also standing for itself. Unlike the dynamic presented by motion pictures, still photographic narratives allow for individual readings. The images resonate with each other and together generate meaning in the "interstices between pictures, in the movement from one picture to the next."[14]

This book focuses on the era that began when the provincial capital of Prussia was chosen to be the capital of the united German Empire. This period, which lasted until the outbreak of World War I, shaped Berlin from a modest, provincial capital into a powerful industrial metropolis. This transformation process was complicated and not without significant growing pains. The picture of the ever-evolving city that Karl Scheffler had minted is strikingly similar to definitions of modernity in general. It recalls Charles Baudelaire's famous characterization of modernity that was inspired by Paris of the second half of the nineteenth century as "the ephemeral, the fugitive, the contingent, the half of art whose other half is the eternal and the immutable."[15]

For quite some time, the imperial era, during which Berlin rose to being a burgeoning multimillion metropolis, was assigned a secondary rank within German studies and the urban histories of Berlin. Berlin's image became closely associated with either the "golden" interwar years, and their artistic avant-gardes (Berlin Dada and narratives such as Alfred Döblin's *Berlin Alexanderplatz* or Christopher Isherwood's 1939 story *Goodbye to Berlin*) or Albert Speer's disturbingly grandiose visions for its transformation into Hitler's Germania.

However, Berlin's reunification just over a quarter century ago, as well as the rise of a global understanding of modernity in historical scholarship, have catapulted Berlin onto the stage of public popular and scholarly attention. Berlin is not merely to be understood as a late articulation of European metropolitan developments; instead, it becomes a part of a fascinating, much larger, transnational system of cultural, social, political, and economic developments.

Such impulses for a contextualizing inquiry within contemporary and global histories inspire a comparative look at Paris,[16] which has historically served as Berlin's primary rival. Berlin and Paris each generated quite different images, which is not surprising given their different cultural geographies and the drastically different narratives and circumstances in which each found itself during the nineteenth and early twentieth centuries. The Berlin that emerges from this comparison is a younger, perhaps less "emotional" city than Paris, a city that developed a certain pragmatism and adaptability in dealing with its own realities, given its rapid transformation into a metropolis. Accordingly, Siegfried Kracauer observed in the 1930s that the Berlin visitor returns to the city "conscious here of breathing the air of harsh reality, as they say."[17]

Writers and scholars have long been intrigued with the similarities and differences between both cities, and Walter Benjamin is probably the best-known author who had both a biographical and profound professional interest in both metropoles. His extensive writings on Paris's arcades and his explorations of Baudelaire's work, as well as his texts about his Berlin childhood,[18] have deeply impacted how we think of both cities in the late nineteenth and early twentieth centuries. By the onset of the twentieth century, the reading of Berlin in comparison to Paris, which Benjamin declared the "capital of the nineteenth century,"[19] noticeably shifted. Benjamin's contemporary and friend Kracauer, who was also acutely aware of both cities' imaginaries, made explicit distinctions between both cities. For Kracauer, as Andreas Huyssen concluded, "the street in Paris still functions as site of memory and experience, while streets in Berlin either scream with emptiness or undergo such rapid architectural change that they no longer hold any memory of the past."[20] Max Osborn alluded to this experiential binary of memory and contemporary experience when he imagined for Berlin a harmonious "side-by-side" of old and new as "two tightly connected parts of a large, logical, organic whole." To Huyssen, Kracauer sees Berlin of the 1930s "as the decisive cauldron of modernity in political and social crisis, while Paris is described as a city of the past."[21] Berlin turns out to have a complicated relationship to a past and, as a consequence, to the formation of any coherent collective memory. In light of this understanding, recent scholarship has invoked the label of Berlin as "capital of the twentieth century,"[22] an attribute that used to be reserved for industrializing and fast-growing North American cities such as New York City or Chicago. It is here, situated between Paris and Chicago, that a new interpretation of Berlin must begin.

Photography arrived in Berlin in the 1830s and became both a witness of and collaborator with the modernizing, industrializing, and consuming city. Unlike painting, it was not initially considered an academic or artistic medium and therefore developed outside many of the conventions and controls that the academy posed on its members. In fact, photography quickly developed a status and popularity that threatened other older forms of visual representation. This played out in varying forms, from the architectural photograph, to the panorama, and, later, to the instantaneous street photograph. Photography responded to the urbanite's craving for self-affirmation and reassurance of the preservability of that which seemed to be increasingly threatened by eradication and ignorance: the historical city and the history and identity of its inhabitants. But photography also became an eloquent tool and even a symbol for city boosterism and the celebration and embracing of new technologies.

Portraiture and architecture imagery were particularly affected by the arrival of the (seemingly) truthful photograph. Professional photographers established themselves in Berlin throughout the 1860s, 1870s, and 1880s, working either as generalists in portraiture, architecture, and object photography or specializing in individual genres. They served both a local clientele and an increasing tourist population's hunger for images. During this era, the field was dominated by men, while women's voices were often muted in Berlin's photography culture. Around the turn of the century, as cameras and photographic equipment became more affordable and easier to handle, professional photographers were joined by growing numbers of amateurs, and women became more active in Berlin's photo clubs.[23] The various forms of photographic output multiplied into picture postcards, stereophotographs, illustrated newspapers and journals, portfolios, guidebooks, travel documentations, and family albums.

The groups of photographs discussed in this book were chosen not primarily for their aesthetic or artistic value, but rather for their visual narratives of particular cultural, social, economic, and political practices. They were exclusively collected by the city's most significant museums and archives, some of which began paying attention to photography during this era. Their narratives are therefore shaped by a range of factors: the photographers' strategies, the commissioning institutions' goals, and the collecting entities' intentions.

The photographic image over the past forty years or so has undergone a process of powerful reconsideration across the disciplines.[24] This includes its consideration by art historians and its reevaluation by social scientists and historians as something more than an illustration of historical "fact." It also involves its contextualization by representatives of cultural studies, philosophy, and the social sciences. Photography seen through this lens emerges as a complex form of meaning making and communication. Its sensitivity and receptiveness to the subjectivity and sociality of its creators is understood in terms of their ability to create meaning, as they "manipulate the physical means of production of photography; cameras, film, lighting, objects, people."[25] By serving crucial functions for their time and culture and reflecting the attitudes of their time and place, they become "cultural messengers."[26] Peter B. Hales summarizes the function of photographers in American cities during the era of urbanization as serving "as covert teachers to their information-hungry viewers." Their lessons, Hales points out, "affected not only how Americans saw the expanding and encroaching urban sphere but how they comprehended the terrors and promises offered by its streets and structures—what subjects and themes they judged to be of enduring value or of great shame in these noisy, sprawling human productions known as cities."[27] For many observers during the late nineteenth century, Berlin will have fit this description much better than Europe's other metropolises. It is this paradox of the "American city of Europeans,"[28] as Osborn put it, that photographers were particularly well equipped to tackle. Their language, unlike a writer's, painter's, or musician's, intuitively picked up the changing, exciting, and alienating nature of the modern city.

Baudelaire aptly characterized the mid-nineteenth-century painter's task as "looking for that indefinable something we may be allowed to call 'modernity,' for want of a better term to express the idea in question, the aim for him is to extract from fashion the poetry that resides in its historical envelope, to distill the eternal from the transitory."[29] Baudelaire identifies this tension between the "eternal" and the "transitory" as central to the modern (urban) experience of his contemporaries—a tension that lies at the heart of this project. The two Baudelairian central characteristics of modern urban culture, history and transformation, and the dichotomy they present, are particularly pertinent in these comparative observations about Berlin and Paris. This dynamic also influences the structure of this book, the first half of which discusses the manifestation and articulation of progress and modernization, while its second half examines the formation of a sense of history, historicity, musealization, and preservation. These tendencies unfold in their greater complexity through case studies that engage different photographic technologies as they emerged alongside urban dwellers' growing engagement with visual media: the panorama and the illustrated press (chapter 1); architectural photography and photographic portfolios (chapter 2); documentary "rubble photography" and photogrammetry (chapter 3); and artistic "pictorialist" photography as museum object (chapter 4).

Chapters 1 and 2 examine panoramic photography and architectural photography as a means to construct an affirmative image of the city. Both of these forms of urban imagery are based on long traditions of urban representation that reach back to Renaissance vedutas and architectural drawings. Chapters 3 and 4 outline three scenarios of urban image-making as different forms of spectacle, "ruin porn," and nostalgia: a sequence of measuring images documenting the erection of an equestrian monument, a heterogeneous set of images of urban demolition and construction sites, and a survey project capturing the picturesque "Old Berlin."

Photographers in Berlin, more than in other German-speaking cities like Hamburg, Dresden, Munich, or Vienna, were highly skilled and pragmatically minded but rarely participated in contemporary photo-avant-garde debates. Such dichotomies and individual traits define every grown city's image, but Berlin presents a unique case, as it chronologically inverts the attention to old and new. It was only around 1900 that artistically minded photographers made public statements about Berlin's historic parts, while their predecessors had competed with affirmative imagery of the new metropolis. As the brief comparison with Paris demonstrated, before Berlin began to remember its own historicity, it celebrated its new identity as a city in permanent transition. Unlike any other European metropolis, Berlin's development into a world city coincided with the instrumentalization of photography's technological and aesthetic capacities and their ties to boosterism and historical consciousness. The urban space and its photographic image, in its particular forms of presentation, distribution, and perception, display a unique quality of urban space, one that architectural critic Anthony Vidler identified as "reciprocally interdependent with society."[30] Karl Scheffler's assessment of Berlin further distinguishes it from cities like Hamburg, Dresden, and Munich; he claims that all of these cities, unlike Berlin, became what they are because "they were the heart of the countries, which all forces felt drawn to and returned to inspiredly."[31] Berlin lacked such precondition, as it "literally emerged like a colonial city, like American and Australian cities did deep in the outback in the nineteenth century."[32]

This fascinating and fulminant era of Berlin's history has been launched back into our consciousness in the past quarter century by Berlin's reunification. The city's reconceptualization and the ongoing negotiations of topographic memories, processes of material and cultural overwriting of what used to be East Germany and East Berlin, and the rapid influx of new Berliners bear at times eerie similarities with events and attitudes from more than one hundred years ago. Addressing imperial Berlin's collective conscious and its craving for a holistic urban identity, and their correlation with photographic imagery and challenges, adds to today's still unresolved East–West binary. While East and West became synonymous for communist and capitalist convictions, respectively, they were understood during the imperial era as denominators of working-class (East) and upper-class (West) living. Berlin's urban imagery and its unique story and complex gestalt also put into perspective how the unified Berlin today might develop a narrative for itself. Utilizing the past as a mere branding tool and popular form of contemporary place-making is countered here by a thorough exploration of Berlin's image(s). While some may be reluctant to reconnect to Berlin's imperial history, true identity formation requires looking closely at the past, at archives and collections of images and their context and interrelations. And while it is doubtful that Max Osborn's wish to understand "old" and "new" Berlin as "two tightly connected parts of a large, logical, organic whole" will come true, this book aims at situating Berlin's image within a broader discussion of modernity. Exploring this city's self-generated photographic narratives and the critical voices that contextualize its urban experiences provides a means to reconsider modernity and the city today.

ONE

Crafting the Metropolis

Photo Panoramas in the Illustrated Journal *Berliner Leben*

> Apparently an invariable characteristic of city life is that certain stylized and symbolic means must be resorted to in order to "see" the city. The most common recourse in getting a spatial image of the city is to look at an aerial photograph in which the whole city—or a considerable portion of it—is seen from a great height.
>
> —ANSELM L. STRAUSS, *Images of the American City*

Representations of Berlin, filtered through conventions or framed through language, were increasingly employed for the sake of creating narratives for visitors, starting in the 1880s and peaking around 1900. The aerial or panoramic view was well suited to convey these narratives. Tourist albums, illustrated journals, stereographic images, and large panoramic or dioramic installations were the technically generated manifestations of this distanced overview. A series of eighteen wide-angle panoramas called "Neu-Berlin" ("New Berlin"), published in 1901 and 1902 in *Berliner Leben: Zeitschrift für Schönheit und Kunst* (*Berlin Life: Journal for Beauty and Art*), this chapter suggests, embodied a new type of panoramic vision. These images represented the growing complexity of the relationship between the city and its image as it was shaped by advancements in optical technology and the experience of growing anonymity in the city. They present a type of "grand-style photography," revealing both "vistas too extensive for the witness" and "order hidden to the walking presence."[1] Beyond such structuring and orienting qualities, panoramic photography in Berlin, and in the expanding metropolises in North America, distorted and omitted detail to present a city that seemed to care primarily about a highly selective representation of growth and progress.

However, the celebratory subtext of such panoramic imagery coalesced with the ambivalent and critical voices of Berlin: Friedrich Fuchs, in a short text accompanying the "New Berlin" panoramas, soberly acknowledged that Berlin would never qualify to match Emperor Wilhelm II's proclamation of becoming the "most beautiful city in the world."[2] A flat and motionless city "above which hovers a layer of smog," it lacked Paris's natural elevations and its gripping views. "Here, one has to climb city hall or to make the effort to climb Kreuzberg mound to enjoy a panorama and is then indeed rewarded by a sea at one's feet that stretches all the way to the horizon." Despite such disadvantages, Fuchs proposed embracing the city's modern features: its architecture and new districts; the inner city of "stone, iron and glass" with "light, air, spatial generosity, fire safety and practical elegance"; its "long, dead-straight streets" with colorful shop windows and the residential boulevards on the city's outskirts. According to Fuchs, such circumstances that "defy even American conditions" had blindsided Berlin's architects.[3] This city's "tidiness" and artificiality was paired with a fitting representation in the abstracting and distancing perspective of the panoramas' eighteen wide-angle views. The more the photo panorama removed the observer from the city and the greater its claims for comprehensiveness, the more palpable the sense of alienation famously described by Berlin-based urban sociologist Georg Simmel in "The Metropolis of Modern Life." Andrew Lees and Lynn Hollen Lees remarked at the universality of a sense of alienation among contemporaries, who "looked anxiously at 'world cities,' which for them embodied modernity in its many forms." A city like Berlin, which had grown so quickly over such a short period, "seemed uncontrollable and unfamiliar. The scale of its diversity overwhelmed contemporaries, who worried about the physical and political problems generated within urban environments."[4]

Berlin's striking "newness," was sensed not only by its inhabitants on a daily basis and over years of witnessing change incrementally, but even more acutely by tourists and foreign observers. Their reporting also put into perspective any attempts at self-promotional narratives in Berlin by pointing at its fractured identity in comparison with other European capitals. The French travel writer and illustrator Charles Huard, echoing Mark Twain, described Berlin as "new, clean, and without character, completely new, newer than any American city, newer than Chicago, the only city that can be compared to Berlin in respect to the surprising speed of growth."[5] French critic Luc Gersal, who visited Berlin in 1892, assessed the city from the top of city hall (the Rotes Rathaus), pointing out the city planners' and architects' failure to create an aesthetically coherent modern city. "It is palpable that we are in a city that was equally built on (military) command and with respect for utility. This is the textbook modern city; no other European capital is as young. But she has not volunteered to be modern, practical, and American. Instead of following her nature, she wants to dress up elegantly, which suits her badly."[6] These types of critical assessments date back as far as 1810, when the socialite and public intellectual Germaine de Staël wrote that she "would welcome new cities and laws in America: there, nature and freedom resonate enough with one's soul, so that memory is dispensable; on our old continent, however, we rely on traces of the past. Berlin, this entirely modern city, does not make a ceremonial, serious impression, as pretty as it may be: One neither feels the imprint of the country's history, nor of its inhabitants' character."[7]

Some of these perceptions reflect Berlin's rhythm and time, which was noticeably changing by the turn of the twentieth century. Due to new technological standards, time seemed to pass more quickly, and life was becoming more intense. Its rapid urban development could not have been predicted in the early nineteenth century. In the 1830s Berlin was a quaint city of about 230,000 inhabitants, but by 1871 it already had more than tripled in size to over 800,000. It passed the one million mark by 1877, had two million inhabitants by 1905, and grew to a robust 3.8 million by 1920.[8] The city's geographic expansion mirrored the population growth, expanding from 63.26 square kilometers in 1871 to 878.1 square kilometers by 1920 after the formation of Greater Berlin (Groß Berlin).

One of the earliest signs that the modern age had arrived was the opening of the first Prussian railway line between Berlin and Potsdam in 1838 (Figure 1.1). Because of the city's increasing separation of workplace and home, expanding transport was not simply a matter of quantitative spread triggered by a general urban growth; instead, it was determined by entirely new conditions of separated urban functions. The city's early nineteenth-century public transportation system was based primarily on horse-drawn carriages, but by 1900 horses had been joined by a range of bus, electrical tram, subway, elevated, and rail-train systems, all of which had to complement each other in response to the city's growth.

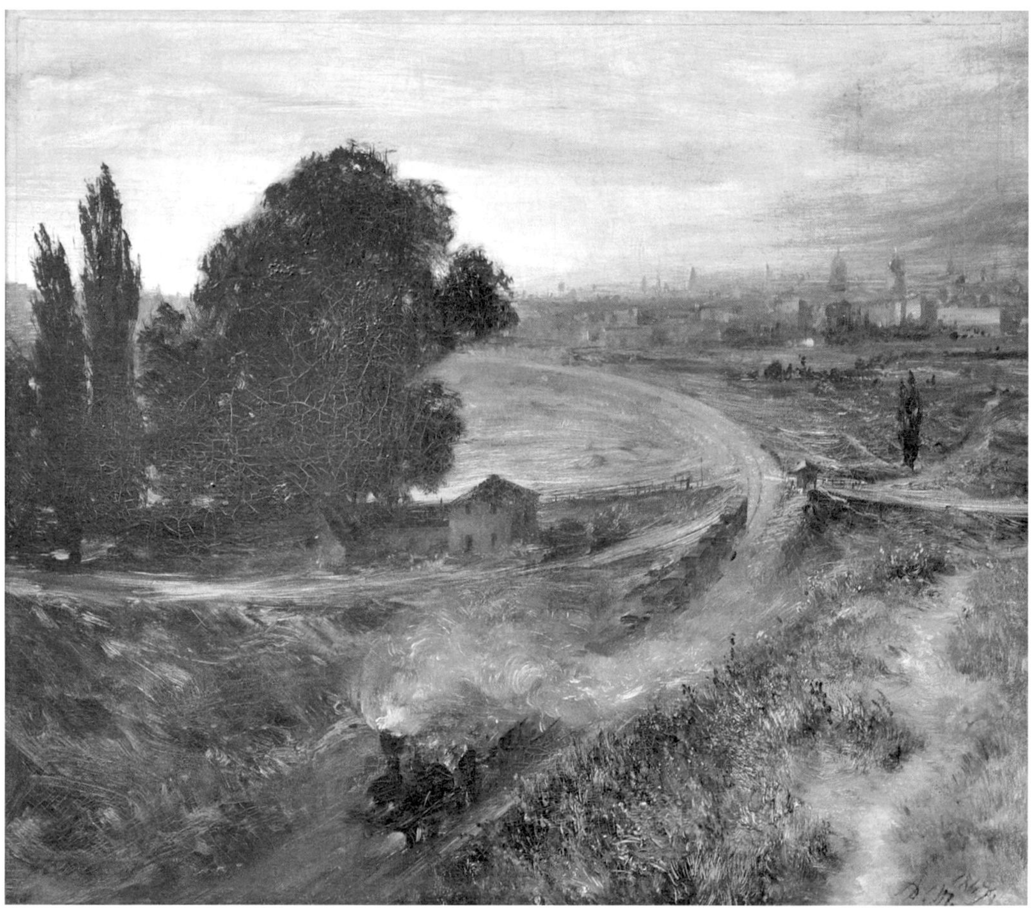

Figure 1.1. Adolph von Menzel, *Berlin–Potsdam Railway*, 1847. Oil on canvas, 42 × 52 cm. Alte Nationalgalerie, Berlin. A/643 Nationalgalerie, Berlin. Wikimedia Commons.

The driving force behind attempts to bring order into planning efforts in Berlin was based on "city technology developed by engineers."[9] The state stepped back from the charge it had taken throughout the earlier part of the nineteenth century and left the playing field to private initiatives: housing associations and widespread terrain speculation beyond the inner city. Any solution to the drastically changing new city was left to chance, and neither the city nor private investors attempted to generate a comprehensive concept for growth. It was not until the period 1908–10, during an exhibition and competition for the development of Greater Berlin that a systematic projection of the city's expansion beyond its historic walls was drawn up.[10]

The city's industrial growth was heavily impacted by the development of technology. Electrical and machine industries were among the strongest in the city and attracted thousands of laborers from Prussian provinces, Poland, Russia, Galicia, and Romania, who began flooding the city by the 1870s. In 1895, people of non-German origin made up 17 percent of the population.[11] By the 1860s, Berlin city officials sensed that the city's growth required a coordinated response and commissioned the civic engineer James Friedrich Hobrecht (1825–1902) to conceptualize its first projection for the city's expansion in 1862 (Figure 1.2). Despite the official commission, Hobrecht did not deliver a detailed street plan, and his design only allowed for a general division of land around Berlin's city center.[12] This approach granted great flexibility in terms of use, ownership,

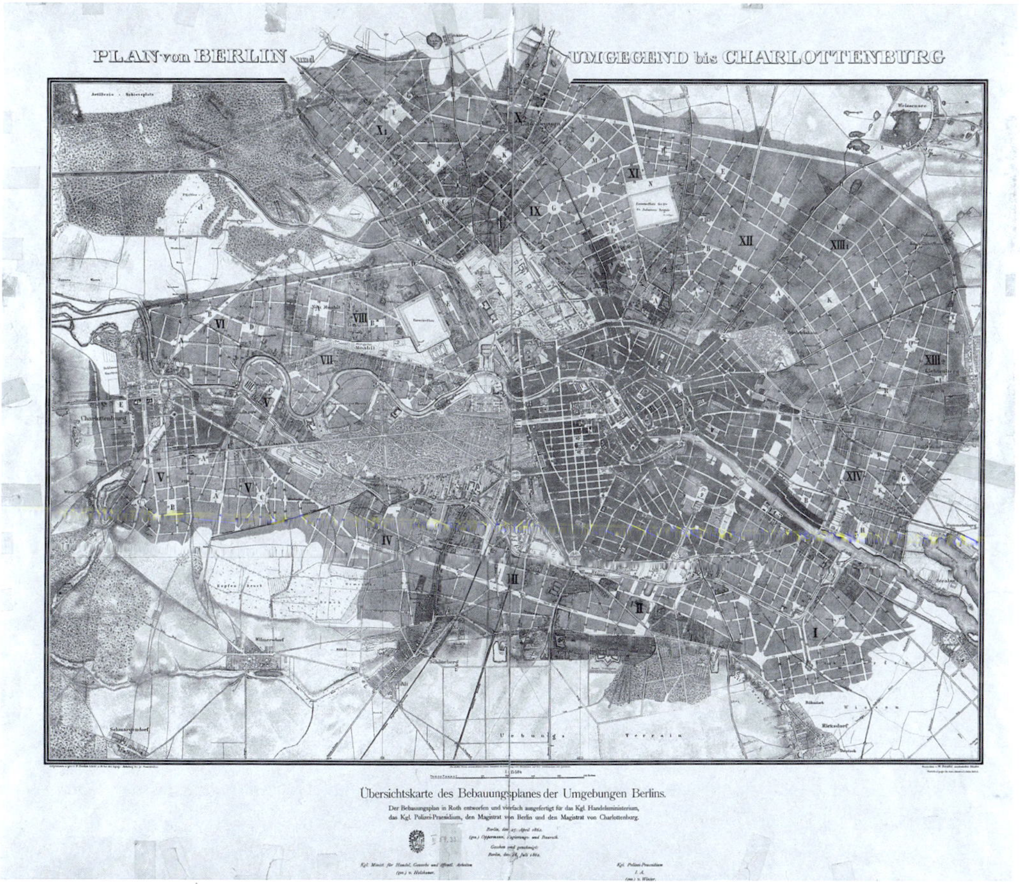

Figure 1.2. Ferdinand Boehm, *Plan von Berlin und Umgegend bis Charlottenburg* (Hobrecht Plan), 1862. Zentral- und Landesbibliothek Berlin. Wikimedia Commons.

and occupation, but also relinquished control over the city's plan to whoever had the means and ambition to take it.

Berlin's Urban Imaginaries

The panoramic view, or "all view" as derived from the Greek term *pan* (all) *horama* (see), was an indispensable feature of both traditional city representation and nineteenth-century visual culture. Stephan Oettermann, in his comprehensive account of its development, explains that panorama "is an artificial, technical term, in other words, created for a specific form of landscape painting which reproduced a 360 degree view and was invented independently around 1787 by several different European painters" (Figure 1.3).[13] Painted panoramas

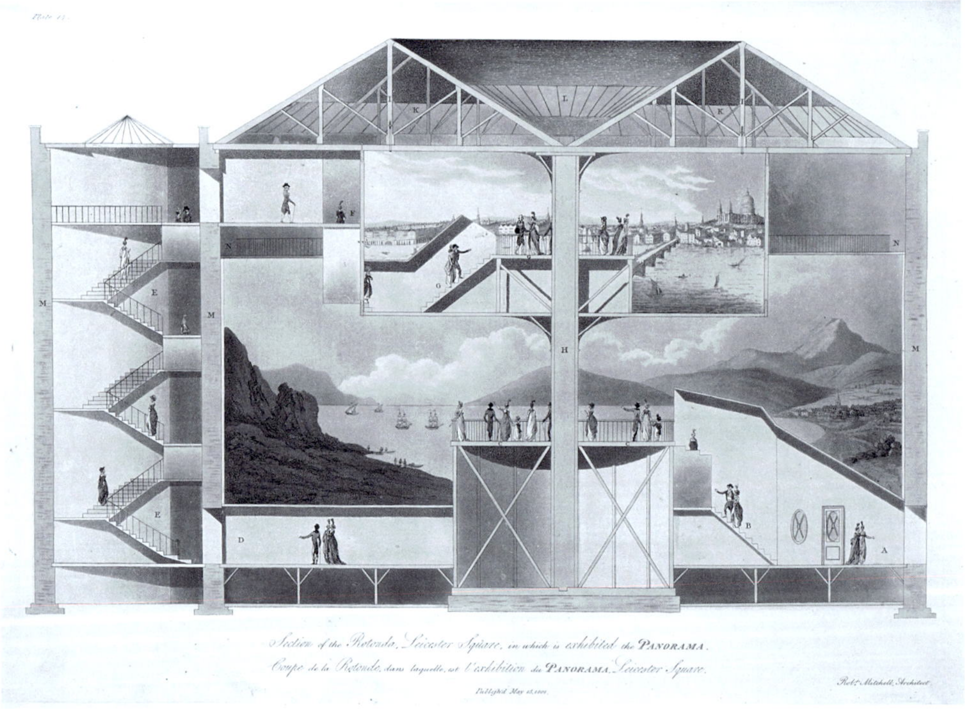

Figure 1.3. Robert Mitchell, section of Burford's Panorama, Leicester Square, London. From *Robert Mitchell's Plans, and Views in Perspective, with Descriptions of Buildings Erected in England and Scotland; and . . . an Essay to Elucidate the Grecian, Roman, and Gothic Architecture (Plans, descriptions et vues en perspective, etc.)* (London: Oriental Press, 1801). Etching, colored aquatint. British Library, call number 56.i.12 (Plate 14). https://www.bl.uk/picturing-places/articles/the-spectacle-of-the-panorama.

and dioramas were not simply "imitations of the panoramas that have existed as natural formation" but rather served as "an apparatus for teaching and glorifying the bourgeois view of the world." As a device that was deeply linked to the emerging middle class, the panorama was not employed to simply give the view of a random horizon from an elevated spot; its purpose was also highly symbolic.[14] In Oettermann's words, it "served both as an instrument for liberating human vision and for limiting and 'imprisoning' it anew." The panorama became the "first true visual 'mass medium' before photography."[15]

The well-known Berlin-based landscape painter Eduard Gärtner created several Berlin panoramas during the 1830s, capturing the city at the onset of industrialization. Their serenity and unhurried Biedermeier air were far removed from photographic panoramas created sixty years later, but they give important clues to the perceptional shift between the Prussian and German capitals. Gärtner drew and painted several versions of this stunning panorama of Berlin from the rooftop of Schinkel's Friedrichswerder Church. In its final version, he integrated a depiction of himself and other figures, including the Berlin science luminary Alexander von Humboldt, who looks through a telescope. Gärtner's infant child is climbing the church's roof unguarded (Figure 1.4).

As in his other city images, but more expressively in his interiors, Gärtner depicted the city as a place inhabited by, and in the service of, its residents. City dwellers on the streets and squares are often recognizable as individuals

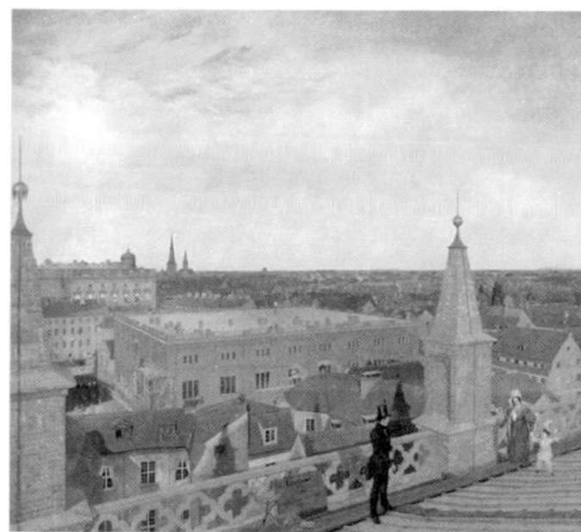
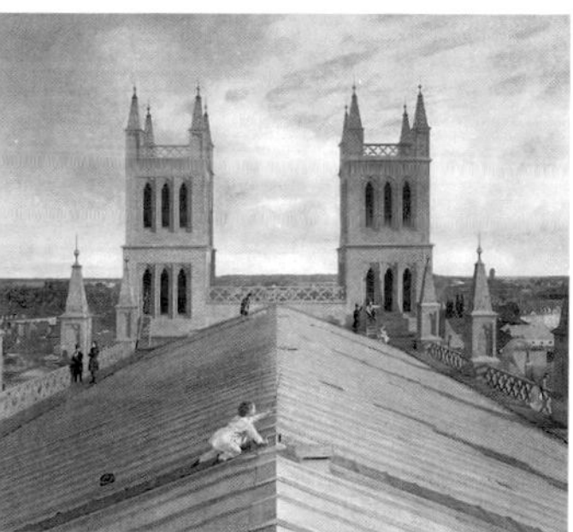
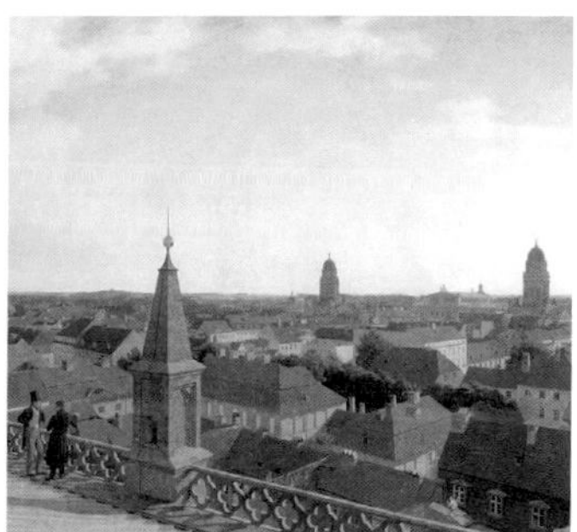

Figure 1.4. Eduard Gärtner, *Ein Panorama von Berlin, von der Werderschen Kirche aus aufgenommen* (Panorama of Berlin, captured from Friedrichswerder Church), 1834. Oil on canvas; two three-piece panels, middle piece 91 × 93 cm, side pieces each 91 × 110 cm. These are the three panels looking south (southeast, south, southwest). Inv. GK I 6179, Property of the Hohenzollern Estate, Stiftung Preußische Schlößer und Gärten, Berlin. Wikimedia Commons.

in his panels. Gärtner captured his urban scenes (some of them likely aided by a camera obscura) with a photographic accuracy and atmospheric effect that would not have been achievable by the then-limited photographic techniques. As photography officially entered the stage shortly after 1839, and as popular interest in topographical painting slackened after 1840, Gärtner was forced to make artistic decisions that would allow him to adjust his work to the taste of a middle-class clientele. Slowly losing the court's patronage, he began to enhance his cityscapes with romantic, atmospherically colored suggestions (Figure 1.5).[16] Such creative freedom was not at the center of photographers' interests, nor were consumers of photography anticipating or hoping for artistry: they expected and craved utmost accuracy and an exact likeness of the depicted subject.

While Gärtner painted a tranquil, romanticized Berlin for king and court, the next generation of panoramic images were sweeping, mechanically generated,

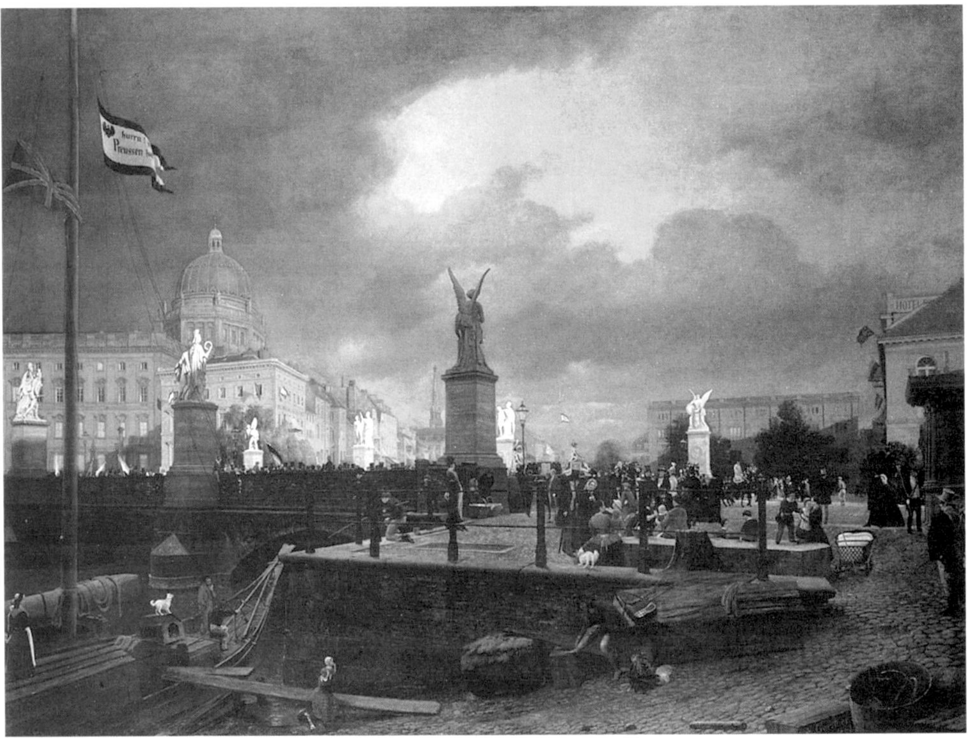

Figure 1.5. Eduard Gärtner, *Ansicht der Schloßbrücke hierselbst* (View of Berlin's Castle Bridge from the north), 1861. Tempera on wood. Stiftung Preußische Schlößer und Gärten. Wikimedia Commons.

and mass-disseminated views for tourists. Travel and tourism, common as "grand tour" among the northern European nobility, became an increasingly popular and affordable practice among the educated and affluent middle classes by the second half of the nineteenth century.

Reflecting Berlin's growing popularity among travelers and indicating the normalization of the concept of travel for a growing segment of society, the German publisher Karl Baedeker (1801–59) developed a Berlin edition of his popular travel guidebook in the early nineteenth century. His practical, red-clad volumes set the standard for authoritative guidebooks for tourists in Germany and abroad.[17] The 1904 German edition of the Baedeker travel guidebook for Berlin (Figure 1.6) described the "New Berlin" panorama site and gives a sense of the excitement at the measures that the city was taking to replace old structures with new ones and to give some old tourist destinations an overhaul:

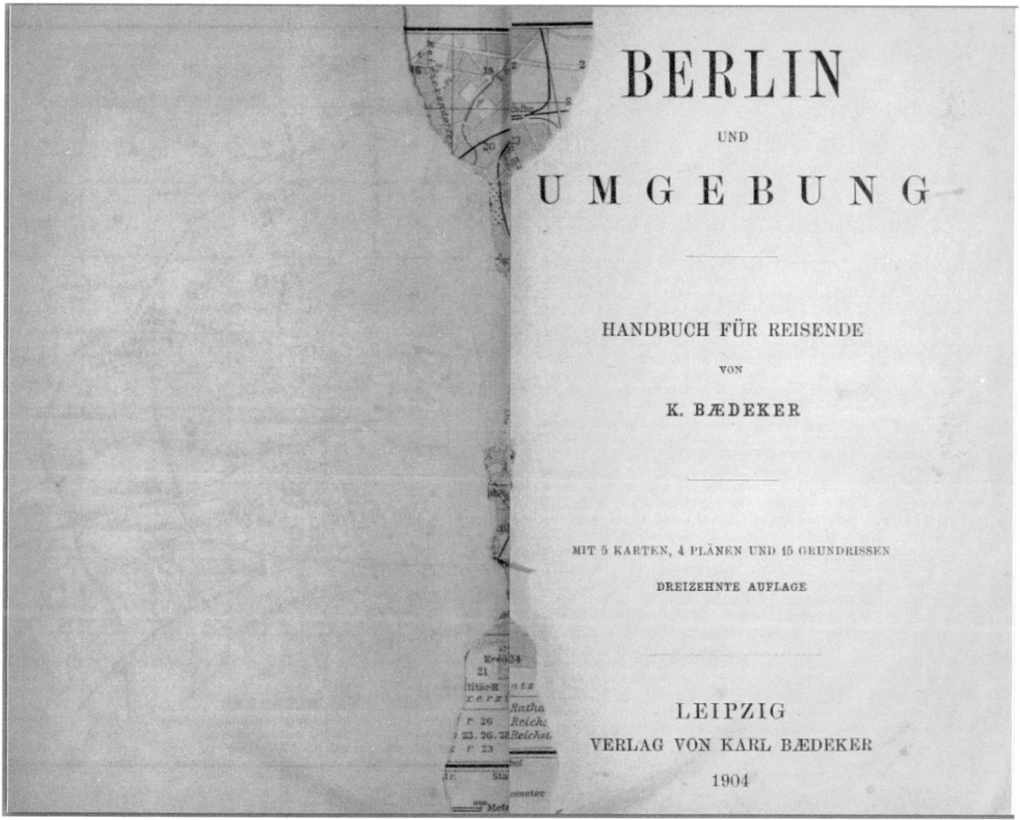

Figure 1.6. Baedeker guidebook for Berlin, 1904. German edition from Baedeker Publishing.

> The surroundings of the castle have been redesigned according to the castle's baroque building type. Now, Lustgarten, Opera Square, and Linden Boulevard truly form a monumental promenade of the first order, a similar example of which can be found in Vienna but is lacking in Paris and London. In the Linden Boulevard, which did not reflect its old reputation anymore, old buildings are increasingly replaced by more and more magnificent buildings for hotels and stores; the rows of trees and walkways have been reorganized.[18]

This sort of metropolitan monumentality and grandeur was the result of twenty years of fervent demolition, building, and restructuring measures, and led to the formation of a representational city center and this center's simultaneous depopulation.[19] The Collegiate Church and the National Monument, which had been commissioned by Emperor Wilhelm II, were both new additions to Berlin's skyline. Built in Berlin's breed of Prussian neobaroque, they were indicative of the emperor's desire to give this burgeoning metropolis a historical varnish in order to aesthetically reinforce values that he feared were lacking or vanishing. The older buildings marked peaks of Prussian political and cultural power and, in unison with the city's modern buildings, formed a narrative of continuity and growth. Thanks to Baedeker's assertion that "from (city hall) tower [one has the] best round-view of Berlin,"[20] the view of the city from that spot became well known from written descriptions, photographs, and photo panoramas.

During the 1880s, the popular early nineteenth century spectacle of the spatial panorama experienced a revival in Germany, and Berlin became the epicenter of this revival. According to Bernard Comment, "six rotundas exhibited twenty-four panoramas between 1880 and 1914. The first to open was the National Panorama in 1881."[21] One such panorama, which was on display between 1890

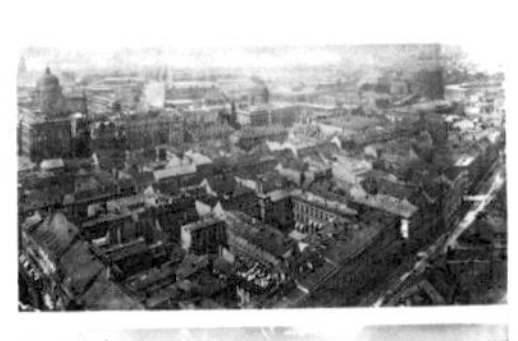
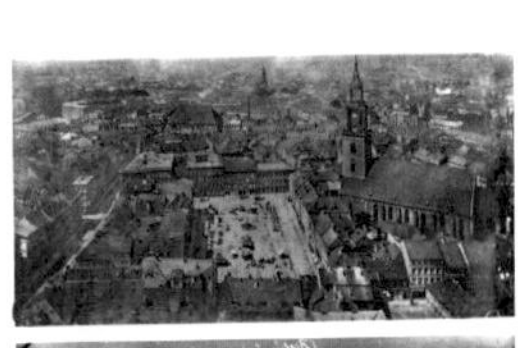
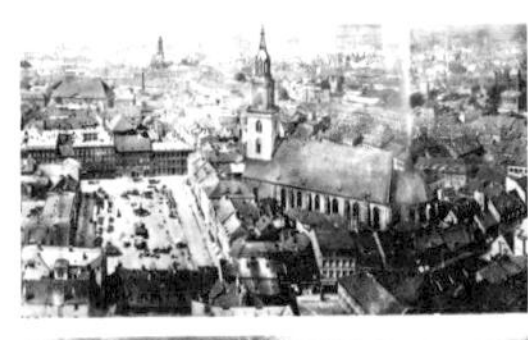
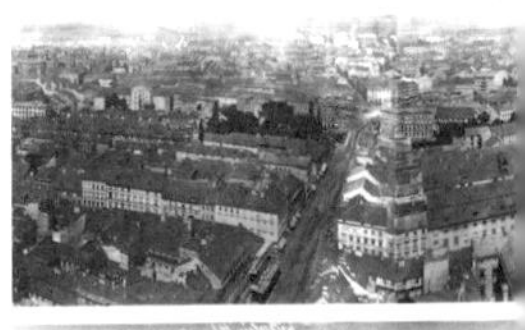

Figure 1.7. Albrecht Meydenbauer, *Panorama vom roten Rathaus* (Panorama of Berlin from City Hall), 1868. Eight photographic plates. Brandenburgisches Landesamt für Denkmalpflege, BLDAM, Bildarchiv, negative numbers 38 e 20/5556.1–38 e 27/5556.8.

and 1891, depicted an idealized re-creation of Rome from a standpoint amid the ruins of the emperors' palace on the Aventine Hill.[22] It both exemplified the panorama's symbolism and demonstrated the long-standing German fascination with Italy. Its display in the late nineteenth century also suggested an affinity deriving from its model function for a yet-unachieved German national unity.[23]

Grand-Style Photography

This desire for unity is on display in the first photo panorama of Berlin viewed from its new city hall, which employs a 360-degree view and was created in 1868 by Albrecht Meydenbauer, the inventor of photogrammetry (Figure 1.7). Photographed from the tower of city hall in the year before the building's completion,[24] this eight-panel set of prints is a fascinating "sequel" to Gärtner's painted view.[25] Stark shadows and sunlit southern façades suggest that these photos were taken during the early afternoon, and the pronounced black-and-white contrasts of the busy city's rooftops and its misty sky depict a self-assured urbanity. While technical limitations of the era constricted the ability to include people and other moving elements in the photograph, some mobile objects, such as a horse carriage and vendors on the market in front of St. Mary's Church, do come into focus. A fast-paced stream of traffic leaves all but a fading line indicating its path past city castle; such traces of traffic were the result of the technical challenge of capturing objects in motion. Once photographic technology was able to react faster and exposure times became shorter in the 1880s, such blurring became a thing of the past.

The grainy texture of Meydenbauer's prints echoes Gärtner's romantic interpretation of the city, while their astounding detail also points to Meydenbauer's

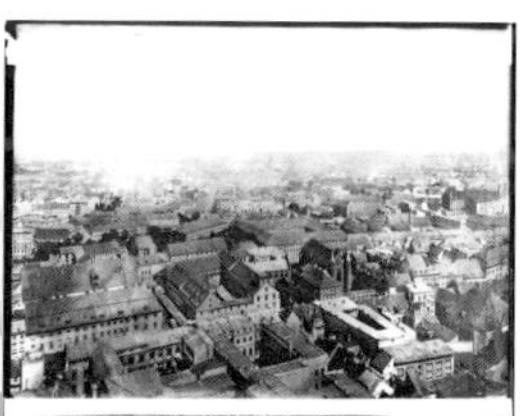

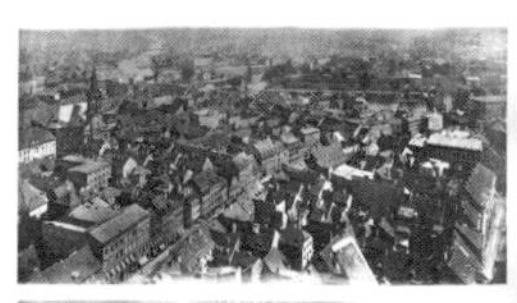

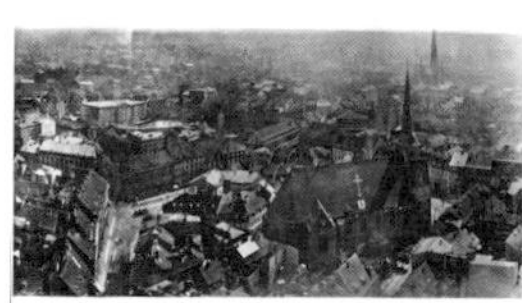

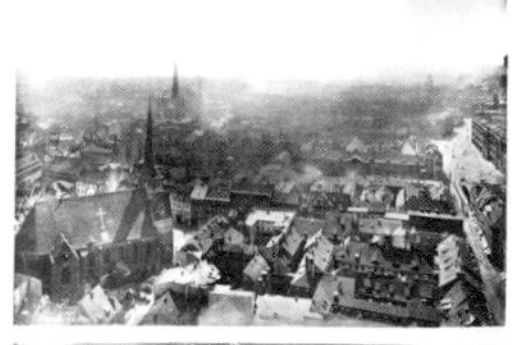

documentary intentions. Meydenbauer's photogrammetric camera, which he had begun to market one year earlier, was based on the wide-angle Pantoskop lens, which had been invented by Emil Busch in 1865 and was crucial technology for panoramic photography.[26] Meydenbauer had a keen interest in systematic architectural and urban documentation, given his primary goal of eternalizing historic monuments for posterity at the service of historic preservation. Photographing as both a documentarian and chronicler, he was most likely the first to photograph from the recently erected city hall tower, which Baedeker would later suggest to be the city's finest vista. In this panorama from city hall, Meydenbauer sets the stage for a new image of Berlin, which suggested, through its contrasting representation of the city's buildings in great focus and its accelerating pace in blurred traces, the urban transformations to fully set in after 1871.

Thirty years later, another spectacular panoramic photographic project was undertaken by the professional photographer Max Ziegra (1852–1923; verifiably worked in Berlin). He photographed Berlin from the tower of city hall in a set of three plates in 1896 (Figure 1.8). Given the horizontally elongated format of each individual image (17.1 × 49.1 cm), Ziegra most likely used a panoramic camera to generate a 180-degree view. Ziegra's distribution strategies and commissioners are not known. However, technically his photograph is clearly a direct precursor to, and link between, the traditional painted panorama, the multipanel/plate photograph of Meydenbauer's, and what would become a fashionable

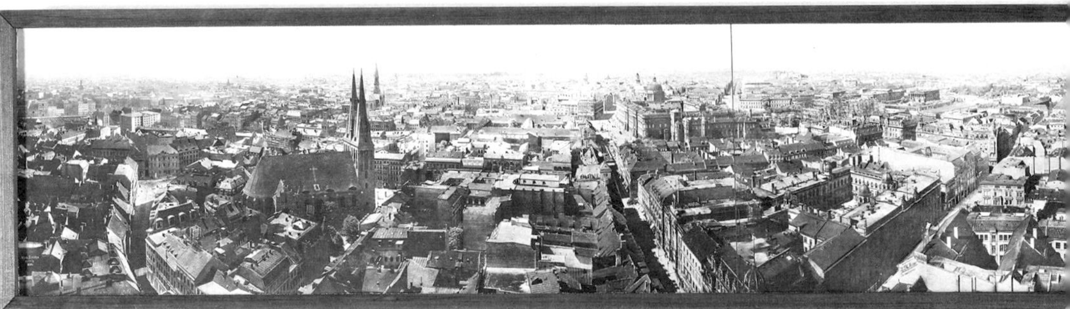

Figure 1.8. Max Ziegra, *Berlin-Panorama Seen from the Tower of City Hall* (three parts, view from Molkenmarkt to Parochialkirche), 1896. Photograph on carton, collodion print. Measurements of the joint three images: 17.1 × 147.5 cm (individual measurements: 17.1 × 49.1 cm). Inventory number SM 2010–0911. Copyright Stiftung Stadtmuseum Berlin. Photograph by Michael Setzpfandt, Berlin.

type of photographic panorama around the turn of the century. This was a noticeably distorted panoramic vision, which was featured prominently in the *Berlin Life* "New Berlin" series. Ziegra's panorama, taken with the new panoramic camera, already featured such a distorting and quasi-summarizing effect on his motif, which appeared bundled together in each of its three parts.

Panoramic photographs of modern and monumental urban sites, taken in this kind of promotional spirit by professional photographers, typified what the American photo historian Peter B. Hales termed "grand-style photography." Discussing the photographs of the Chicago World's Columbian Exposition's "White City" (Figure 1.9), he described them as a "work of visual rhetoric, fabricated to be seen, to be consumed by the eye, not read but witnessed."[27] These images generated a particular aesthetic and presented a unique urban experience. Grand-style photography conveyed the message of the World's Fair, this "utopian sermon in space and structure." It would make graspable what could not be "fully understood by simply being there, especially in the often-crowded, always-hurried atmosphere of nearly every visitor's experience."[28] Not surprisingly, panoramic and bird's-eye depictions experienced a popular revival during the last quarter of the nineteenth century, particularly in the United States, where lithographs and photographs of fast-growing industrial towns and cities were being produced.[29] Berlin's photographers and journalistic and publisher entrepreneurs eagerly employed an equally grand language in their depictions of the "American" metropolis of Berlin.

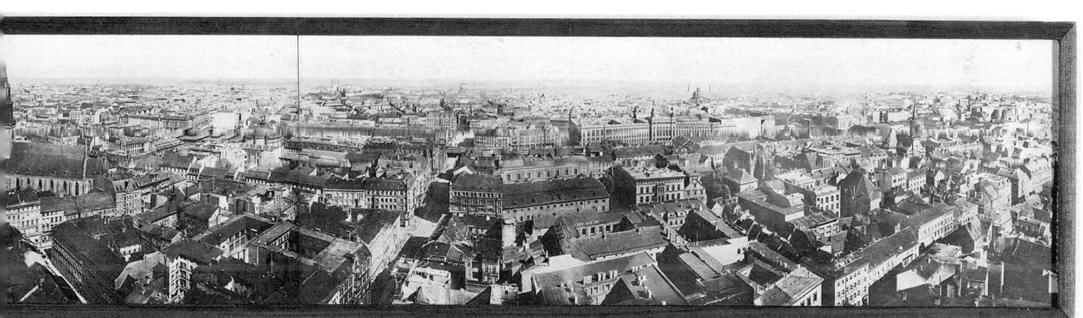

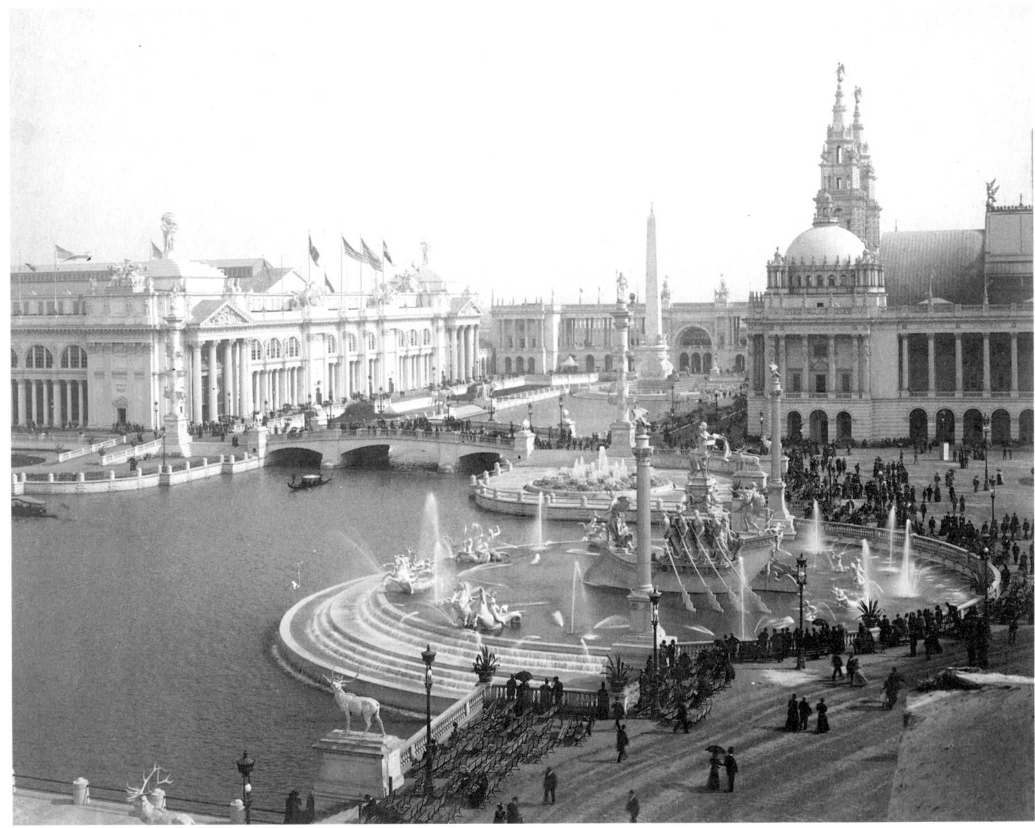

Figure 1.9. Charles Dudley Arnold, *Court of Honor, World's Columbian Exposition, Chicago*, 1893. Photograph by Chicago History Museum, inventory number ICHi-18013.

Similar to photographers in the burgeoning cities of North America, architectural and urban photographers in Berlin of the 1870s through the 1890s picked up on material transformations of the city and registered shifts in the ways in which the city was experienced. They began to photographically "map" Berlin, driven by either public and private commissions or their own interest in the city's changing appearance and nature. They captured new public buildings, main traffic axes and nodes, train stations, and other infrastructural sites, as well as the city's new residential neighborhoods and street life. The daily and illustrated press soon began to play a crucial role in the city's cultural climate and self-promotional rhetoric.[30] Once image and text could be jointly reproduced and mass disseminated, these "theaters of modern life" became affordable entertainment for the entire family and forceful voices in urban identity formation.[31]

Along with urban and event photographs, stories of city life were now seen by thousands, if not millions, of readers.

The initial challenges in mass production, and the high costs for the dissemination of early photographic panoramas through wood-engraved reproductions in illustrated magazines,[32] were overcome by the 1880s with the invention of the autotype—the first printing technology that allowed for a synchronal printing of text and image. Popularized during the 1890s, when it replaced xylograph and collotype technologies, the autotype, which was based on the halftone printing process, had become the established printing process for the illustrated press and picture postcards by the turn of the century.[33] Meisenbach, Riffarth and Company was Berlin's, and one of the European continent's, "largest graphic artistic compan[ies], which encompassed all reproduction techniques."[34] Photo agencies such as Ullstein publishers and image services (*Bilderdienste*) became crucial instruments and promoters of photography's mass consumption. Photo technology made great strides as the photographic manufacturer Agfa in Rummelsburg near Berlin constantly updated and advanced its photographic products, cameras, lenses, and film. Berlin's fulminant rise as a bastion of mass publication, and of commercial and journalistic photography, started these crucial decades around the turn of the century.

"Neu-Berlin"—New Berlin

The series of photo-panoramic views called "Neu-Berlin" were published in 1901 and 1902 in the popular Berlin illustrated weekly *Berliner Leben: Zeitschrift für Schönheit und Kunst* (*Berlin Life: Journal for Beauty and Art*) (Figure 1.10). This journal, published between 1898 and 1928, functioned as a platform for the latest news and gossip about town and also worked to instill a sense of the beauty and culture of the city into its readers. In order to achieve that, it addressed events in Berlin's cultural and political life through essays, but primarily through single photographs and arrangements of celebrity photographs, instant event photographs, and photographs of the city itself. This "lifestyle magazine" of the early twentieth century was explicitly geared toward a middle-class audience ("housefriends in the city and country, in palaces and bourgeois dwellings"). It depicted, in the words of its publishers, "in a refined artistic manner . . . everything [the radiating life in Berlin] has to offer in respect to beauty, inspiration, curiosity, and importance, be it at court and in society, in the sciences, arts, and literature."[35]

Originally, each issue published a brief essay called "our images" (*unsere Bilder*), which commented on a respective issue's illustrations (see Figure 1.13). Later editions omitted such explanations and introduced short stories, poems, and anecdotes that were dispersed between photographs. Image editors began to experiment with the layout: it might display one image per page, sometimes two to four images were shown on one page, or photographs of different sizes were arranged in a collage-like fashion (see Figures 1.11 and 1.12). Each issue sold for 50 pfennigs, which was about twice the price of a liter of milk or a loaf of bread, and thus was a pleasure affordable only for the upwardly mobile and better-to-do middle class.[36] Not all photographers who published here were mentioned by name, although a number of well-known urban photographers,

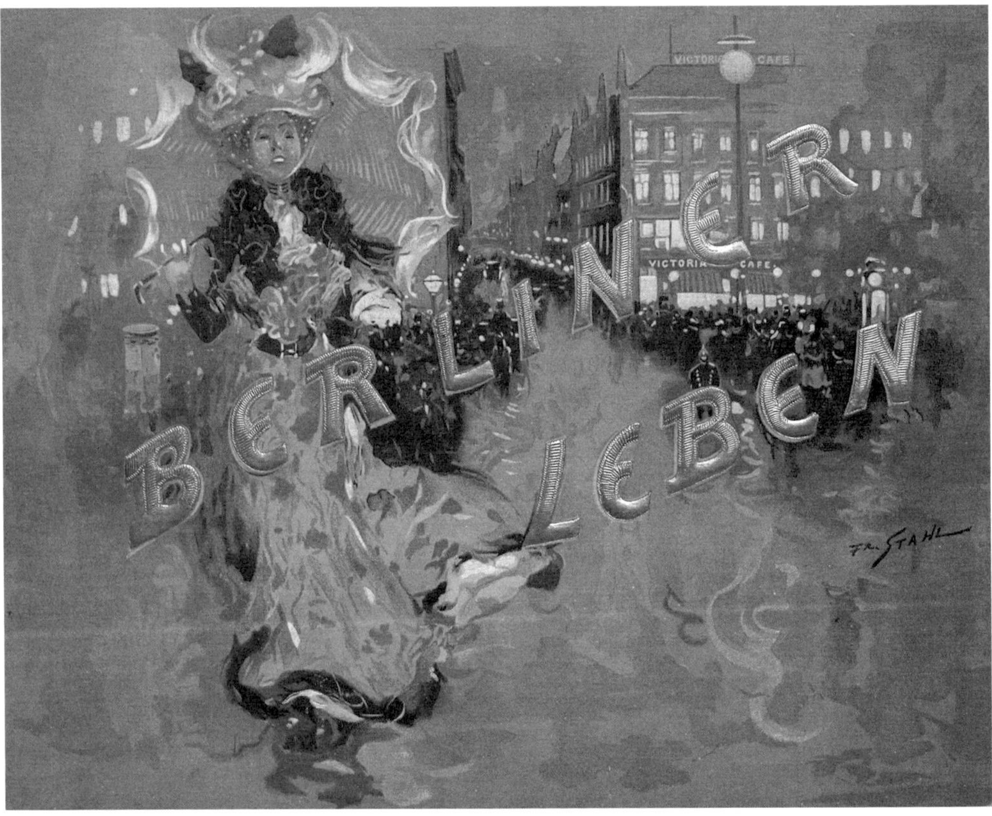

Figure 1.10. Cover for the 1901 volume of *Berliner Leben: Zeitschrift für Schönheit und Kunst*. Digitized by the Zentral- und Landesbibliothek Berlin, 2016. https://digital.zlb.de.

142

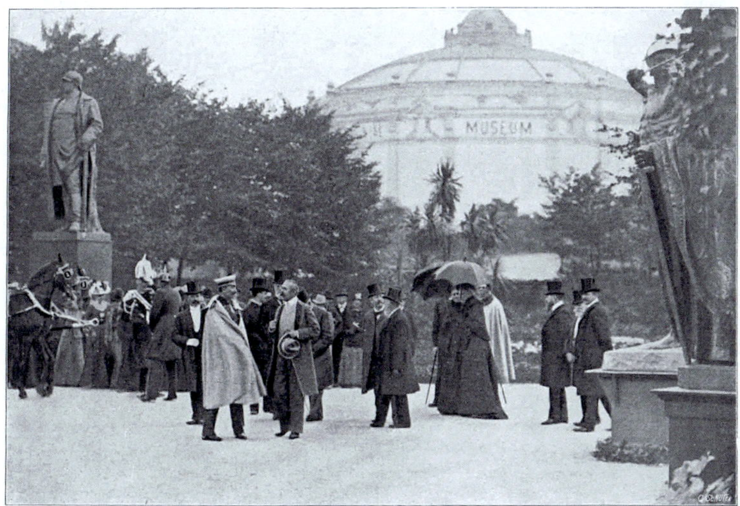

Kaiser Wilhelm II. in der Grossen Berliner Kunstausstellung

Original-Aufnahme für „Berliner Leben" von Hofphot. Boll, Berlin.

Figure 1.11. Photographic illustration, "Kaiser Wilhelm II. in der Grossen Berliner Kunstausstellung," *Berliner Leben* 3 (1900): 142. Digitized by the Zentral- und Landesbibliothek Berlin, 2016. https://digital.zlb.de.

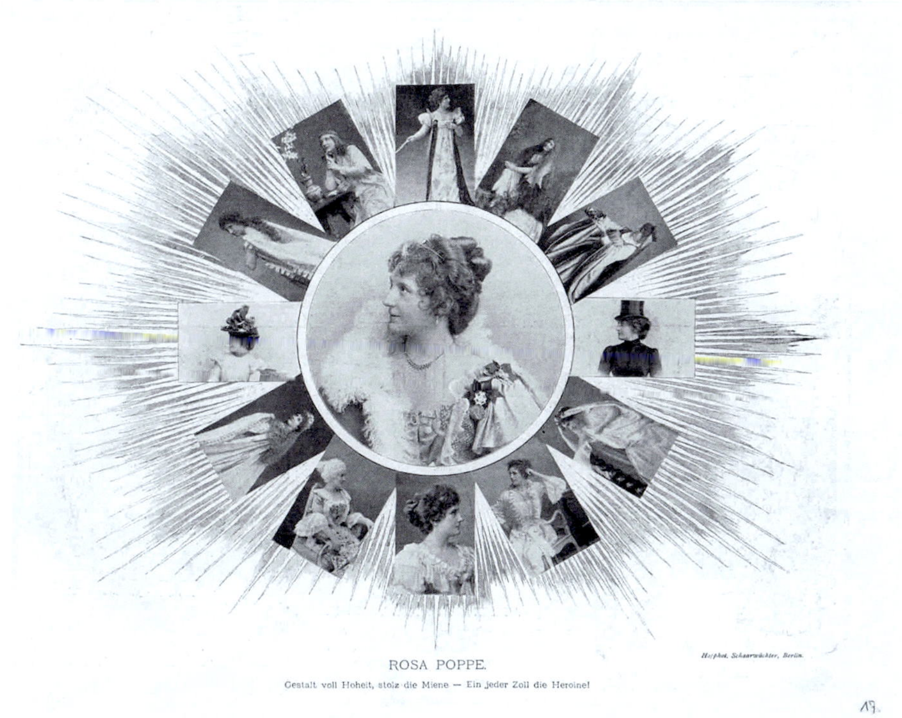

Figure 1.12. Photographic illustration, "Rosa Poppe. Gestalt voll Hoheit, stolz die Miene— Ein jeder Zoll die Heroine!" *Berliner Leben* 1 (1898): 19. Digitized by the Zentral- und Landesbibliothek Berlin, 2016. https://digital.zlb.de.

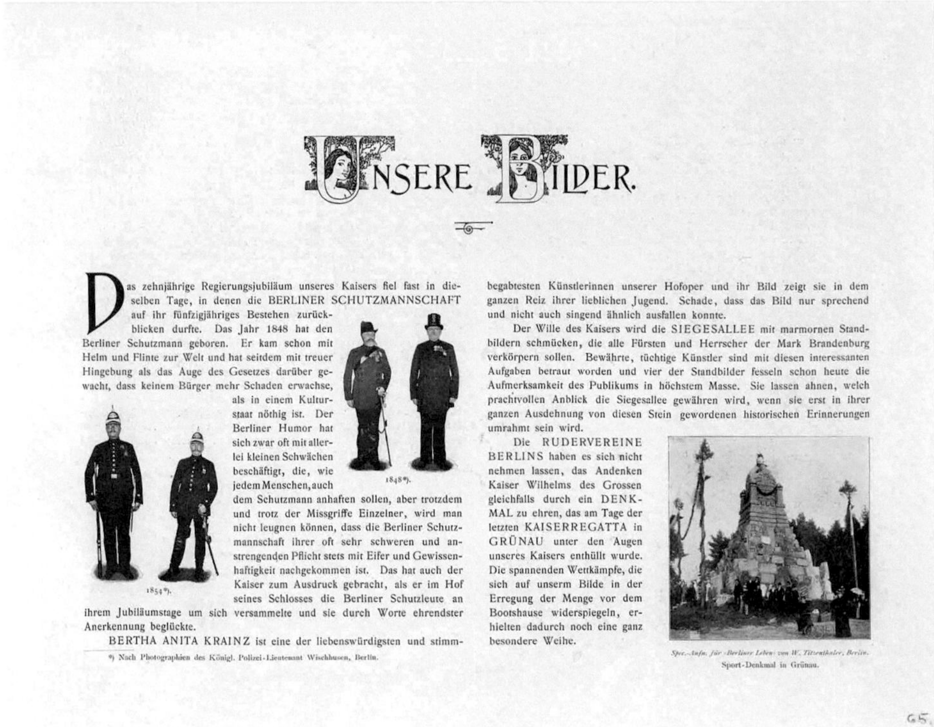

UNSERE BILDER.

Das zehnjährige Regierungsjubiläum unseres Kaisers fiel fast in dieselben Tage, in denen die BERLINER SCHUTZMANNSCHAFT auf ihr fünfzigjähriges Bestehen zurückblicken durfte. Das Jahr 1848 hat den Berliner Schutzmann geboren. Er kam schon mit Helm und Flinte zur Welt und hat seitdem mit treuer Hingebung als das Auge des Gesetzes darüber gewacht, dass keinem Bürger mehr Schaden erwachse, als in einem Kulturstaat nöthig ist. Der Berliner Humor hat sich zwar oft mit allerlei kleinen Schwächen beschäftigt, die, wie jedem Menschen, auch dem Schutzmann anhaften sollen, aber trotzdem und trotz der Missgriffe Einzelner, wird man nicht leugnen können, dass die Berliner Schutzmannschaft ihrer oft sehr schweren und anstrengenden Pflicht stets mit Eifer und Gewissenhaftigkeit nachgekommen ist. Das hat auch der Kaiser zum Ausdruck gebracht, als er im Hof seines Schlosses die Berliner Schutzleute an ihrem Jubiläumstage um sich versammelte und sie durch Worte ehrendster Anerkennung beglückte.

1848*).

1854*).

BERTHA ANITA KRAINZ ist eine der liebenswürdigsten und stimmbegabtesten Künstlerinnen unserer Hofoper und ihr Bild zeigt sie in dem ganzen Reiz ihrer lieblichen Jugend. Schade, dass das Bild nur sprechend und nicht auch singend ähnlich ausfallen konnte.

Der Wille des Kaisers wird die SIEGESALLEE mit marmornen Standbildern schmücken, die alle Fürsten und Herrscher der Mark Brandenburg verkörpern sollen. Bewährte, tüchtige Künstler sind mit diesen interessanten Aufgaben betraut worden und vier der Standbilder fesseln schon heute die Aufmerksamkeit des Publikums in höchstem Masse. Sie lassen ahnen, welch prachtvollen Anblick die Siegesallee gewähren wird, wenn sie erst in ihrer ganzen Ausdehnung von diesen Stein gewordenen historischen Erinnerungen umrahmt sein wird.

Die RUDERVEREINE BERLINS haben es sich nicht nehmen lassen, das Andenken Kaiser Wilhelms des Grossen gleichfalls durch ein DENKMAL zu ehren, das am Tage der letzten KAISERREGATTA in GRÜNAU unter den Augen unseres Kaisers enthüllt wurde. Die spannenden Wettkämpfe, die sich auf unserm Bilde in der Erregung der Menge vor dem Bootshause widerspiegeln, erhielten dadurch noch eine ganz besondere Weihe.

Spec.-Aufn. für »Berliner Leben« von W. Titzenthaler, Berlin.
Sport-Denkmal in Grünau.

*) Nach Photographien des Königl. Polizei-Lieutenant Wischhusen, Berlin.

65.

Figure 1.13. Photographic illustration, "Unsere Bilder," *Berliner Leben* 1 (1898): 65. Digitized by the Zentral- und Landesbibliothek Berlin, 2016. https://digital.zlb.de.

such as Max Missmann, Waldemar Titzenthaler, and Hugo Rudolphy, were credited by the journal.[37]

By the time *Berlin Life*'s first edition was published, mass-disseminated panoramic photo albums featuring promotional urban images had become common. Typical photo albums of Berlin contained urban imagery and often panorama photographs similar or identical to the ones in *Berlin Life*, such as the series of photo albums published by Globus Publishers around 1900 called *Album von Berlin* (see Figure 1.14). Besides the panoramic series discussed here, *Berlin Life* published larger panoramas, which covered two entire pages and were often retouched, photo-collaged, and captured from street level.[38] *Berlin Life* was one of a number of German journals around the turn of the century that were dominated by photographic illustrations such as *Berliner Illustrirte Zeitung*, *Münchner Woche: Aktuelles illustriertes Blatt für Literatur, Kunst und Stadtrundschau*, and *Deutsche illustrirte Zeitung*.

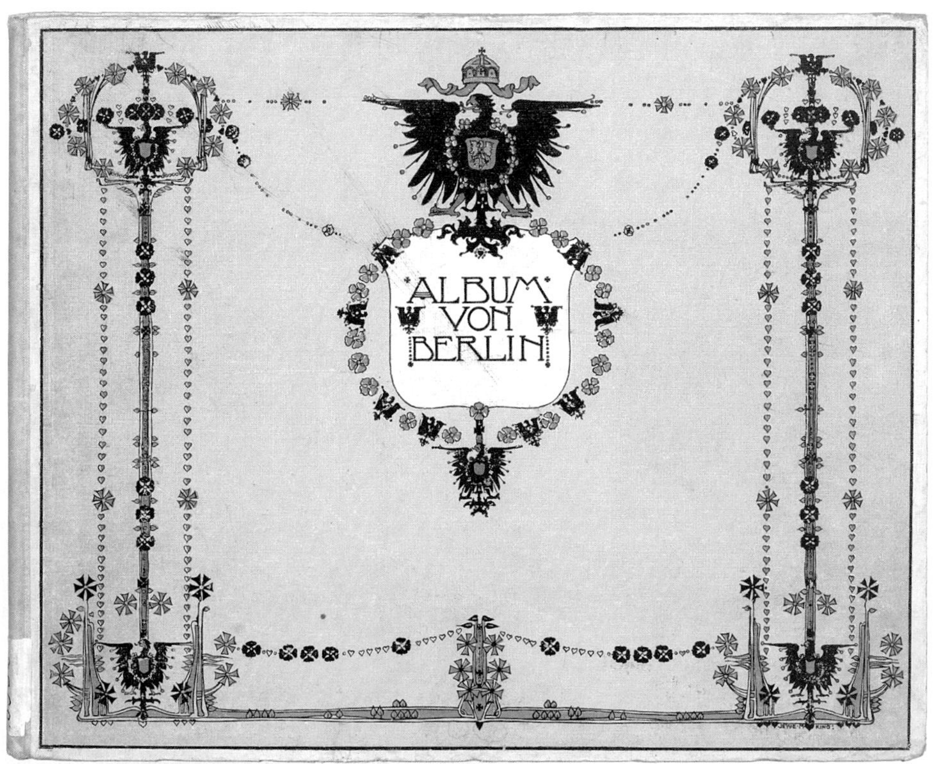

Figure 1.14. Cover of *Album von Berlin* by Globus Verlag, circa 1905. Private collection.

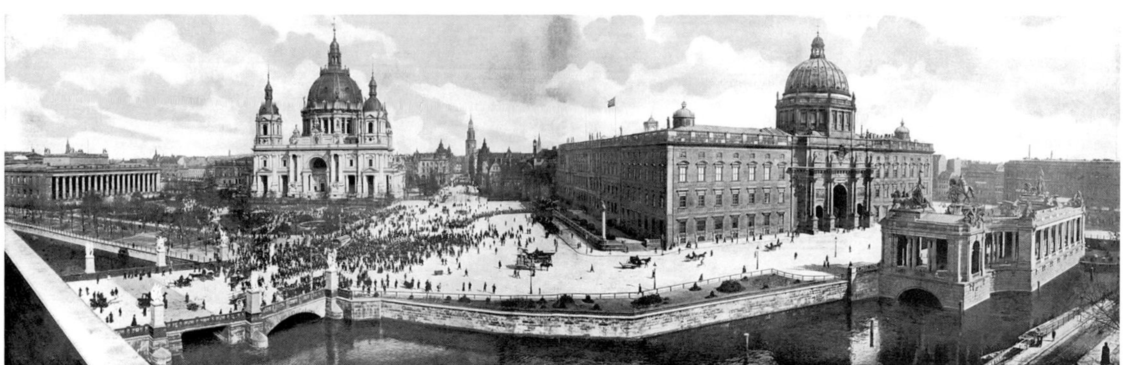

Figure 1.15. Panoramic image of Lustgarten, city castle, and monument from *Album von Berlin*, circa 1905. Private collection.

The sweeping photographic views in *Berlin Life*'s "New Berlin" series took the panorama—and with it the image of Berlin—to a new level of grandiosity. While demonstratively serving as an "economical surrogate for travel,"[39] its drastically distorted vista omitted details and its essentializing interpretation prevented any real identification with the city (see Figure 1.15 and the upper panorama of Figure 1.17b). Unlike Meydenbauer's and Ziegra's photo panoramas, this photograph of Lustgarten, city castle, and the Wilhelm I monument did not aspire to communicate points of reference and a sense of belonging but rather made a forceful and selective claim for the city's central historical and modernized features and its new sense of importance among European metropolises. While Ziegra, through his methodical and detail-oriented approach, achieved a more comprehensive and "democratic" view of Berlin, the *Berlin Life* panorama effectively functioned as "optical simulator." An initially unfamiliar and strongly experienced sensual impression could be practiced again and again until it became a matter of course and a common part of human vision.[40]

Eighteen wide-angle panoramic images (7.62 × 25.40 cm) of different sites were published in five different issues of *Berlin Life*. Four sets of four images were published in 1901, each one displaying two panoramas on two opposite pages. Under each image, individual buildings and sites of historic and touristic importance were labeled in small font. One set of two panoramas appeared in a 1902 issue of the journal. The groups of four images were titled "New Berlin I" through "New Berlin IV"; the set of two was labeled "Panoramas of Berlin V." Unlike traditional panoramic devices, the panoramic camera used for these images was supported by a wide-angle lens, which lent the distinctive distorting effect to its images. They were either swing-lens cameras, where the lens rotated while the film remained stationary, or 360-degree rotation cameras, where both the camera and the film rotated.[41]

Each set of four images covered a different track and took the observer across town: "New Berlin I" (Figure 1.16) sent the viewer from Berlin's historic center, with its royal endeavors of Mühlendamm, Kurfürstenbrücke (Elector's Bridge), stables (Marstall), and castle (Schloß), all the way to the affluent far western suburb of Halensee and its brand-new subway station.[42] In between, the traveler stopped at the elevated train station at Hallesches Tor (Halle Gate), south of the city center, and then at Savigny Platz (Savigny Square) in Berlin's affluent Charlottenburg district.

"New Berlin II" (Figure 1.17) spanned from the modern Alexanderplatz adjacent to the city's historic center into the new southern territory of the city and the newly erected elevated train track at Skalitzer Straße and Oranienstraße. The series then traveled back to the centrally located city castle, with the cathedral and Museum Island, and finally to Potsdamer Platz, which was the busiest and most trafficked Berlin square.

"New Berlin III" (Figure 1.18) also gave a glimpse of both old and new Berlin. The iconic Brandenburg Gate met the Lehrter Railway Station, which had been completed in 1868. The traveler zigzagged back east to the opera, university building, and Hedwig Church along the eastern stretch of the famous boulevard Unter den Linden and ended up northwest from there at Kronprinzenbrücke (Crown Prince's Bridge) at the Spree River.

"New Berlin IV" (Figure 1.19) maneuvered the track between Jannowitz Bridge and its elevated train lines and station, adjacent to the Spree, in the eastern city center and three prominent city squares. Two of them, Moritzplatz and Mariannenplatz, were located in the city's new southern expansion, the Kreuzberg district. The other, Lützowplatz, was located in the western suburb of Charlottenburg.

The two images of "New Berlin V" (Figure 1.20) returned to Blücher Platz (Blücher Square) and Hallesches Tor, and the photographer captured both the elevated train track and the column on Belle-Alliance Plaza behind it. The second image was taken from Waisenbrücke (Orphan Bridge), which overlooked the Spree River westward toward Neukölln am Ufer.

At a first glance, the new Berlin, according to the *Berlin Life* image editors, seemed to rely on both the remnants of its history as the home of the Prussian court and on its new developments and expansions. This image correlated with the more affirmative city assessments by travelers and the language of tourist guidebooks, but it also revealed and celebrated what foreign correspondents had criticized, the city's new developments and neighborhoods. Photo editors and photographers consolidated old and new and sent the viewer on a quasi-chronological trip through town, from old city to new. The entire series's choreography across the Berlin city map suggested a dynamism of motion that exceeded Paris's leisurely and *flaneurial* pace. These panoramas facilitated a quick grasp of essential sites and helped process the era's sense of a shifting dynamic between space and time.

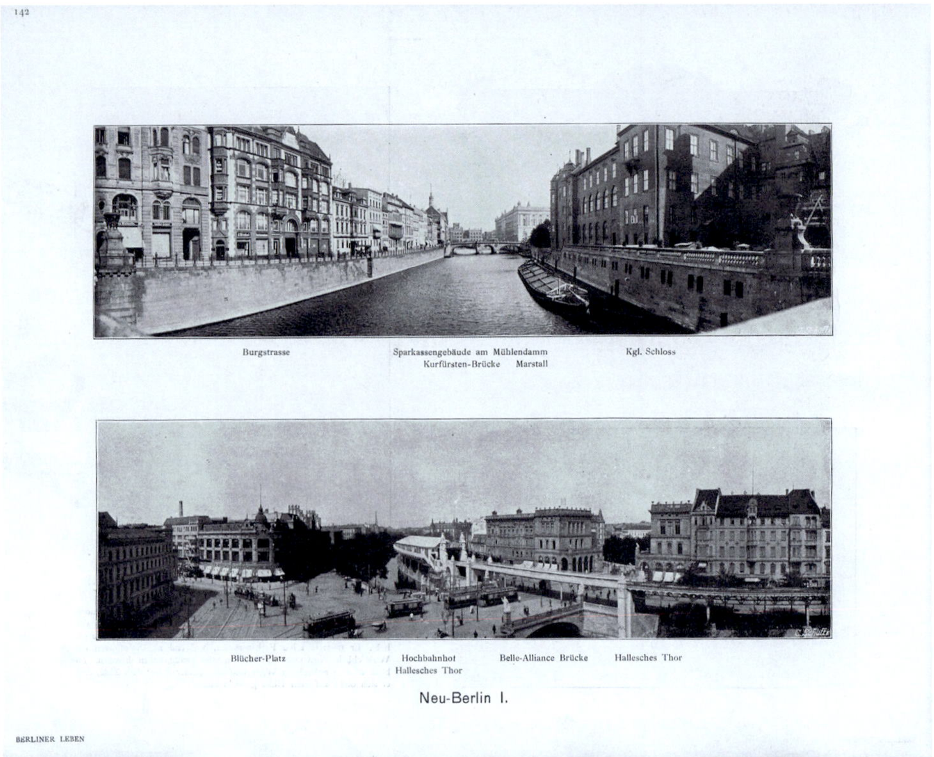

a

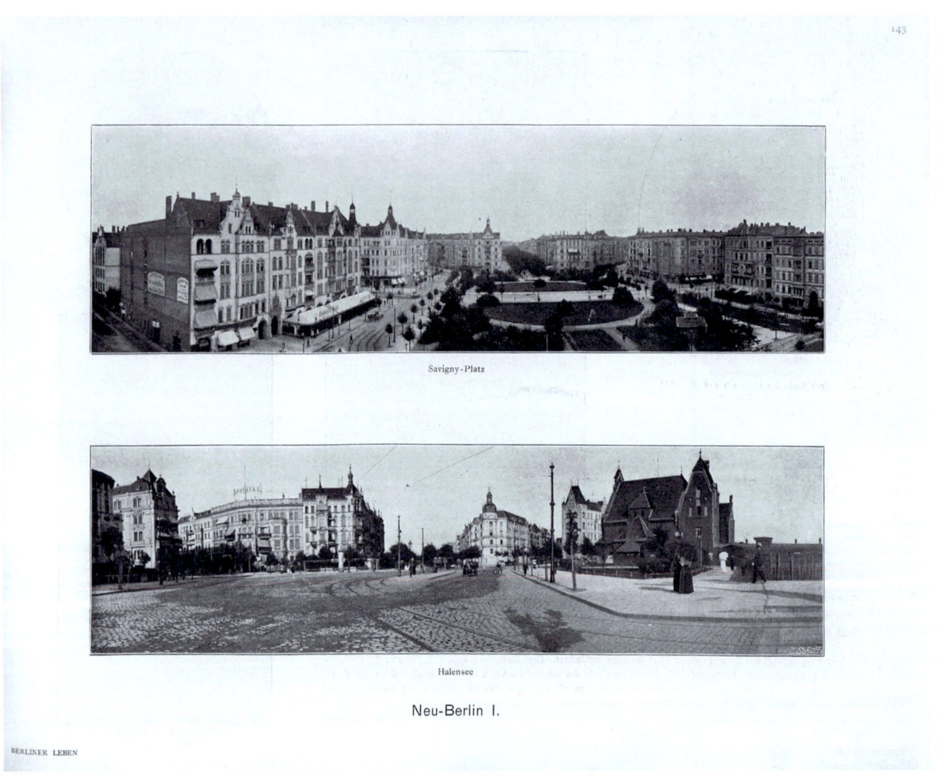

b

Figure 1.16. Four photographic panoramas, "New Berlin I," *Berliner Leben* 4 (1901): 142–43. Digitized by the Zentral- und Landesbibliothek Berlin, 2016. https://digital.zlb.de.

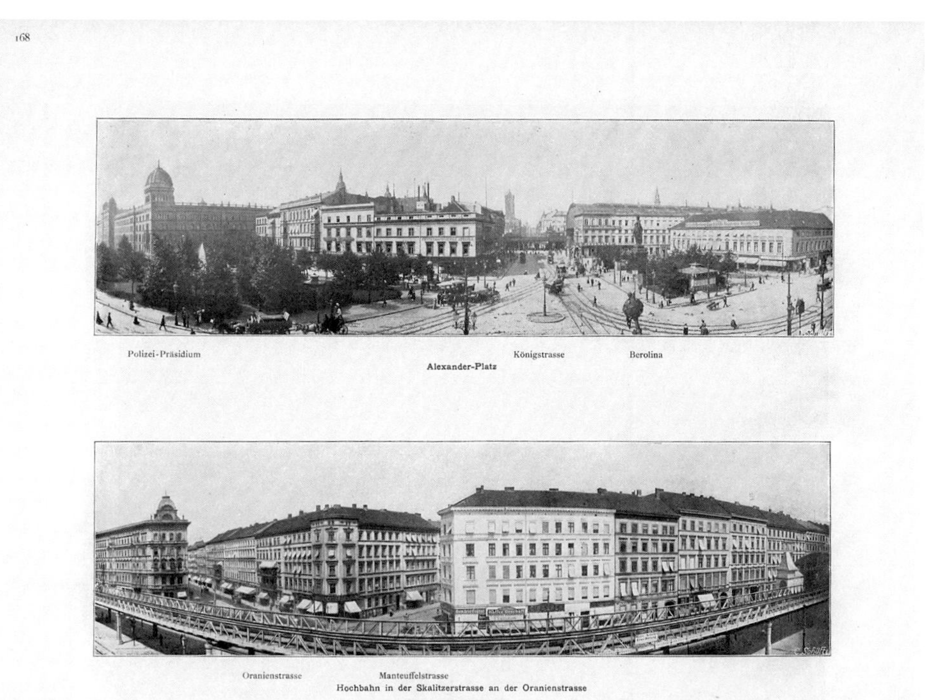

a

169

Altes Museum Schloss-Brücke Dom Lustgarten Königliches Schloss National-Denkmal
Schlossfreiheit

Königgrätzerstrasse Leipzigerstrasse Königgrätzerstrasse
Potsdamer Platz
Neu-Berlin II.

BERLINER LEBEN

Originalaufnahmen des „Berliner Leben".

b

Figure 1.17. Four photographic panoramas, "New Berlin II," *Berliner Leben* 4 (1901): 168–69. Digitized by the Zentral- und Landesbibliothek Berlin, 2016. https://digital.zlb.de.

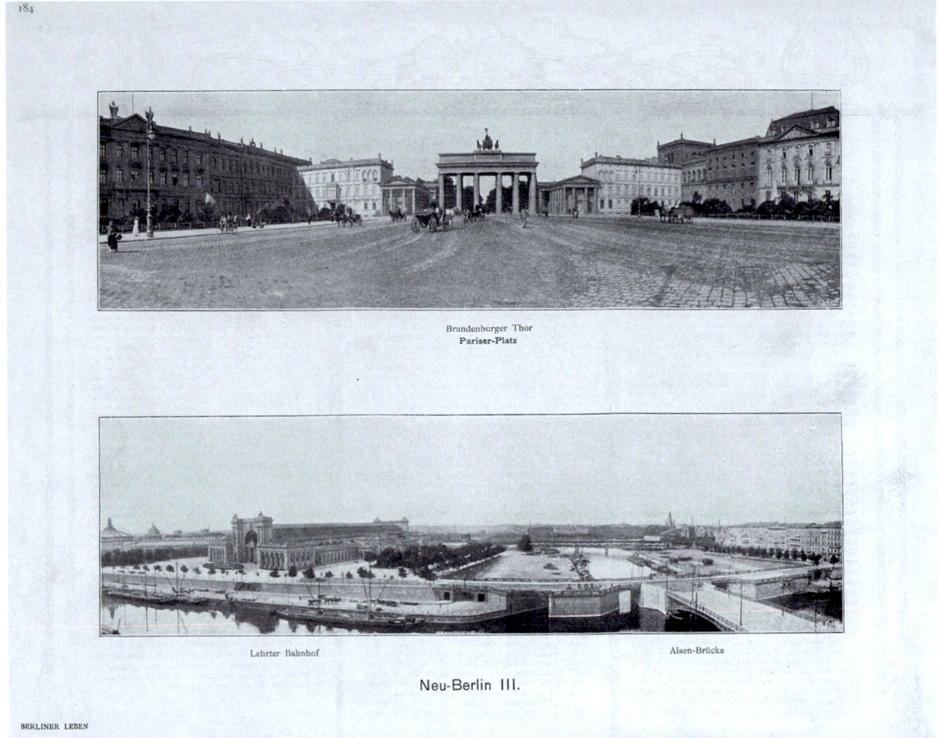

a

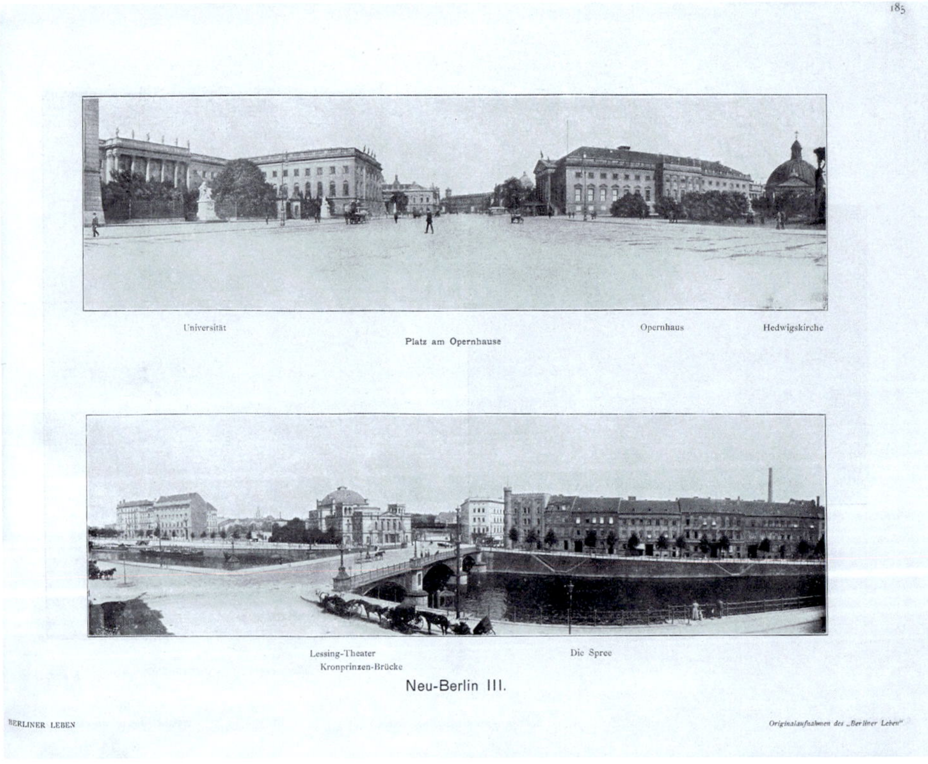

b

Figure 1.18. Four photographic panoramas, "New Berlin III," *Berliner Leben* 4 (1901): 184–85. Digitized by the Zentral- und Landesbibliothek Berlin, 2016. https://digital.zlb.de.

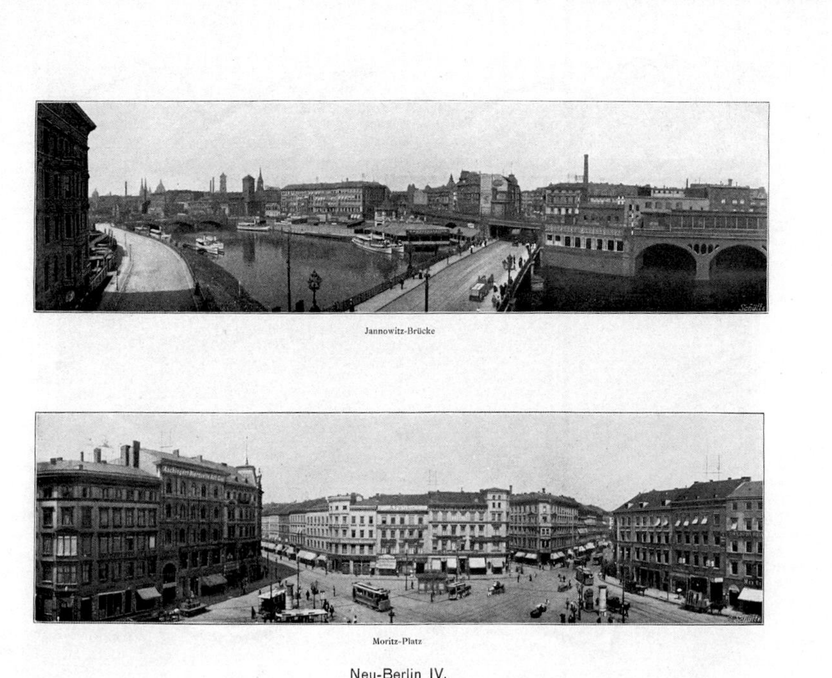

BERLINER LEBEN

Originalaufnahmen des „Berliner Leben“

a

211

Mariannen-Platz

Lützow-Platz

Neu-Berlin IV.

BERLINER LEBEN

Originalaufnahmen des „Berliner Leben“.

b

Figure 1.19. Four photographic panoramas, "New Berlin IV," *Berliner Leben* 4 (1901): 210–11. Digitized by the Zentral- und Landesbibliothek Berlin, 2016. https://digital.zlb.de.

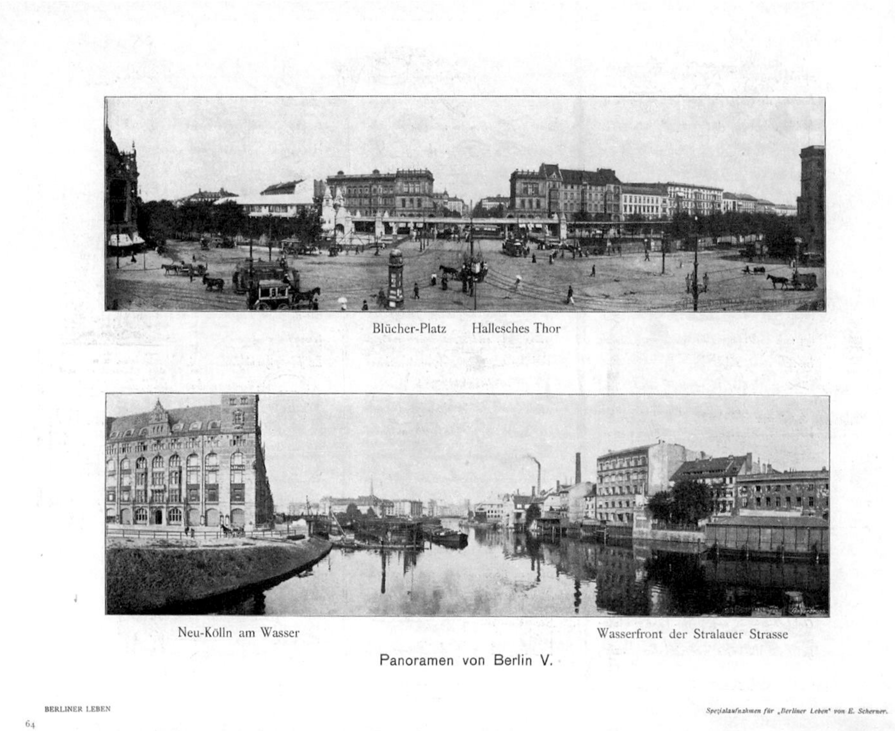

Figure 1.20. Two photographic panoramas, "New Berlin V," *Berliner Leben* 5 (1902): 64. Digitized by the Zentral- und Landesbibliothek Berlin, 2016. https://digital.zlb.de.

A new consciousness for Berlin's official aesthetically refined city center and the modern new traffic infrastructure emerges when one takes a closer look at two of these panoramas. One shows a sweeping view that surveyed the Museum Island and the city castle (see the upper panorama of Figure 1.17b).[43] This image belies a noticeable pleasure taken by its photographer in embracing the distortions generated by the convergence of the wide-angle lens and the panoramic camera. The photographer chose a dramatically elevated standpoint, and created, thanks to the camera's technology, a sweeping, 180-degree aerial view. This look at the heart of Berlin was, like the other images in this series, featured in an extreme horizontal format and captured the most important historical monuments and contemporary structures of this era: starting on the left with Karl Friedrich Schinkel's Old Museum (1823–30), the Berliner Dom (Collegiate Church, 1893–1905), Lustgarten (Pleasure Garden), Schloßbrücke (Castle Bridge), the city castle, and ending with the National Monument to Wilhelm I

(1895–97) on the far right. While the photographer's exact viewpoint was hard to determine, it was most likely taken from the rooftop of a bank building across the Kupfergraben waterway as the balustrade to the very left indicates, as well as the vicinity to the water.[44]

The convincing choice of elevated viewpoint, use of camera, and pictorial effect in this image becomes apparent when comparing it with the more comprehensive panoramas by Meydenbauer and Ziegra discussed earlier. Their more traditional panoramic pursuit depicted 180- and 360-degree views of the city but lacked the symbolic charge of the "New Berlin" image, which was obtained by the contrasting topography of Berlin's most important architectural monuments and their almost textbook-like display and chronological ordering of architectural styles.

Georg Bartels's wide-angle panoramic view of the same site from the 1890s is instructional in comparison as it was created with an entirely different intention (Figure 1.21). Focusing on the immediately visible buildings and capturing the site of the Wilhelm monument, the Schloßfreiheit, before its demolition from street level, his was a survey photograph rather than a promotional grand-style image. Bartels was interested in the city's historic layers, its vanishing and transforming neighborhoods. His pursuit of Berlin was both as professional photographer and at times as an amateur preservationist, which led to a diverse body of work that encompassed the old, the new, the center, and the fringe of the city.

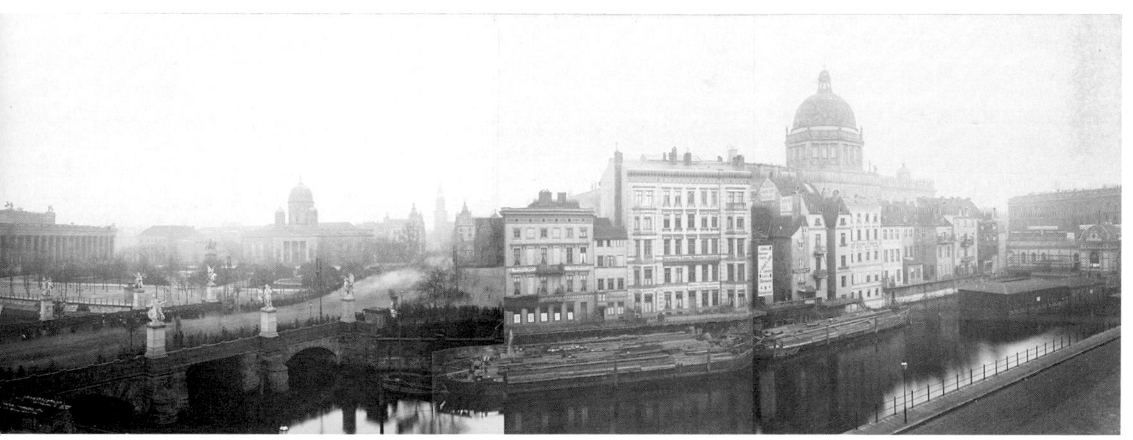

Figure 1.21. Georg Bartels, *Schloßfreiheit Wasserseite* (Waterfront of *Schloßfreiheit* building complex), 1890. Photograph, 17.1 × 23.1 cm. Inventory number XI 3808. Copyright Stiftung Stadtmuseum Berlin. Photograph by Michael Setzpfandt, Berlin.

Another *Berlin Life* panorama features the intersection of old and new Berlin. It shows the Blücher square, the Hallesches Tor elevated train station, Belle-Alliance Bridge, and Hallesches Tor (see the lower panorama of Figure 1.16a).[45] Hallesches Tor station was one of a handful of exceptionally elaborate designs for elevated stops that were conceptualized according to more ambitious aesthetic guidelines than most of the other stations, which followed a standard, practical design. Originally assigned to esteemed architect Alfred Messel (whose design seemed not to have fulfilled the funders' expectations), architects Solf & Wichards created a design that per its clients' wishes, did not divert attention away from the two modern gate buildings that had recently replaced the original Hallesches Tor. The potentially distracting station hall was rendered less dominant by decorative elements on gables and pillars.[46]

The wide-angled image of the station and gate particularly benefits from the photograph's pronounced horizontality. Here it is marked by the elevated railway, which is further emphasized by the photographer's raised viewpoint. Its elongated lateral form is intersected by the tram tracks crossing Belle-Alliance Bridge and framed in the center right by the two cubic markers of the new Halle Gate buildings. The rondelle of Belle-Alliance Plaza is faintly visible, tucked behind the gate's opening, though the plaza can be seen more clearly in the second panorama of this site in the 1902 volume (see the upper panorama of Figure 1.20). This was one of three *Berlin Life* panoramas that depict Berlin's brand-new elevated train line. By 1900, Berlin, according to Baedeker's 1904 guide, had turned into "the most important railway center and one of Germany's eminent trading places and perhaps the first industrial city on the continent."[47] This development, as well as the city's rapid growth beyond its original borders, placed significant pressure on the city to manage and expand its public transportation system.

Formally and aesthetically, the photograph's distinctly horizontal orientation was contrasted by the iconographies of two historic and contemporary paintings that focused on the circular shape of the Belle-Alliance rondelle instead. Belle-Alliance Plaza was depicted in paintings in the eighteenth and early twentieth centuries. Dismar Degen's painting of Friedrichstadt rondelle and Halle Gate from a bird's-eye perspective (1734) (Figure 1.22) projected the absolutist "Soldier King's" vision of a controlled expansion of the city,[48] while, two hundred years later, Ernst Ludwig Kirchner's *The Belle-Alliance Plaza in Berlin* (1914) (Figure 1.23) was an expressionist "aestheticization of urban life."[49]

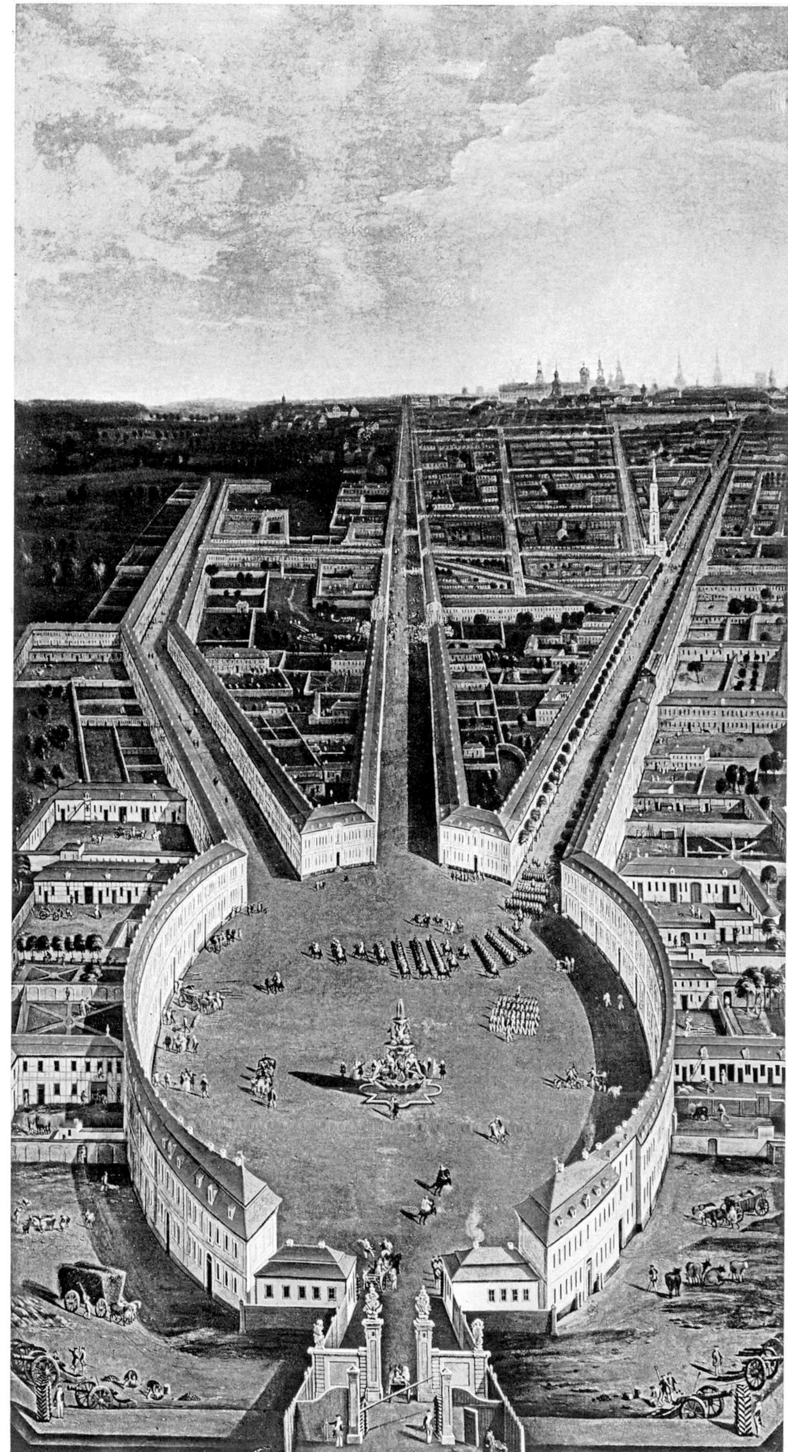

Figure 1.22. Dismar Degen, *Das Rondell in der südlichen Friedrichstadt* (The plaza [Belle-Alliance Platz] in southern Friedrichstadt, Berlin), 1734. Oil on canvas, 232 × 123 cm. Former property of Märkische Museum, XI 28093, war loss. Reproduction of a heliogravure from Franz Jahn, *Drei Jahrhunderte Baukunst in Berlin*, 1939. Staatliche Museen zu Berlin, Preußischer Kulturbesitz, Berlin. bpk Bildagentur / Staatliche Museen zu Berlin, Preußischer Kulturbesitz, Berlin / Art Resource, NY.

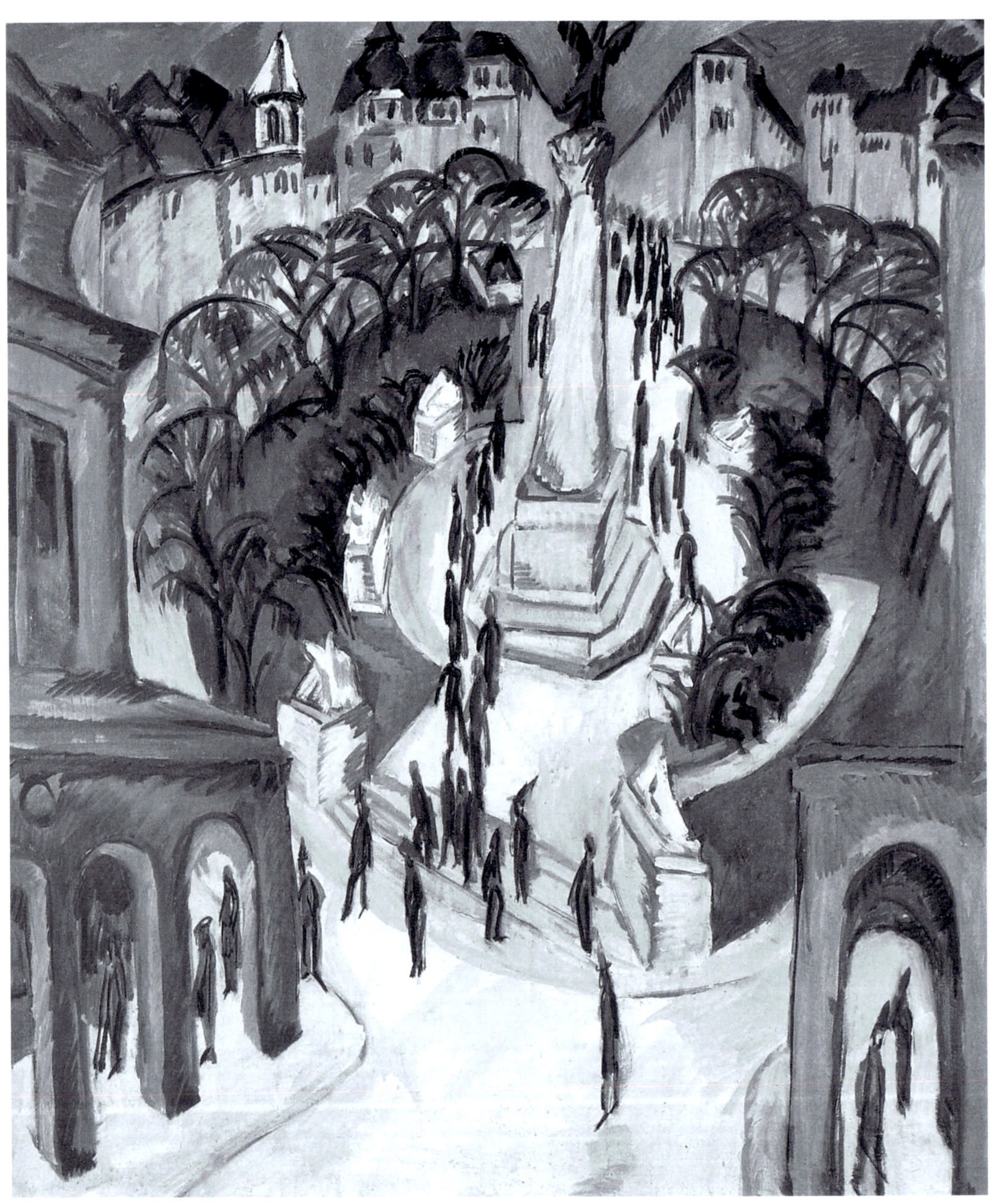

Figure 1.23. Ernst Ludwig Kirchner, *Belle-Alliance-Platz*, 1914. Oil on canvas, 96 × 85 cm. Berlin Nationalgalerie, SMPK. Inv. B 129. Wikimedia Commons.

The photograph in *Berlin Life* was neither able to nor interested in reciprocating Degen's projection or echoing and anticipating a consciously aestheticized impressionist, pictorialist, or expressionist approach. The panoramic, wide-angled image was a complex fusion of a faithful representation and its deliberate dramatization through technical means. The photograph's emphasis here shifted away from an iconic urban marker to the dynamic of the elevated line and station, which, at the time of the photograph's creation, was still under construction. Like Degen and Kirchner, the photographer took an elevated standpoint, but the photograph suggested neither an orderly and well-structured nor an emotionally charged urban situation. Instead, it displayed a vibrant dynamism and liveliness. The image's deliberate distortion dramatized the event, and the elevated train tracks appear to be slightly bent. The plaza and formerly constricting gate lost its centrality as one gazed cityward, toward the exciting action of urban commerce, entertainment, and spectacle.

This strategy completely shifted the viewer's focus away from a centralized plan and toward the former periphery. The city, this photograph suggested, was no longer determined by its strategic function or its inner order, but by its well-functioning infrastructure, accessibility, and connectivity with other places. This photograph emphasized that via the elevated trains, the urban dweller could have a high-speed experience of Berlin as he or she flipped through *Berlin Life*. The Berlin metro ("U-Bahn") was designed as a "place of contact and turnover" for business.[50] It was a means of transport that was popular until the motor car became common among the better-to-do members of the middle class. However, such infrastructure was exclusive in its way, as it benefited only a fragment of the city's populace; the elevated passengers were predominantly businessmen and higher-ranking government employees.

Berlin Life's mass-reproduced panoramas linked Berlin with American cities and produced a visual rebuke to critics like Mark Twain. In the sweeping, dynamic *Berlin Life* panoramas, the viewer's position differed from any spectator experience of a classic panorama or diorama. As viewers "read" these images, they were engaged with the city without any physical action. With the "New Berlin" image of Berlin's inner city through the photographic fish eye, the photographer achieved the projection of a field of vision into the flat plane, which only fifty years earlier would have required a presentation in the round and kinetic action on the part of the observer.

The elevated perspective and the use of the wide-angle lens, which distanced the image's subject matter, enhanced the possibility of an all-encompassing image, a kind of ordering and organizing of what had become the city's "incoherent form."[51] Motion was reintroduced to the visual experience in the form of the dance-like circuits of the sites' location sequence on Berlin's map for *Berlin Life* readers who traced the sites of the different panoramas both according to their appearance and from volume to volume. Following the editorial suggestions of *Berlin Life*, such chronology was not determined by the age of the architecture or city quarters depicted, but rather by the sequence of images and volumes. Beauty was reintroduced into the modern city through the meandering motions of the urban explorer on his way between city castle and Halensee, Lehrter Railway Station and Halle Gate Elevated Station, and back to Brandenburg Gate. This new urban "ornament" or image-editorial choreography might have been what the educator and critic Willi Warstat had in mind when he thought about the city as a "restless, yet strong and lively creature."[52]

As readers of *Berlin Life* opened a new issue with four more panoramas, they embarked on a journey across a city that was overwhelmingly busy and ever changing. Images of modern and historic sites created the illusion of comprehension—an ability to negotiate this "unintelligible mess,"[53] which must have been simultaneously consoling, exhilarating, and distressing. Urban orientation seemed to be defined through new parameters. Instead of focusing on reading the city based on its significant urban monuments that were anchored in a consistent urban fabric, as Meydenbauer and Ziegra had done, or visualizing the passage into the city or within it, a strategy the Baedeker recommended, *Berlin Life*'s cityscapes suggested that its readers split their attention between monuments and important sites and—seen from the window of an elevated train—the city's modern edges. This strategy intended to raise the city's "imageability," as urban historian Kevin Lynch terms it in his seminal book *The Image of the City* (1960),[54] but the strategy required an observer's *divided* attention.

This new spatial experience and novel visual language corresponded with the leveling effect of the turn of the century's *Zeitgeist*. Georg Simmel described a kind of emotional flattening as communication became more rationalized in urban environments, and a certain degree of indifference toward individual qualities and traits affected aesthetic expression. The city formed the urban dweller through new impressions; the city's dynamic "seeped into the pores of existence and detached one's identity from a way of life focused on nature."[55] This echoes the annihilation of space while accelerating time that Wolfgang Schivelbusch has identified in early nineteenth-century literature and scholarship.[56]

But photographers were not daunted by their reconfiguring environment; they appropriated the city to their creative advantage via the panoramic camera and wide-angle lens. They invented the city anew and successfully managed to sell it to the masses as reality. A song in *Berlin Life* celebrating the illustrated journal's claims for truthfulness and authenticity made its intentions clear and revealed its editors' acute awareness of their command over the city's image:

> If you never saw the Residence of the King but would like to see it, fulfillment is nearing, and you needn't even go there; as an ultramodern journal evolved to truthfully depict Berlin in nature-like images, elaborate and made by artists' hand. It shows you copies of it all, elevating your heart and spirits; through truthfulness and without fabrication, that is *Berlin Life*, through truthfulness and without fabrication, that is *Berlin Life*.[57]

The notion that *Berlin Life* presented images objectively, untouched by "fabrication," or "*Phantasie*," as the German text called it, was of course a stylization and conscious interpretation of the city according to the journal's editors. This rhetoric, editorial image-layout, and powerful iconography constructed a vital, holistic, organic image of a city that in actuality was fragmented and heterogeneous.[58] Foreigners like Twain, Huard, Gersal, and de Staël, along with local observers such as Karl Scheffler, Friedrich Fuchs, and Werner Hegemann, sensed this disconnect, but panoramic imagery's expression of tidiness held sway over the majority of its viewers.

TWO

Framing Progress

Ludwig Hoffmann, Ernst von Brauchitsch, and Berlin Architectural Photography, 1902–1912

> Seeing is thinking, in the sense that it is a discriminating and constructive activity: it creates patterns of reality adapted to human purposes.
>
> —YI-FU TUAN, "Place: An Experiential Perspective"

Architectural imagery—the elevation, plan, or perspectival representation of buildings—is a kind of fiction, fabricated like the image of a city, as discussed in the previous chapter. Architects have used such pictorial conventions for centuries, and photographers have adopted and adjusted them to their advantage.

Seeing, Thinking, Building

Architectural photography in Berlin at the turn of the twentieth century opened a new chapter in the understanding of both mediums. The city architect Ludwig Hoffmann's civic architecture and his exclusive photographer Ernst von Brauchitsch's depictions produced a unique image of the city that redefined the meaning of architectural representation. Their close collaboration embodies Yi-Fu Tuan's astute observations of how seeing and thinking constitute space. Their joint "purpose" was the creation of a measured and sovereign Berlin image; of a city ready to be counted as peer to other metropolises in Europe. However, without the interpretation through Brauchitsch's photographs, Hoffmann's work would most likely have fallen even more readily into oblivion than it already did after World War I. This collaborative project demonstrates that the "urban image," as human geographers and urban sociologists have come to understand it, can be interpreted through architectural photography as both a creative and a generative process.

Soon after Ludwig Hoffmann, the city architect of Berlin since 1896, published the first volume of his heavily illustrated publication *Neubauten der Stadt Berlin* (*New Buildings of the City of Berlin*) in 1902 (Figure 2.1), the volume became an important promotional tool for the city. The city magistrate generously sent *Neubauten*, and subsequent issues by Hoffmann, to the royal court, national and local governments, several state agencies, and architects and critics.[1] They were also nationally and internationally distributed to architecture schools, building and planning agencies, and libraries.

Ludwig Hoffmann and Ernst von Brauchitsch's collaboration conveys the profound changes that both photography and architecture underwent during these decades, as well as the deep shifts in these men's respective professions. The volatility of turn-of-the-century Berlin culture became the backdrop for

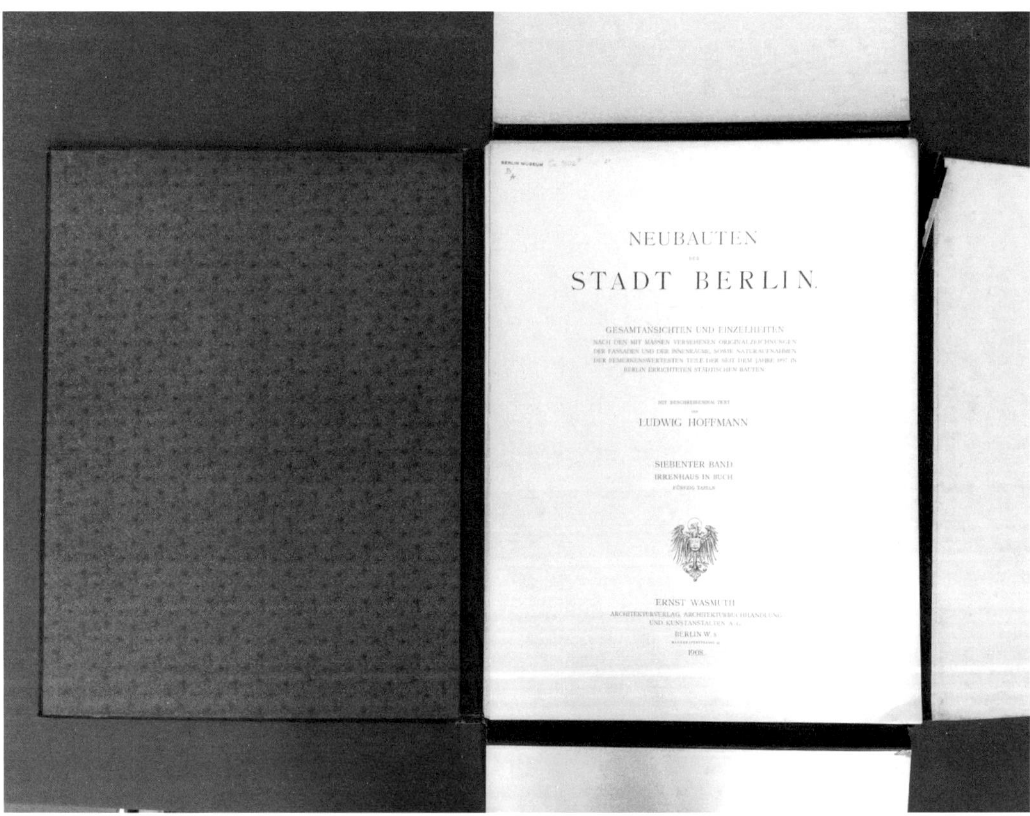

Figure 2.1. Ludwig Hoffmann, with photographs by Ernst von Brauchitsch, *Neubauten der Stadt Berlin*, cover of vol. 7, *Irrenanstalt Buch* (Berlin: Wasmuth, 1908). Stiftung Stadtmuseum, Bibliothek. Photograph by the author.

Hoffmann's rise to fame and enormous recognition, but also to his fall from grace and the emergence of Bauhaus modernism after World War I, which rejected his work as "refined eclecticism" and "mediocre."[2] Brauchitsch's style combined the matter-of-fact language of architectural photography with a subtle and poetic pictorialism, an approach that faded after the war, replaced by more instantaneous and journalistic approaches and an understanding of photography as a medium with its own inherent aesthetic language.

Hoffmann's power, and limitations, set the framework for architectural development in Berlin, and he found a "congenial interpreter of his work" in Brauchitsch.[3] For decades, their close collaboration produced a symbiotic relationship, as Brauchitsch became the eloquent translator for Hoffmann's architectural vision.[4] Brauchitsch carefully chose his viewpoints and lighting conditions and managed to isolate buildings or building complexes and details in a way that affirmed their exquisite and tightly planned character. Brauchitsch emerges as a photographer who employed his artistry as a mediating tool that at times seemed to preempt the criticisms that Hoffmann's work received in the second half of his tenure. Instinctively anticipating public responses to Hoffmann's buildings, Brauchitsch created a second architectural narrative that bolstered Hoffmann's work—and the city image—by adding pictorial and scenographic oomph.

Pursuing Architecture and Photography circa 1900

The appreciation for and documentation of Berlin and its architecture date back to the eighteenth century, when the coauthors Johann Christoph Müller and Georg Gottfried Küster as well as Friedrich Nicolai first described and illustrated Berlin's historic churches, castles, bridges, and public and residential buildings.[5] Later on, several illustrated guidebooks and inventories used both etchings and photographs, indicating a shift in purpose from a representational to a more preservationist agenda. Publications of urban photographs in special portfolios created after the turn of the century often enhanced such preservationist intentions through a distinctly aestheticized presentation.

Since the first daguerreotypes and talbotypes of buildings, architectural photography had been understood as immediately attached to the architecture that it depicted, and thus inherently determined by that architecture (Figure 2.2). By the 1850s, the use of architectural photographers on construction sites was fairly

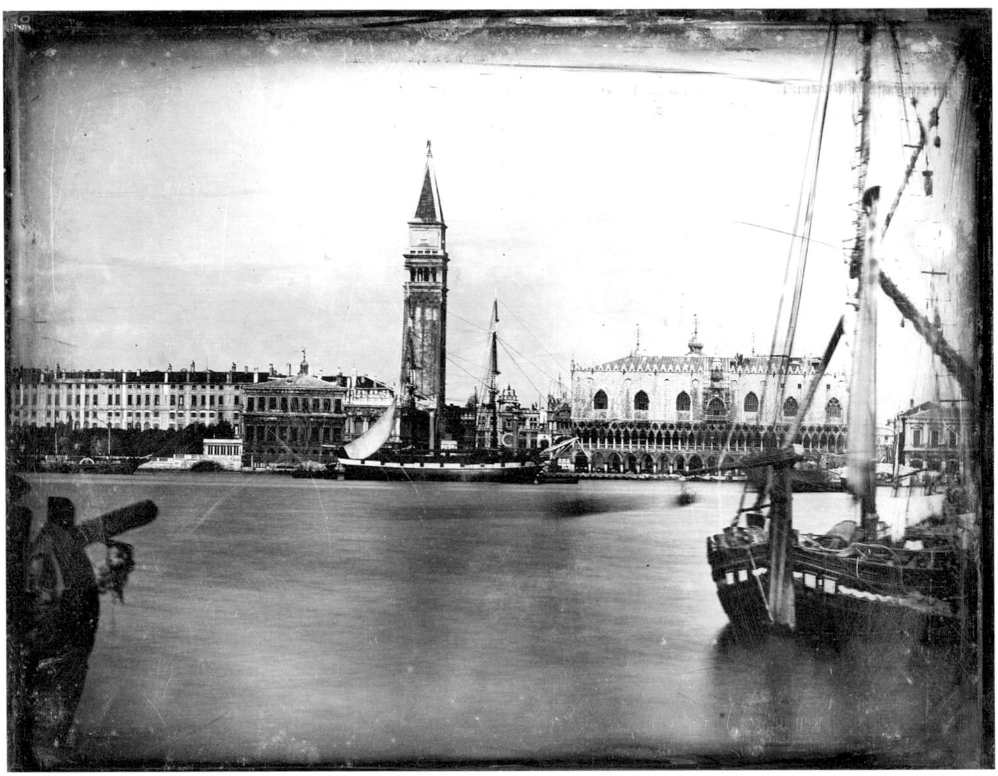

Figure 2.2. John Ruskin and Le Cavalier Iller, *Venice: The Ducal Palace, the Zecca, and the Campanile with Moored Ships in Foreground,* circa 1851. Half-plate daguerreotype. Le Cavalier Iller was a professional photographer who collaborated with Ruskin. Photograph by and copyright K. and J. Jacobson, Essex, UK.

common.[6] The basic dynamic between photography and architecture, in which architecture was understood as the main protagonist and photography as the capable, yet indifferent, aid, would persist for at least the next five decades.

Architectural photography production in Germany was a well-formed and well-established enterprise by the late nineteenth century. In Berlin, Leopold Ahrendts (1825–70) (Figure 2.3), a contemporary of the Frenchman Édouard Baldus, photographed the most important monuments of the baroque and neoclassical eras and received overwhelming praise for his command of photo technique and the clarity, tonal range, and "artistic" quality of his stunning albumen and salted paper prints.[7] Ahrendts was a former draftsman, painter, and lithographer, a training and background that was typical for the first wave of entrepreneurial photographers.

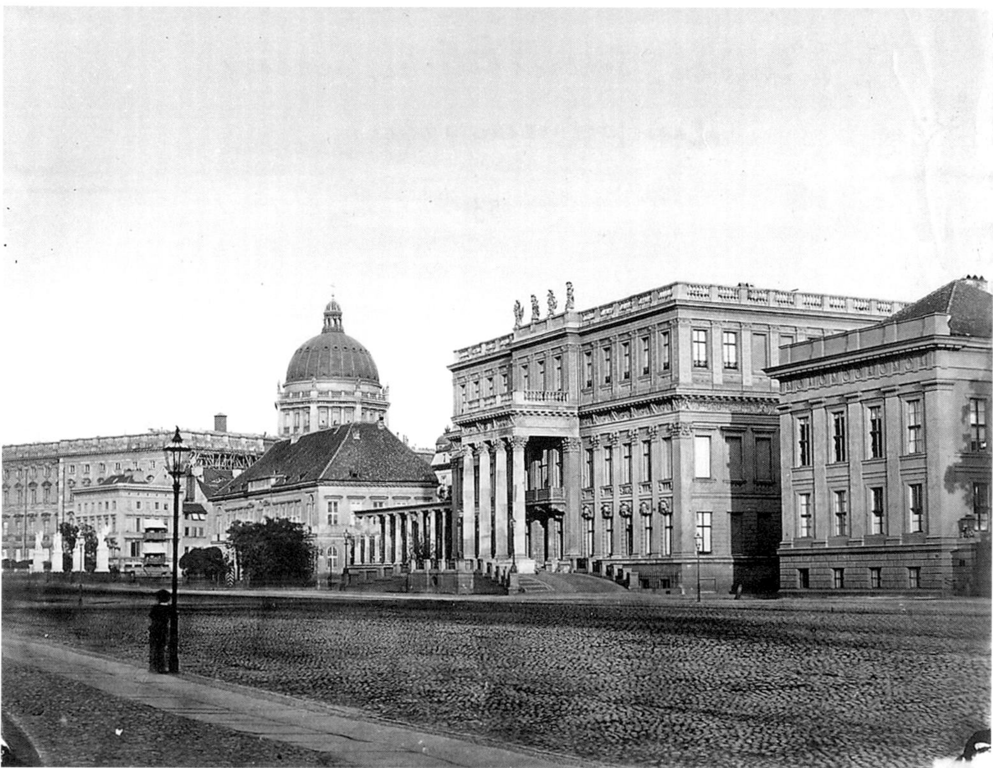

Figure 2.3. Leopold Ahrendts, Unter den Linden with the Palais of Count Friedrich Wilhelm von Preußen, the Commandantura, and the city castle, 1857. Photographic salt print. Copyright Stiftung Stadtmuseum Berlin. Photographic Collection, inventory number GE 2004/254 VF.

Hermann Rückwardt's (1845–1919) architectural photography also played an important role in the discourse of the medium at the end of the nineteenth century (Figure 2.4). His great commercial success was indicative of a new type of professionalism that employed and embraced modern photographic and reproductive technologies to their fullest capacity. The works of Ahrendts and Rückwardt demonstrate that a successful career as an architectural photographer required sensitivities to pictorial conventions of architectural representation and a keen awareness of both photographic and photo-reproductive technologies. Ahrendts's and Rückwardt's other successors include F. Albert Schwartz, Georg Bartels, Max Missmann, and Waldemar Titzenthaler, all of whom were crucial in transmitting distinct interpretations of the city and its architecture from the late 1870s to the early 1900s. These photographers all

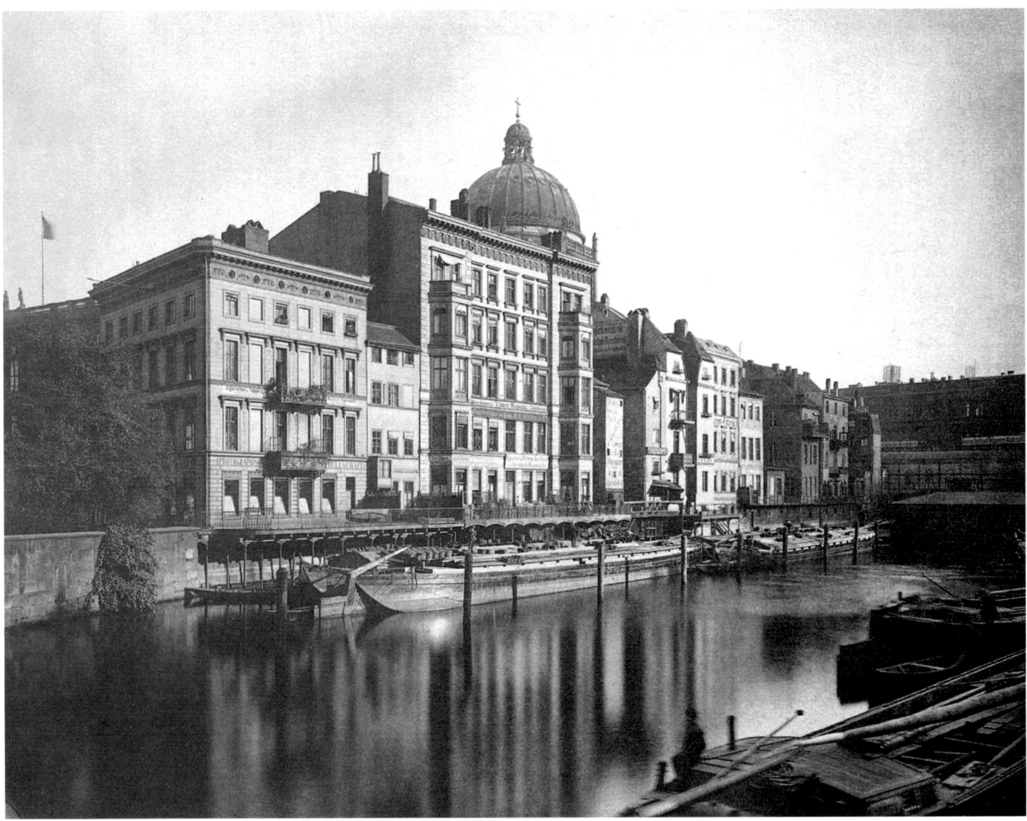

Figure 2.4. Hermann Rückwardt, the Schloßfreiheit building complex's waterfront at Kupfergraben, with the city castle's dome in background, circa 1890. Photograph on carton, 13.7 × 19.9 cm. Wikimedia Commons.

shared the professional routine of dragging large, tripod-supported cameras and handling fragile glass-plate negatives in order to perform their work. Such work rituals began to shift as more affordable handheld cameras and roll film entered the market by the 1890s.

Around 1900, photographers struggled to situate their medium within technological and artistic discourses. Disciplines and genres such as architectural photography and landscape photography were regarded as parts of different professional and aesthetic realms and practices. Both genres were akin to, and imbued with, old pictorial conventions. However, architectural photography was regarded as objective, scientific, and generated mostly through technical procedures, while landscape photography was practiced by affluent amateurs and assisted by new elaborate printing techniques and was therefore elevated into the realm of art.[8]

By the time that Ludwig Hoffmann (1852–1932) was elected as Berlin's official city architect in 1896, Ernst von Brauchitsch (1856–1932) had already photo-documented Hoffmann's first large and significant project, Leipzig's Imperial Court House (1887–95).[9] Brauchitsch became central to crafting an image, and eventually to creating a legacy, for Hoffmann (Figure 2.5). Hoffmann, who urban historian Dieter Hoffmann-Axthelm once labeled a "city-image architect" (*Stadtbild-Baumeister*),[10] would not have been understood with the same depth as his contemporaries if not for Brauchitsch's meticulous, exacting, and

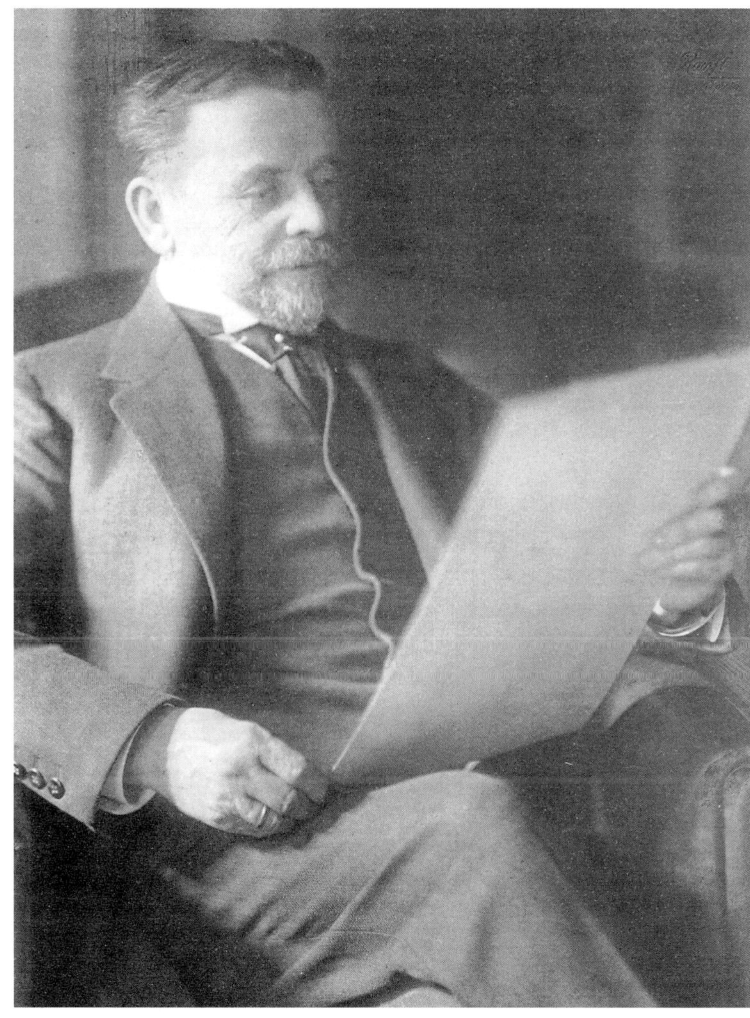

Figure 2.5. Ernst von Brauchitsch, photograph of Ludwig Hoffmann, circa 1910. Photogravure. Wikimedia Commons.

aesthetically stunning photographs, which were disseminated, besides in the volumes for Hoffmann, through portfolios and architectural publications.

Photography's appropriation by the architectural profession was part of a larger shift in photo-aesthetic debates of the 1880s, 1890s, and early 1900s—this process corresponded with changes that were taking place within architecture. Hoffmann was chosen as city architect based on his style, reliability, and professionalism. His relationship to his photographer was shaped by the conditions for public architecture that he faced when starting his job in Berlin. Hoffmann was part of the last generation of what his biographer Dörte Döhl calls "bureaucrat-architects," state-employed architects *(Beamte)* who had been the sole recipients of public project commissions. During the 1890s, these conditions changed as the architectural profession in Prussia and Germany increasingly opened such commissions to private architecture firms. Their new, more competitive approach to city contracts introduced experimentation with innovative material, aesthetic, and architectonic concepts that were funded by private sponsors. This shift, while not directly threatening Hoffmann's work, would have impacted his standing among his peers and most likely inspired Brauchitsch's impetus to explore new creative imaging strategies to establish the significance of Hoffmann's work.

During Hoffmann's twenty-eight-year tenure, he was solely responsible for determining the scope and aesthetics of a project; he faced no competition from rival architects. In exchange for this power, Hoffmann was not allowed to have a private practice. This tight professional framework afforded Hoffmann a great deal of authority within his department, and he used this quasi-monopoly over public architecture to completely restructure his department and to create a tightly controlled system in which he determined working standards and formal rules.[11] Hoffmann's microcosm did not leave much space for dissent, which meant that conflicts with subordinates occasionally led to dismissal or transfer to another department. Those who adopted the new rules stayed and were rewarded by, among other things, having their buildings included in the *Neubauten* portfolio publications.[12]

Hoffmann formulated his own understanding of contemporaneous architecture in an era when architectural historicism was ceding to the advance of art nouveau, the beginnings of a functional, more austere modernism, and other, more pronouncedly regionalist historicisms in the architectural language of "homeland preservation" (*Heimatschutz*). An avid student of Italian Renaissance and baroque architecture, Hoffmann appreciated what he considered their authenticity for their own eras and the exquisite craftsmanship that each exhibited. While he emphatically rejected any form of superficial historicism as a form of façade decoration and was indifferent toward the latest art nouveau or German Jugendstil aesthetic, he embraced a rejuvenation of architecture through the reconsideration of traditional models of historic styles. To Hoffmann, substantiating a contemporary sensibility and experience through the employment of historic forms and building methods, rather than simply copying previous expressions, was the best approach for designing hospitals, schools, public baths, and other public structures. Hoffmann's core focus was a "clear, unceremonious plan disposition, which would address needs in the simplest fashion." Crucial for the artistic impression was the "absolute scale, material treatment, and alignment of the profiles."[13]

Hoffmann aimed to erect buildings that would operate as visual markers and signifiers of bourgeois taste and of a civilized and cultured society. But unlike his contemporaries in private practice, such as Alfred Messel or Peter Behrens, who are known today for groundbreaking design, Hoffmann's executive range was limited to specific building projects; planning was the public works service office's responsibility. This role also distinguished him from Paris's city planner, Baron Haussmann, who had the authority to make major incisions into the city's structure. More than other official architects or planners, Hoffmann staged effects through composition and the use of historic components. Hoffmann-Axthelm describes Hoffmann's realm of influence as being limited to the "strategic occupation of important spots for the city image."[14] As a consequence, Hoffmann relied on buildings that "through their emblematic character spoke of state, history, urban community, of dignity and history, of fate and the past."[15]

Neubauten der Stadt Berlin—New Buildings of the City of Berlin

Over a period of ten years, Ludwig Hoffmann put together a series of eleven portfolios titled *Neubauten der Stadt Berlin* (*New Buildings of the City of Berlin*) and employed Brauchitsch as his photographer. Between 1902 and 1912, Brauchitsch produced one new volume of *Neubauten* almost annually, depicting "total views and details . . . of the most remarkable urban buildings erected in Berlin since 1897."[16]

This generously produced publication was a unique documentation of communal building efforts. It differed from other architectural publications in that it did not concentrate on information about costs, duration of construction, details or unique qualities of construction, materials, and building necessities, but rather on the aesthetics of the buildings and sites.[17] This focus was also made apparent through Hoffmann's comments, which continuously strove to rectify a common notion that publicly used architecture (*Nutzarchitektur*) was only to be judged according to its functionality.[18] Hoffmann aimed for architectural clarity and comprehensibility and the avoidance of unnecessary elements, both of which directly figured into his editorial concept.[19]

Each large-format, dark-brown-clad volume (ca. 51 × 45 cm) included fifty collotype plates (40 × 30 cm) and an insert with a few pages of introductory text by Hoffmann that was accompanied by smaller, cropped images by Brauchitsch. Hoffmann's drawings and Brauchitsch's photographs of various structural details were displayed side by side in the plates section. Images alternated with plans, sections, and detail drawings (*Bauzeichnungen*) (Figure 2.6). Occasionally, a double-page-size foldout elevation or plan was included.

Hoffmann very deliberately chose a large format and complex design, which featured different visual and text materials. He also made a point of not distinguishing between small and large tasks and projects, and to assign entire volumes to exceptional projects such as the Rudolf Virchow Hospital (volume 6), the Insane Asylum in Buch (volume 7), the Märkische Museum (volume 8), and the new City Hall, or Stadthaus (volume 10). Smaller projects included an asylum for children, a public bath, the street-cleaning depot, several middle and high schools, a residential building, two fire engine houses, two wedding registries (volume 1), the candelabra in front of Brandenburg Gate, two public service buildings (volume 4, among others), an "old-folks home" (volume 9), and a vocational school.

Each volume's arrangement of views and drawings followed a similar pattern of movement through these spaces. In the case of important single buildings, Brauchitsch began by capturing the exteriors, alternating more comprehensive shots with detailed views, and then moving inside to focus on individual rooms, corridors, wall decorations, and sculptural ornamentation. In the case of larger

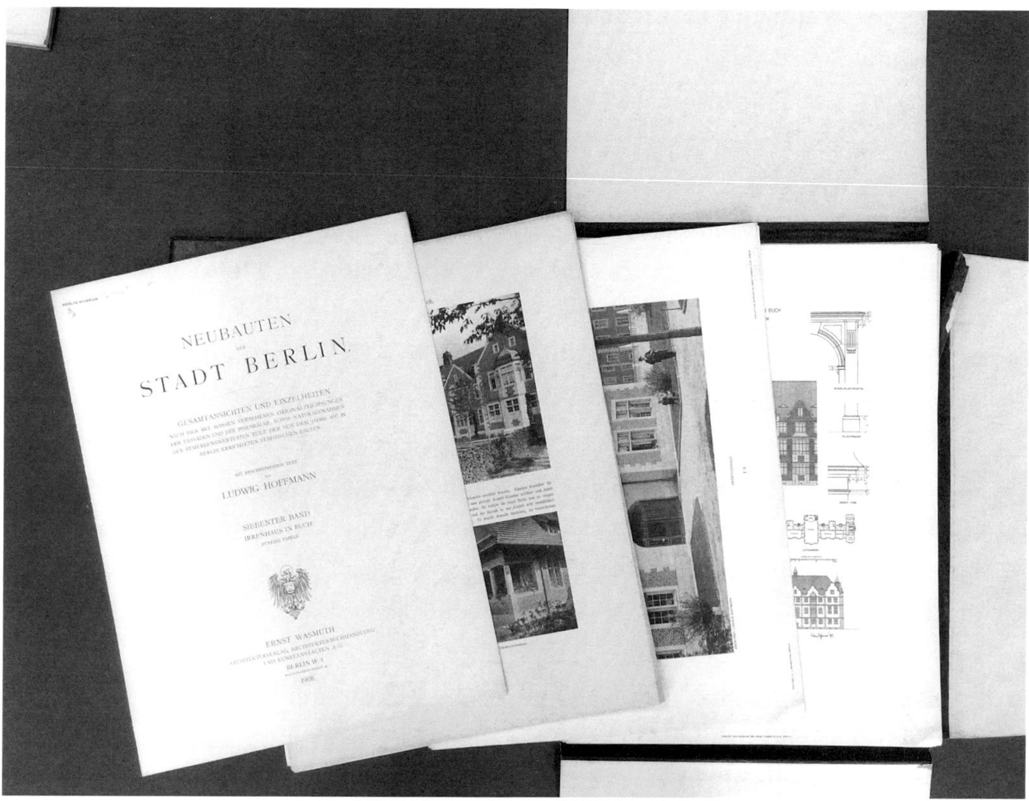

Figure 2.6. Ludwig Hoffmann, with photographs by Ernst von Brauchitsch, *Neubauten der Stadt Berlin*, parts of a portfolio. Stiftung Stadtmuseum, Bibliothek. Photograph by the author.

compounds, such as Virchow Hospital and Buch Insane Asylum, both of which were ensembles of several pavilions and residential, administrative, and infrastructural buildings, he entered through the complex's portal and progressed toward the main building, to smaller functional buildings, and, finally, to each location's chapel. Over the years, Brauchitsch created a total of about eight hundred photographs for this endeavor.

Hoffmann, who is listed as author and editor, had tight control over the project's agenda. His close management of these images was revealed in his introductory statement in the series' first volume and in a letter between the two publishing houses that were involved in printing Hoffmann's portfolios, Ernst Wasmuth and Bruno Hessling.[20] In the letter, Wasmuth, who took over the role of publisher from Hessling with the third volume in 1904, surrendered editorial control to Hoffmann. Hoffmann was to determine what Brauchitsch would photograph and would select the final set of images. In the event that a picture didn't suit Hoffmann, he was free to reject it. Wasmuth also accepted Hoffmann's request to be presented with test prints of "photographic prints as well as collotypes" before execution of the actual prints.[21]

An indication of Hoffmann's understanding of the role of Brauchitsch's illustrations can be derived from this letter and a formulation in Hoffmann's introductory text, in which he called them "renderings after nature" (*Naturaufnahmen*) of the "most important civic buildings in Berlin." Using a common and very general expression for any pictorial capture of a phenomenon, Hoffmann most likely meant by *nature* both the *environment* in a broader sense and the *naturalness*, meaning the *veracity*, of the photographic image.[22] His request to review such renderings prior to publication demonstrates his acute awareness of their importance for shaping and refining his city image. Hoffmann's trust in Brauchitsch as quasi-translator of this tightly controlled image, while never made explicit, is evident in the refined end product of the portfolios.

In 1900, Hoffmann was working on his two most ambitious projects, both of which he would conclude in 1906: the Rudolf Virchow Hospital in the Wedding district north of the city center, and a complex of several medical institutions in Berlin-Buch, a rural northern suburb of the city.[23] Both projects were developed as "hospital cities," which was the predominant form of architectural and urban design for hospital facilities around the turn of the century. It was based on the pavilion system, which had been developed during the second half of the nineteenth century. It was guided by progressive understandings of recovery and organized hospital complexes into groups of well-ventilated and light-flooded buildings that were surrounded by nature. They were operated on the outskirts of urban conglomerations and were run like autonomous economic, logistic, and urban centers.[24]

Hoffmann's design of Buch and Virchow required a logistical scope that no individual building project in the city had ever demanded. Virchow, named after the famous physician, pathologist, writer, and politician Rudolf Virchow (1821–1902), was praised as an outstanding example of a progressive and aesthetically convincing translation of the latest medical research findings into a reform-minded institutional philosophy for treatments and patient care. Emperor Wilhelm II, who bonded with Hoffmann early on, praised the Virchow Hospital as outstanding.[25] Although Buch and Virchow were created in the hospital campus spirit,[26] in Buch, Hoffmann decided against patient pavilions, pointing out that this approach was not suitable for its large number of mentally ill patients. Instead, he built larger buildings that would each house up to 175 patients.[27] Hoffmann deliberately countered the potentially unfriendly appearance of such larger buildings by choosing lively red brick combined with white seams and window frames as well as oriels and gables to emphasize this character. Architectural historian Julius Posener characterized both Virchow and Buch as "part of social reform" despite the fact that Hoffmann wasn't officially participating in the contemporary reform architecture movement.[28]

Brauchitsch's photographs, carefully tracing all aspects of Virchow (volume 6, 1907), Buch (volume 7, 1908), and later of other larger projects such as the Märkische Museum (volume 8, 1909) and City Hall (volume 10, 1911), demonstrated a consistency in quality and approach and an understanding of the vastly different characters and challenges of these projects. Virchow and Buch were captured with great attention to each project's natural context, whereas most images of other more pronouncedly urban sites were depicted in isolation from their urban context. All of Brauchitsch's images framed the architecture, choreographed each project's image sequence, deployed human figures, and responded to editorial circumstances. One of Brauchitsch's approaches for depicting large buildings was to frame them at an angle from street level and from varying distances.[29] Each of these photographs was paired with a sheet that rendered an elevation and plan and sometimes also included ornamental or building details.[30] The photograph replaced the older architectural sketch as a more efficient and faster-working instrument, while the elevation continued pictorial traditions of architectural representation, which clarified the proportions, dimensions, and details of the building.

An echo of such drawn elevations—and a manifestation of Brauchitsch's familiarity with architectural photographic conventions practiced by Rückwardt a few years earlier—can be found in Brauchitsch's full frontal photographs of buildings or façade details, such as the entrance portals for both Buch and Virchow Hospitals, as well as the City Hall's façade on Stralauer Straße (Figures 2.7 and 2.8).[31] While the previous generation of architectural photographers would have attempted to entirely isolate and rectify as much as possible any distortions in order to provide photogrammetric accuracy and accountability,

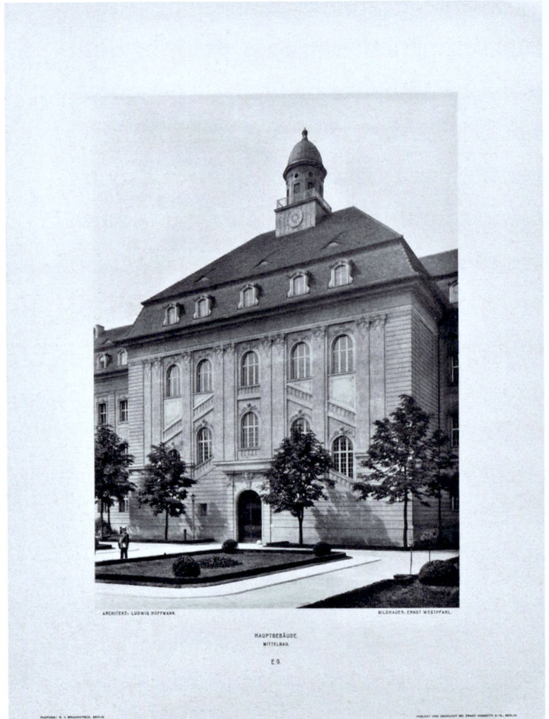

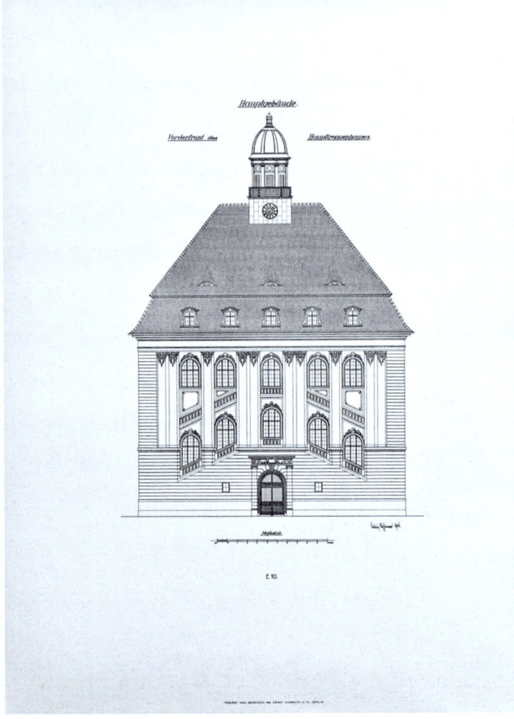

Figure 2.7. Ludwig Hoffmann, with photographs by Ernst von Brauchitsch, *Neubauten der Stadt Berlin*, vol. 6, *Rudolf Virchow–Krankenhaus* (Berlin: Wasmuth, 1907), (left) main building (Hauptgebäude), photograph (E9), (right) elevation (E10). Call number 8 693 ÜF. Copyright Stiftung Stadtmuseum Berlin. Photograph by Oliver Ziebe, Berlin.

Brauchitsch dramatized the scene by adding protagonists that seemed to engage in dialogue. Instead of conveying facts about architectural dimensions, form, and aesthetic, Brauchitsch used the same basic frontal template and engaged the scene's aesthetic and landscape-like qualities. This often involved staging people in these settings. Acting both as a choreographer and a photographer, he unlocked both photographic and architectural space for his intrigued observer.

Plate F9 of Buch Insane Asylum's entrance pavilion demonstrates this approach nicely (Figure 2.9). The vertically oriented photograph concentrates on the stark axial symmetry of the gate building, which occupies the center of the image frame. The actual entrance gate, a round-arched passage through a steeply roofed Flemish Renaissance façade portal, is located at the exact position of the image's vertical central axis and sits at the low horizon-mark of the

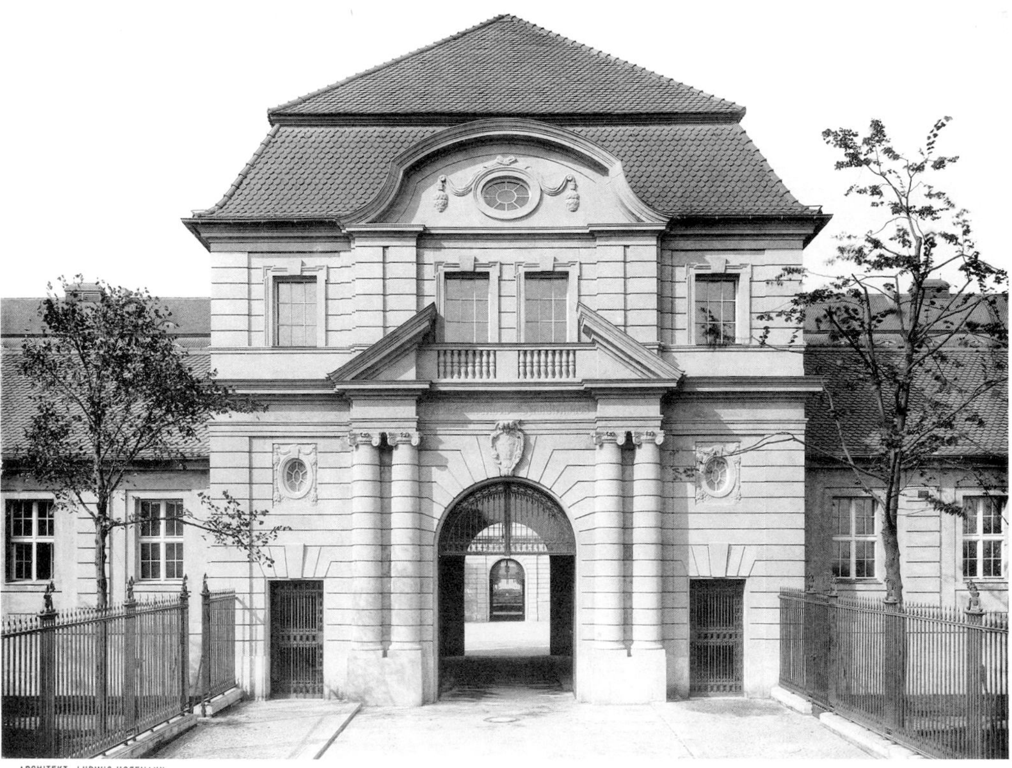

Figure 2.8. Ludwig Hoffmann, with photographs by Ernst von Brauchitsch, *Neubauten der Stadt Berlin*, vol. 6, *Rudolf Virchow–Krankenhaus* (Berlin: Wasmuth, 1907), porterhouse at main entrance (Pförtnerhaus am Haupteingang zur Anstalt) (E4). Call number 8 693 ÜF. Copyright Stiftung Stadtmuseum Berlin.

golden ratio.[32] A casually dressed elderly man on the image's lower left seems to be walking in deep thought toward us; a woman, dressed in simple attire and holding a small child, appears to be waiting for something standing in the central path that leads toward the entrance gate in the image's lower central right. A blonde girl, perhaps seven or eight years old, is occupied with her hands as she stands facing the maid with the child. Young trees frame this scene, which takes place under a cloudless summer afternoon sky.

In two other images, Brauchitsch captured the kitchen building in Buch: one was an environmental shot of the inner access to the kitchen and carriage house;

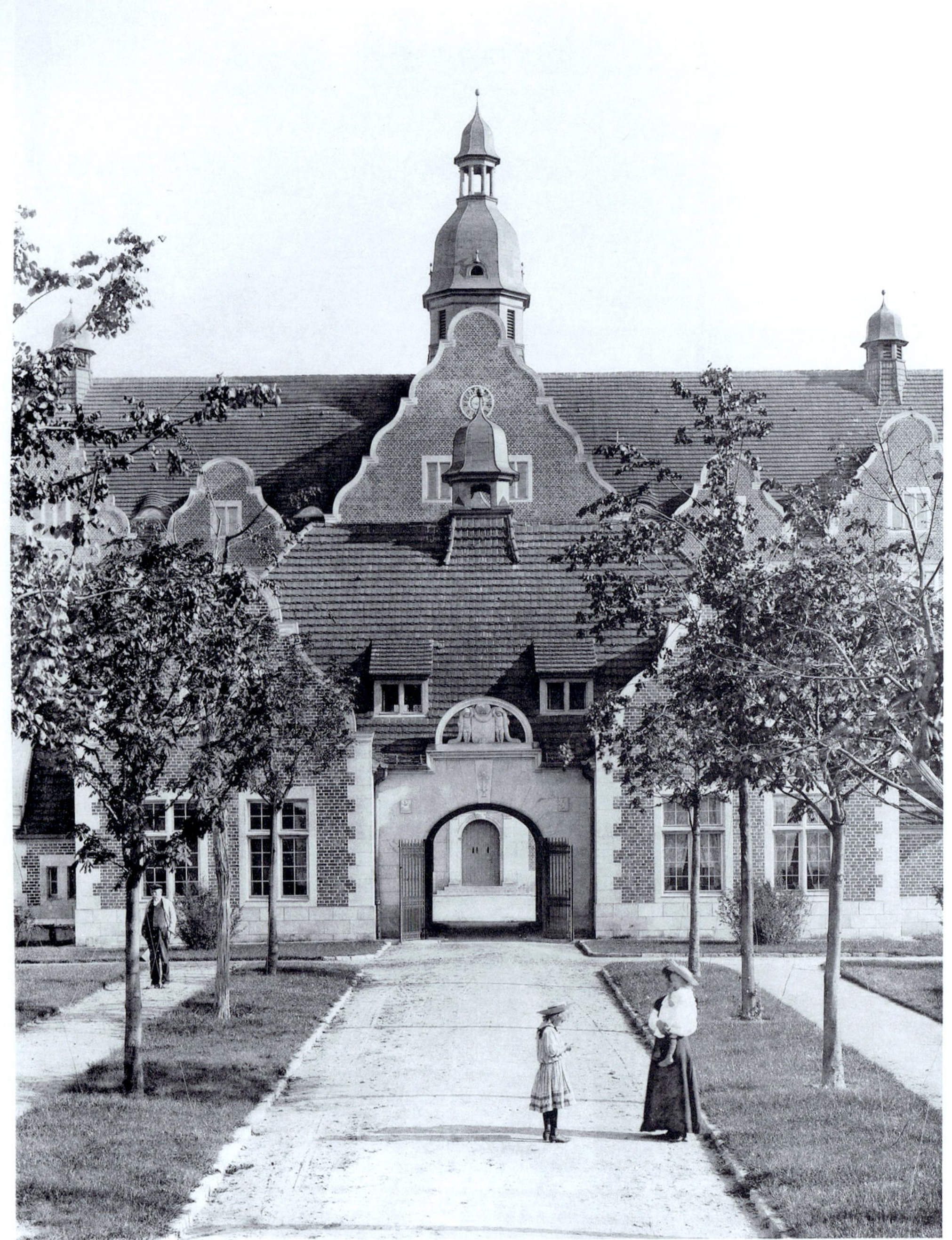

ARCHITEKT: LUDWIG HOFFMANN

ZUGANG ZUR ANSTALT

F 9.

Figure 2.9. Ludwig Hoffmann, with photographs by Ernst von Brauchitsch, *Neubauten der Stadt Berlin*, vol. 7, *Irrenanstalt Buch* (Berlin: Wasmuth, 1908), entrance building (Buch, Zugang zur Anstalt) (F9). Call number 8 693 ÜF. Copyright Stiftung Stadtmuseum Berlin.

the other depicted the façade of the kitchen building and four protagonists, three women and one man (Figures 2.10 and 2.11). The latter image was captured from a similar angle as the former but zoomed in more closely. Showing fewer protagonists (kitchen personnel), it also appears to have been staged more deliberately.

In the more comprehensive view (Figure 2.10), nine male groundskeepers are assembled in front of the kitchen building, and in a style unusual for Brauchitsch, all but one stare at the camera. This sort of crowd arrangement and the curious stares while work was interrupted was common in urban and in

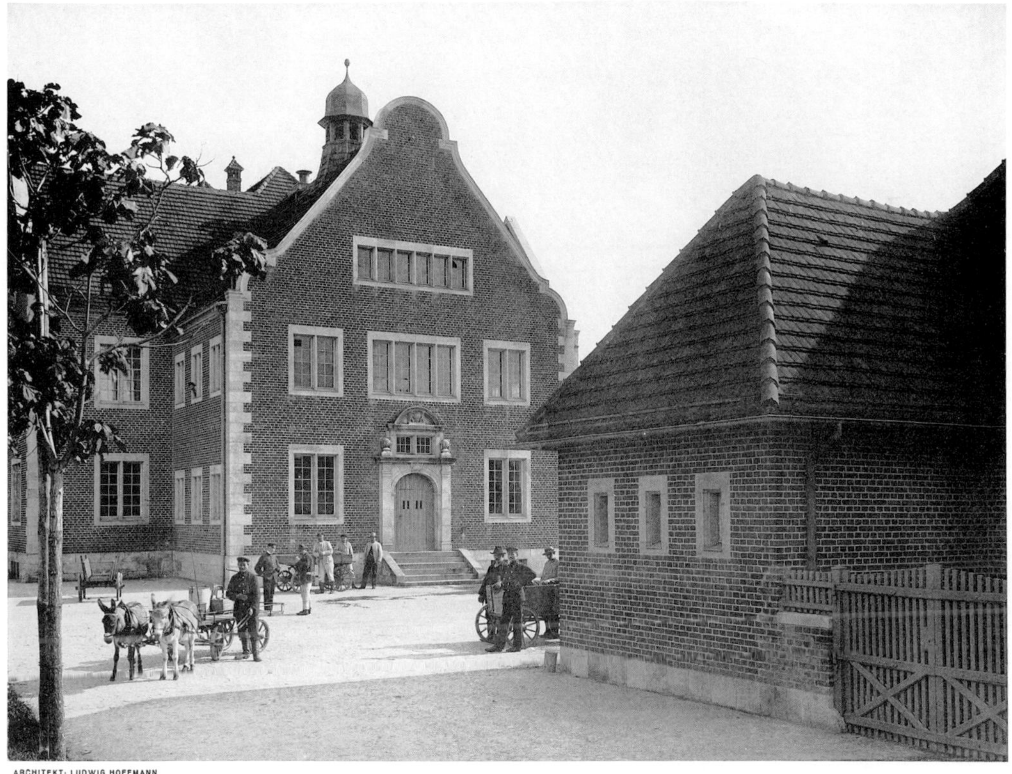

ARCHITEKT: LUDWIG HOFFMANN

INNERER ZUGANG ZUR KOCHKÜCHE UND WAGENSCHUPPEN

F 31.

Figure 2.10. Ludwig Hoffmann, with photographs by Ernst von Brauchitsch, *Neubauten der Stadt Berlin*, vol. 7, *Irrenanstalt Buch* (Berlin: Wasmuth, 1908), inner access to kitchen and carriage house (Buch, Innerer Zugang zur Kochküche und Wagenschuppen) (F31). Call number 8 693 ÜF. Copyright Stiftung Stadtmuseum Berlin.

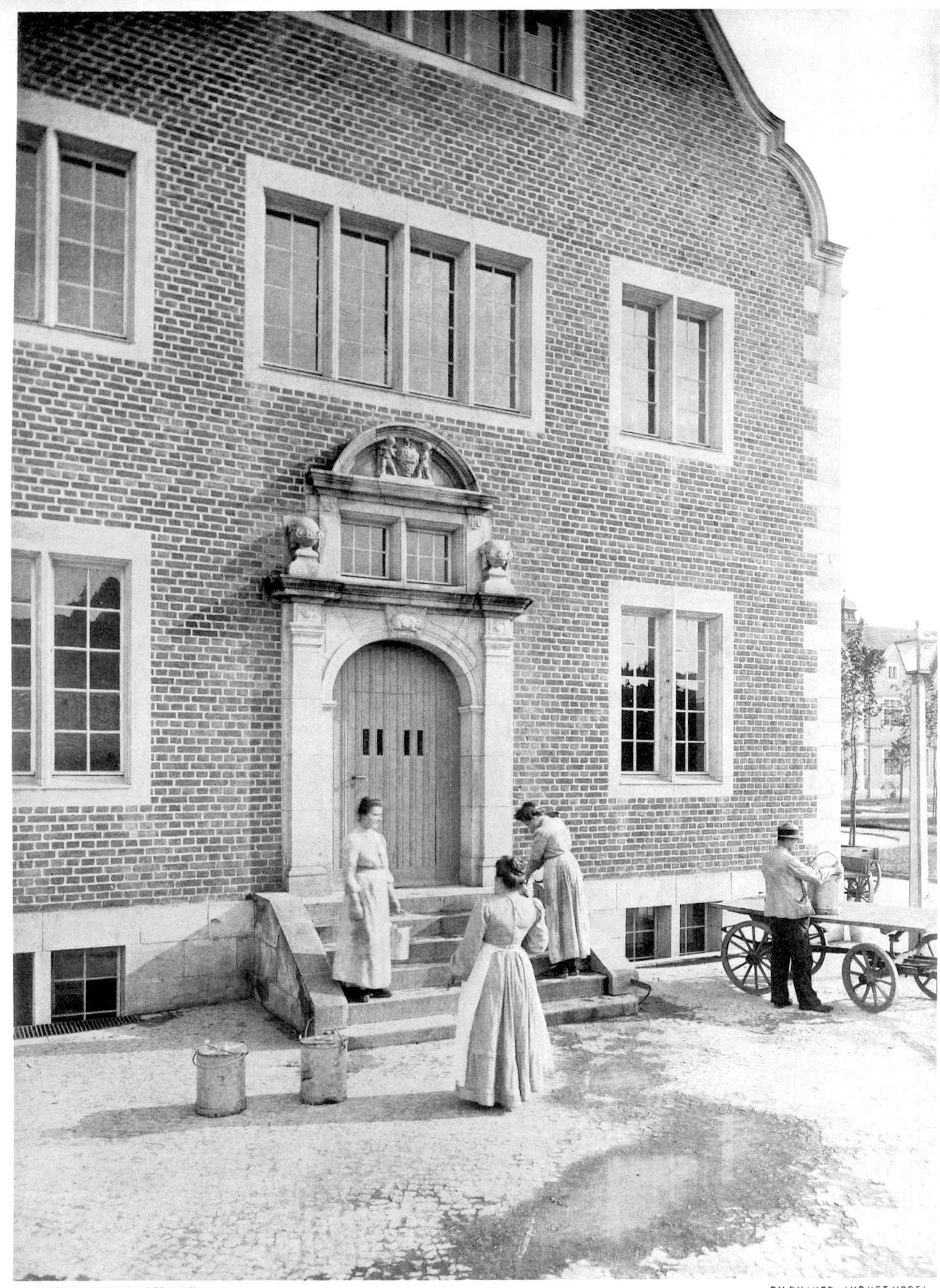

Figure 2.11. Ludwig Hoffmann, with photographs by Ernst von Brauchitsch, *Neubauten der Stadt Berlin*, vol. 7, *Irrenanstalt Buch* (Berlin: Wasmuth, 1908), inner access to kitchen, detail (Buch, Kochküche, detail) (F29). Call number 8 693 ÜF. Copyright Stiftung Stadtmuseum Berlin.

particular types of architectural photographs of the 1860s through 1890s and had a very different effect and connotation than Brauchitsch's inclusion of a few purposefully "coincidental" protagonists in the other image. This photograph is reminiscent of older scenarios, in which photography was such a novelty that crowds gathered and stared, often obstructing the architectural photographer's task, or proudly posing in images of their own property.

A good comparative case is a photograph taken in 1885 by the city photographer F. Albert Schwartz of the insane asylum in Dalldorf near Berlin. Schwartz (1836–1906), the avid documentarian of Berlin's new quarters and historic buildings, photographed the insane asylum's kitchen house in 1885 (Figure 2.12). Like Brauchitsch's overview image of Buch, a number of people (five in front of the building and four visibly inside at an open window) took position side by side and looked out toward the photographer's camera. Schwartz, like Brauchitsch, took a static and formal approach, though he remained further from his subject,

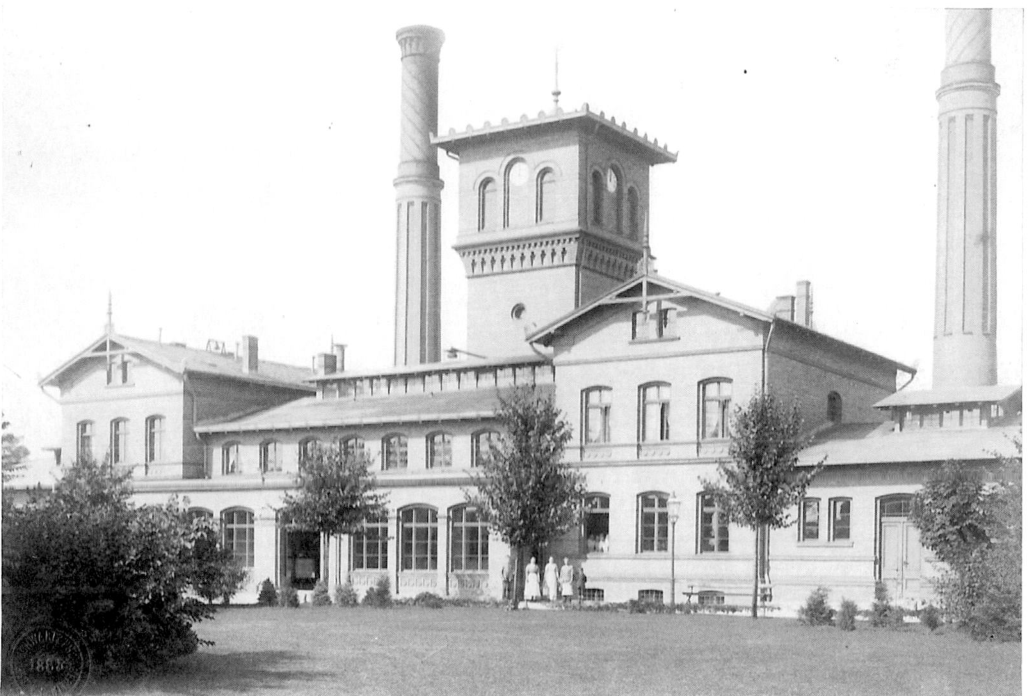

Figure 2.12. F. Albert Schwartz, *Küchenhaus der Irrenanstalt der Stadt Berlin zu Dalldorf* (Kitchen building of the insane asylum of the city of Berlin in Dalldorf), 1885. Photograph (albumen silver print from glass negative). Heimatmuseum Reinickedorf. Wikimedia Commons.

and doubtlessly the people in this image worked in that kitchen and were asked to pose.

Schwartz's light-brown albumen print captured the kitchen building, which had been executed and recently finished by Hoffmann's predecessor, Hermann Blankenstein, in 1881.[33] He framed the central section of this elongated two-story building, photographing it from a position off to the right of the building's middle axis to emphasize its axial symmetry, including the pairs of two high and geometrically decorated chimneys behind the structure. A clock tower that distantly resembled civic Italian Renaissance architectural styles defined and upgraded the appearance of this otherwise modest eighteen-axis building. Schwartz's image plane moves almost parallel to the kitchen building façade; a balance of verticals and horizontals defines his image. His protagonists don't engage with each other but become part of the image as decorative human elements. Film speed was still an issue at the time, as exposure time was about half a second, during which any moving object would have blurred. The elaborate procedure to install a heavy large-format camera contributed to the resemblance between photograph taking and a sacred ritual. In comparison, Brauchitsch's image, while also captured with a large-format camera (an outdated technology when he used it), was defined by dynamic diagonals (the situation of the carriage house in the foreground to the right, the donkey carriage pointing away diagonally from the entrance), pointing altogether toward the kitchen entry.

Schwartz's balanced landscape composition belonged to a far less ambitious project than Brauchitsch's and Hoffmann's. He is best known today not as an architectural photographer, but for the images he created of Berlin's transforming neighborhoods during the 1870s, 1880s, and 1890s. He was most likely asked to take a few images of the kitchen building and the entire complex, and this particular photograph is housed today in the local museum of Reinickendorf, the northern Berlin district in which this building was located.[34] The obvious intentionality of the photograph suggests that Schwartz was commissioned to document the building by the community government.

As part of a large body of work and equipped with different forms of contextualization through other photographs, texts, and the portfolio series, Brauchitsch's photographs revealed much more about the building, its function, its context, and its creator than a photograph by someone like F. Albert Schwartz. As part of a photographer–architect collaboration, Brauchitsch's photographs were part of a richer set of signifiers than Schwartz's, who applied the same photographic conventions regardless of architectural subject matter.

After the primary task of documentation for Hoffmann, Brauchitsch followed the architect's agenda of constructing in balance with nature. He embedded his motif into its natural context, visually integrating the building with its landscaped setting. His photographs also exude a narrative of bourgeois comfort and subtly articulated progress, a focus echoing painterly subjects of the time. His work coincides with that of Berlin impressionist painter Lesser Ury (1861–1931), but it lacks the instantaneous character found in Ury's paintings of leisure and seemingly spontaneous moments in the city (Figure 2.13).[35] Brauchitsch's images, including the kitchen scene, engage space through human figures and their interactions. But particularly when compared to Ury's impressionist approach, they are inhibited by the obvious staging of his protagonists and the need to maneuver his large and heavy camera on a tripod. Brauchitsch's strategy, while indebted to both architectural and landscape-image traditions, comes across as architectural documentation that has been somewhat awkwardly enlivened by human figures. While these image's rhetoric energized and enhanced Hoffmann's architecture and its site, it did not manage (or aspire) to relate to the city experientially. Such an account of urban life became the cornerstone of street photography after World War I. In contrast, Brauchitsch's urban image was concerned with instilling certainty through a clearly framed subject. It was inherently linked to presenting Hoffmann's urban architecture as infallible components of Berlin's urban identity.

Brauchitsch's second, more tightly framed kitchen image had an almost theatrical character (Figure 2.11). The three women in this close-up seemed to be in conversation on the steps to the kitchen entry, one sweeping the stairs (center), another holding a bucket (left), the third, seen from the back, presumably stopping on her way back into the building (between the two others and closest to the photographer). A man standing to the right fumbling with a large metal container on a wooden wagon seems lost in thought. Considered independently from their architectural surroundings, these figures not only look like stage characters in a naturalistic period play by the likes of Gerhart Hauptmann, but they are reminiscent of etchings and photographic depictions of representatives of different professions and segments of German society that were common throughout the eighteenth and nineteenth centuries. The famous

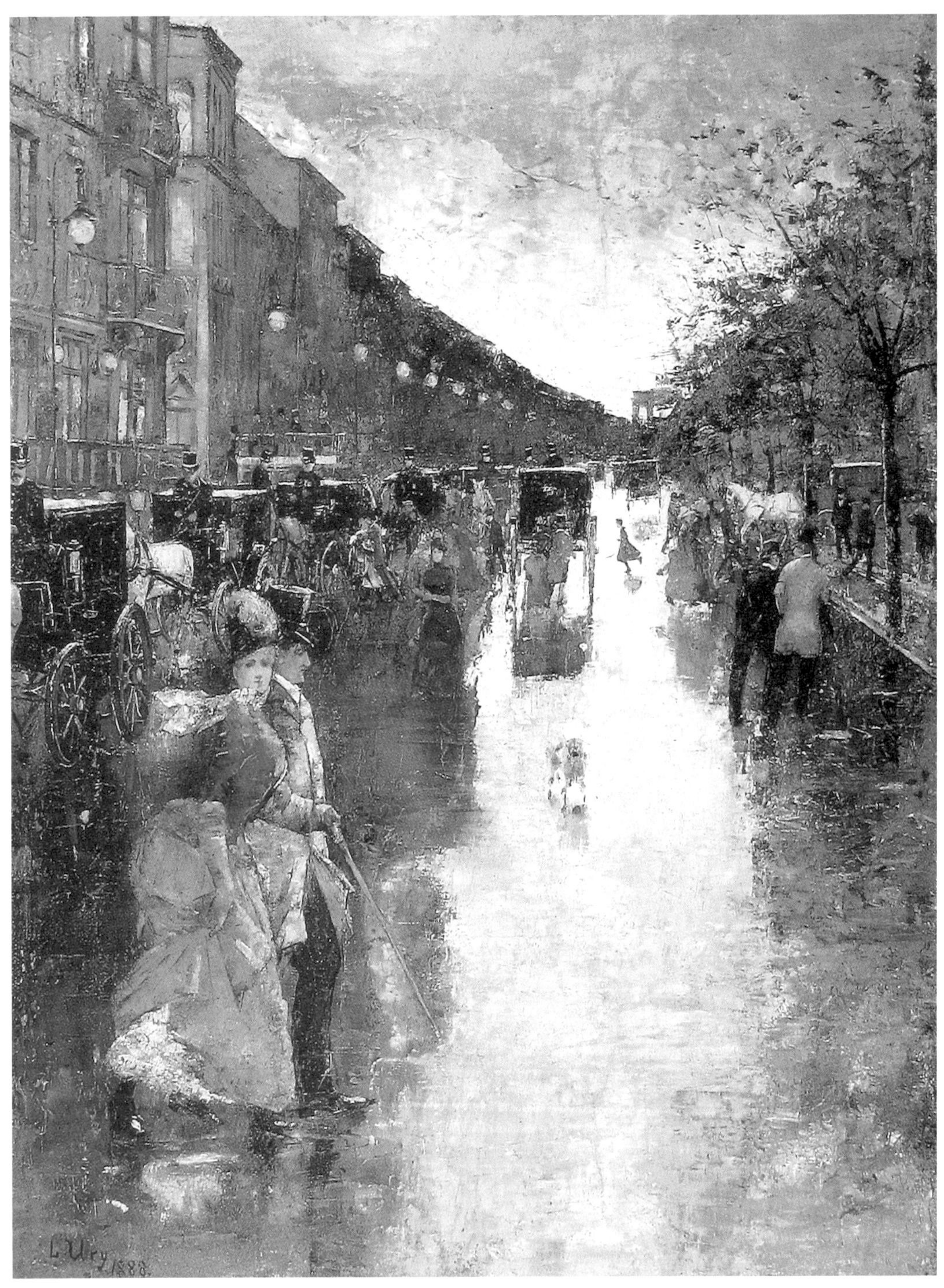

Figure 2.13. Lesser Ury, *Unter den Linden after the Rain*, 1888. Painting. Private collection. Wikimedia Commons.

German photographer August Sander (1876–1964) would pick up such a typological approach to the German class system in his comprehensive portrait project for the book volumes *Menschen des zwanzigesten Jahrhunderts* (*People of the Twentieth Century*).[36]

Bold image-cropping strategies were both a result and a manifestation of technological and aesthetic transformations during the last quarter of the nineteenth century. With the development and application of halftone reproduction by letterpress, images could be adjusted to fit a page with their accompanying text.[37] New forms of image display appeared, and images were most likely "cropped high and narrow to fit between two columns of type."[38] Many of Brauchitsch's images in the introductory text, as well as those published in architectural periodicals, were cropped. This seemingly random and somewhat brutal measure was, however, to the image's eventual advantage, as cropping could "lend a purposefulness to the picture that might well have been lost had the building been shown in the older style, in its totality with room to spare."[39] Such editorial considerations, while taking precedence over image aesthetic ones, contributed to shifting pictorial conventions for architectural representation.

Two of Brauchitsch's images, one taken at the Virchow Hospital and the other one at Buch, serve as examples for such editing and cropping. In the image labeled "recreation park, view toward the chapel" in the Virchow Hospital portfolio, the extra-elongated landscape image displayed what looked like an English park lawn, framed by weeping willows, bushes, and young trees (Figure 2.14). In the central far distance, the chapel building serves as a formal divider; the horizon and a group of three children in the foreground set accents in points of the golden ratio. A family of three stands in the middle ground slightly to the right of the central axis. This image, equipped with staged figures and set in a quasi-pastoral landscape, articulated the idea of the hospital as a site of recovery and nature as counterconcept to the crowded and increasingly unhealthy city. In another image taken in front of the engine house in Buch, two boys pose on the lawn in front of the building (Figure 2.15). In an obviously staged setup, they stretch out on the grass, holding hands, their legs interlocking. The image was cropped into an elongated vertical panel format, fitting it in with the introductory text's layout. The small engine house appears monumental thanks to Brauchitsch's photographic approach from a low viewpoint, capturing the building at an angle. The building, seemingly squeezed into a

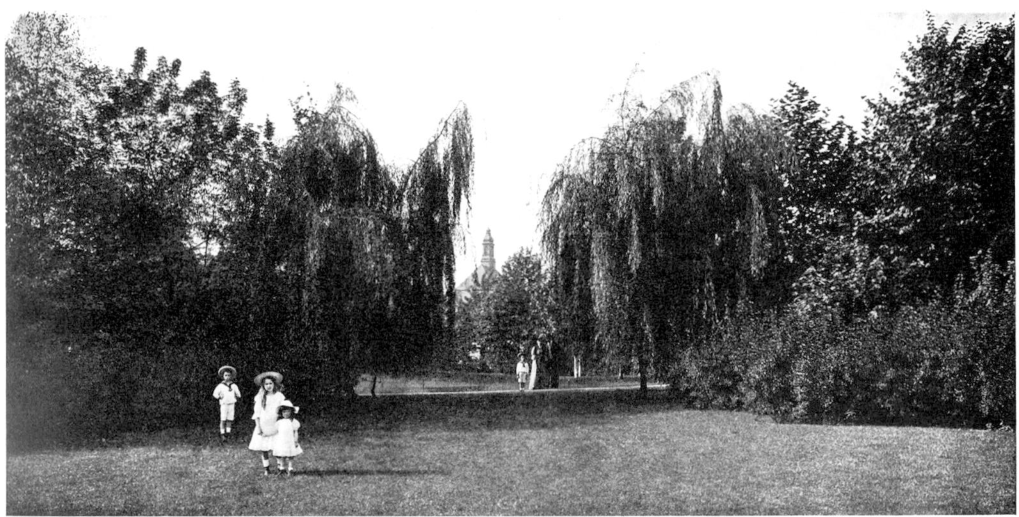

Abb. 71. Erholungspark. Blick nach der Kapelle.

Figure 2.14. Ludwig Hoffmann, with photographs by Ernst von Brauchitsch, *Neubauten der Stadt Berlin,* vol. 6, *Rudolf Virchow–Krankenhaus* (Berlin: Wasmuth, 1907), recreation park, view toward the chapel (Virchow Krankenhaus, Erholungspark. Blick nach der Kapelle), illustration 71, p. xix (detail). Call number 8 693 ÜF. Copyright Stiftung Stadtmuseum Berlin.

narrow picture frame, looms heavily over the two protagonists in the lower quarter of the image.

By the 1890s, largely due to its unprecedented growth, the city administration was in need of a second city hall to complement the Rotes Rathaus, which had been built only thirty years prior. After some deliberations, the magistrate bought twenty-three inner-city parcels and demolished the historical buildings between Parochialstraße, Stralauerstraße, Klosterstraße, and Jüdenstraße. Plans for the building were produced only after the assignment was given to Hoffmann without competition.

Hoffmann proposed a monumental building with five inner courtyards and a large hall that would accommodate approximately 1,500 people for public celebrations. His idea was to create a building that functioned both externally and internally through systems of representation. This effect was secured with a heavy building body on a trapezoidal plan, crowned by a tower almost 80 meters high, which concluded with a 3.25-meter-tall copper statue of the goddess Fortuna.[40] Hoffmann pointed out in his memoirs that the tower was designed to

Figure 2.15. Ludwig Hoffmann, with photographs by Ernst von Brauchitsch, *Neubauten der Stadt Berlin*, vol. 5 (Berlin, 1907), Buch, engine house (Buch, Maschinenhaus), p. viii. Call number 8 693 ÜF. Copyright Stiftung Stadtmuseum Berlin.

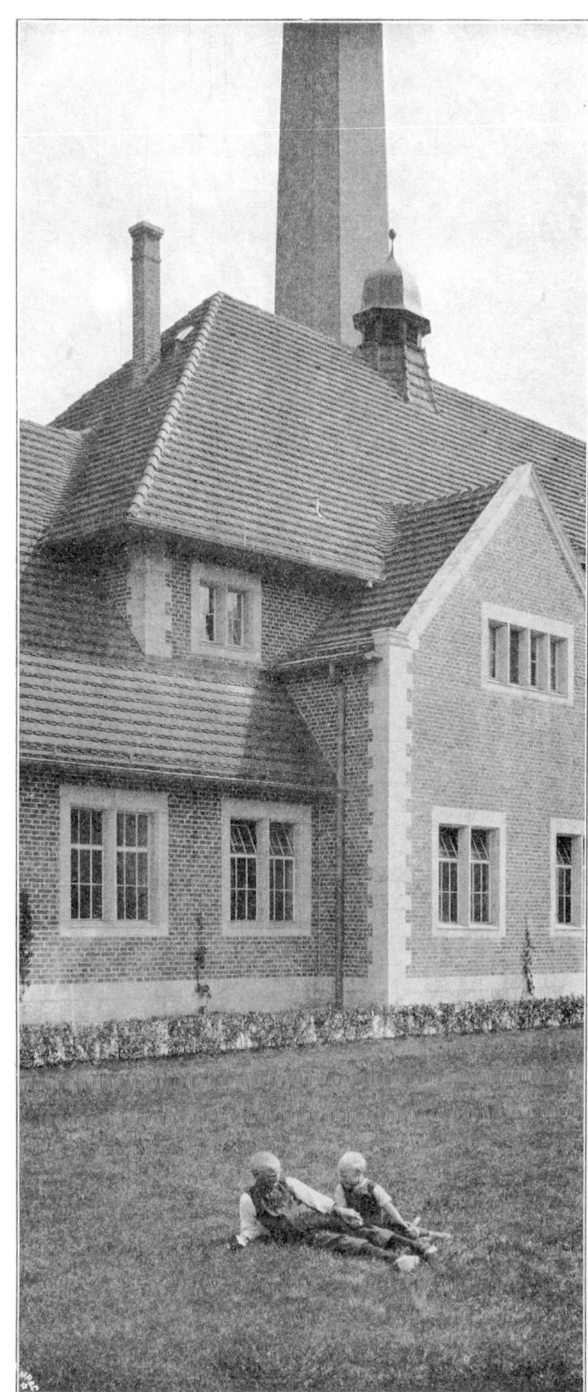

Abb. 30. Maschinenhaus.

link City Hall to important surrounding buildings, citing Carl von Gontard's towers for the nearby French and German Cathedrals at Gendarmenmarkt. This gesture, Hoffmann pointed out, was supposed to demonstrate "Berlin's upward development."[41] The building's style and prominent appearance was inspired by Palazzo Thiene in Vicenza,[42] which was designed by Giulio Romano and completed by the young Andrea Palladio in the 1540s. However, Hoffmann deliberately deviated from the classic proportionality of Palladian façades by stretching the building's pilaster order across two and a half stories, adding a mighty curb roof and the tower.

Brauchitsch's attempts at translating an idea of coherence into a more densely built-out urban realm was manifested in the City Hall portfolio (volume 10, 1911), which framed, cropped, isolated, and elevated this building more strikingly than any of his previous image sets. Brauchitsch's response to the building's location and particular situation was to almost entirely ignore its context and location and focus instead on monumentalizing and elevating the isolated building's materiality and ornamentation. While he had clearly internalized the basic rules of the "factual" style of the 1880s,[43] which depicted buildings in their entirety as free-standing entities, Brauchitsch replaced them by highlighting "fragmentary views" and "an emphasis on qualities of light."[44] This was very much in line with recent photo-pictorialist aesthetic strategies.

Brauchitsch's "frontal façade, middle part" of the City Hall, which appears in the series' City Hall portfolio, was photographed from an elevated standpoint, capturing parts of the classical rigor of Hoffmann's domed building complex (Figure 2.16). As the building was captured at a tight angle, the viewer was cheated of his or her overview and sense of space. By cropping this part of the building in a way that minimized the image's open parts to less than a quarter, one's understanding of the building's dimensions and situatedness in the city was severely inhibited. Instead, the prevailing sense was that of an almost intimidatingly massive and monumental structure. This pictorial pattern was repeated in different variations in images of the building's exterior and interior up to the building's elements (façade, inner walls, ornamental decorations), entirely filling the picture frame into total flatness and abstraction. To some extent, this image appears as decontextualized as older architectural and ornamental details, but its purpose and the motivation for its creation were different from, if not diametrically opposed to, its predecessors. While more traditional

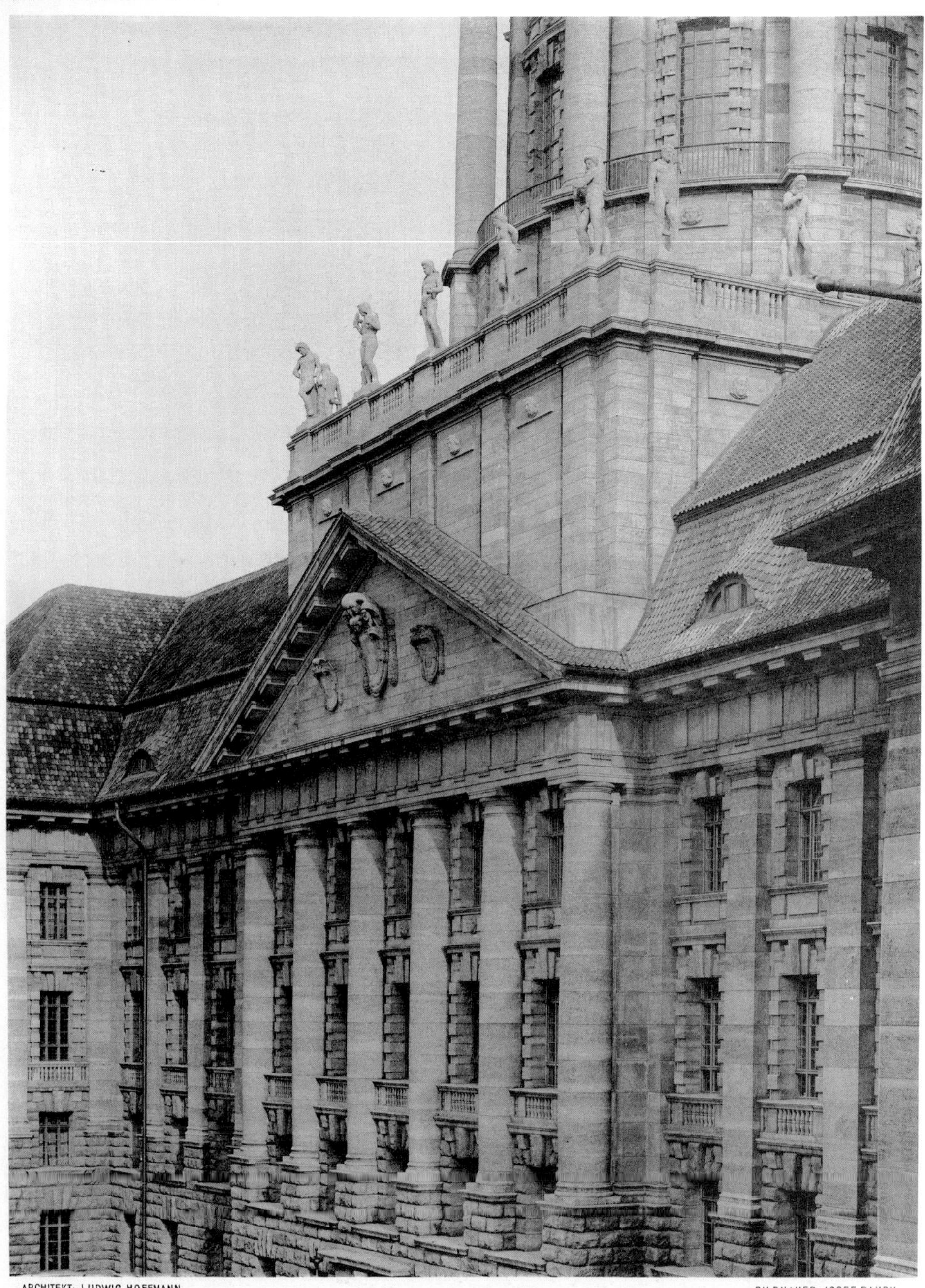

Figure 2.16. Ludwig Hoffmann, with photographs by Ernst von Brauchitsch, *Neubauten der Stadt Berlin*, vol. 10, *Neues Stadthaus* (Berlin: Wasmuth, 1911), City Hall, frontal façade, middle part (Stadthaus, Vorderfassade. Mittlerer Teil. Architekt: Ludwig Hoffmann, Bildhauer: Josef Rauch) (J3). Call number 8 693 ÜF. Copyright Stiftung Stadtmuseum Berlin.

architectural imagery prioritized complete façades or ornamental aspects for pedagogic purposes, the reproduction of Brauchitsch's cropped images promoted stylized views of architecture. The photographer and the architect conspired to monumentalize, even essentialize, the work. Publishing the photographs together with text and cropping them to fit on the same page with an explanatory narrative assured congruence between text and image. Brauchitsch's image of the frontal façade of City Hall confirmed Cervin Robinson's observation about shifting architectural photographic conventions between the 1880s and 1920s: Instead of giving "an air of objectivity to the picture" and the suggestion of "completeness of the information given," as was typical for architectural photography during the 1870s and 1880s, the new generation of architectural photographers proceeded differently.[45] While producing a "compelling impression of the plastic character of the . . . building," a photograph taken in the early 1920s by the well-known architectural photographer Arthur Köster, for example, revealed "virtually no information of its internal organization or its use."[46]

The same is true for a detail shot of the City Hall's lobby, which was captured through a majestic semicircular opening on an upper floor (Figure 2.17). The viewer glances at a rigorously structured inner façade with relief-like pilasters and an attic level above semicircular window openings. Brauchitsch photographed from the dark into the light onto the great inner lobby hall, a move that emphasized the staged nature of the view. Using classical elements, Hoffmann underlined a claim for universality, which would have been appropriate for the building's task. This building (and the photograph through which it was publically presented) was meant to be both functional and timeless.

One particular aesthetic and ideological choice manifested itself in the treatment of space and dimensionality. Brauchitsch's photographs, especially the ones of City Hall, shared with artistic photographers such as Frederick H. Evans a flatness and emphasis of image layers rather than depth of space. Flatness was triggered by a fragmentary approach, which illustrated what Robinson called "the effect of concentrated attention that comes to a view that eliminates all that is inessential."[47] The interior image particularly demonstrated the central role of light in both the abstraction process and in conveying "the atmosphere of a building at the expense of telling anything concrete about its formal organization."[48] Brauchitsch's City Hall interior not only formally reminds one of Evans's pictorialist approach, but it also remarkably resembles his choice of

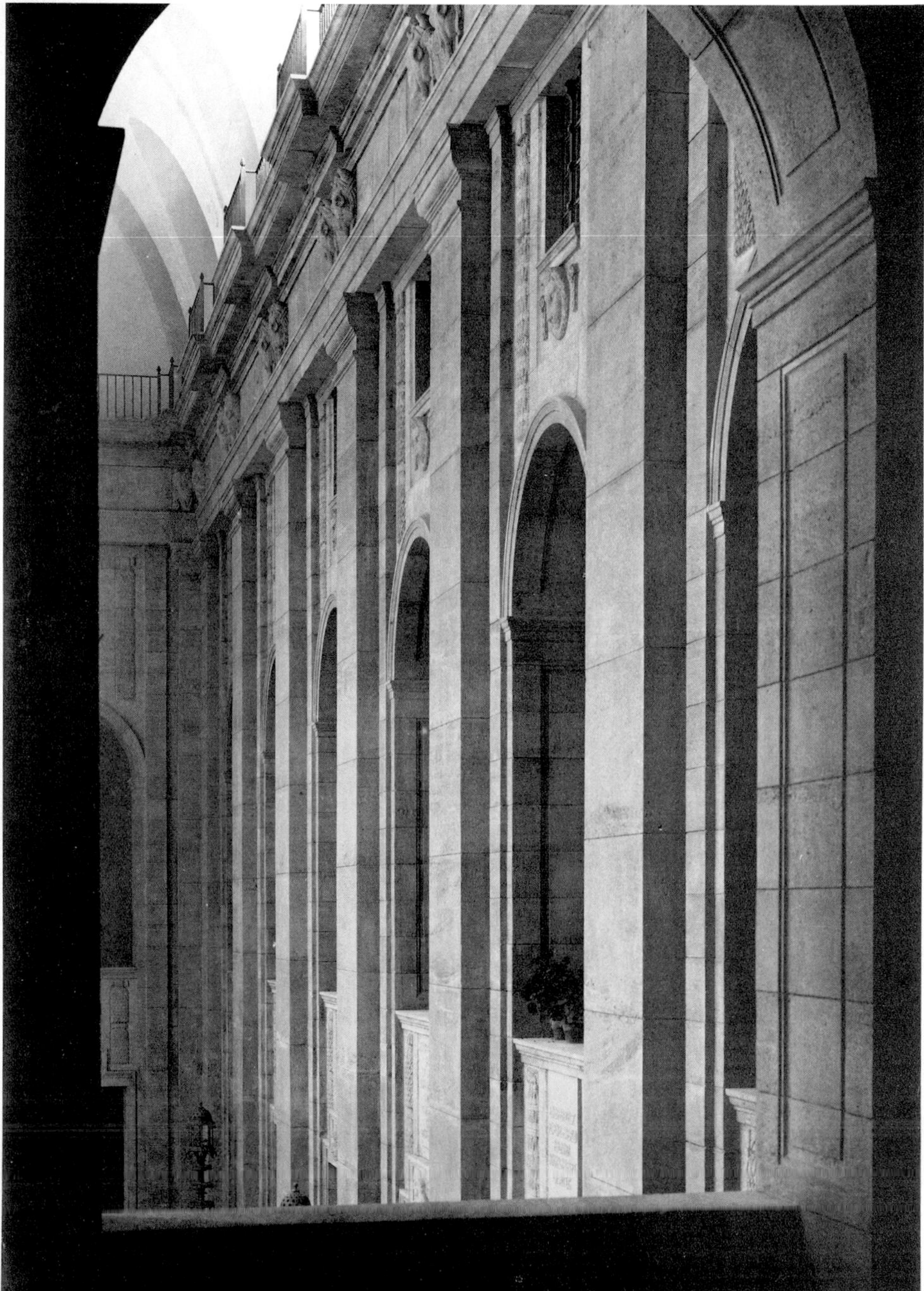

ARCHITEKT: LUDWIG HOFFMANN.

HALLE. DETAIL.

J 44.

Figure 2.17. Ludwig Hoffmann, with photographs by Ernst von Brauchitsch, *Neubauten der Stadt Berlin*, vol. 10, *Neues Stadthaus* (Berlin: Wasmuth, 1911), City Hall, lobby, detail (Stadthaus, Halle detail) (J44). Call number 8 693 ÜF. Copyright Stiftung Stadtmuseum Berlin.

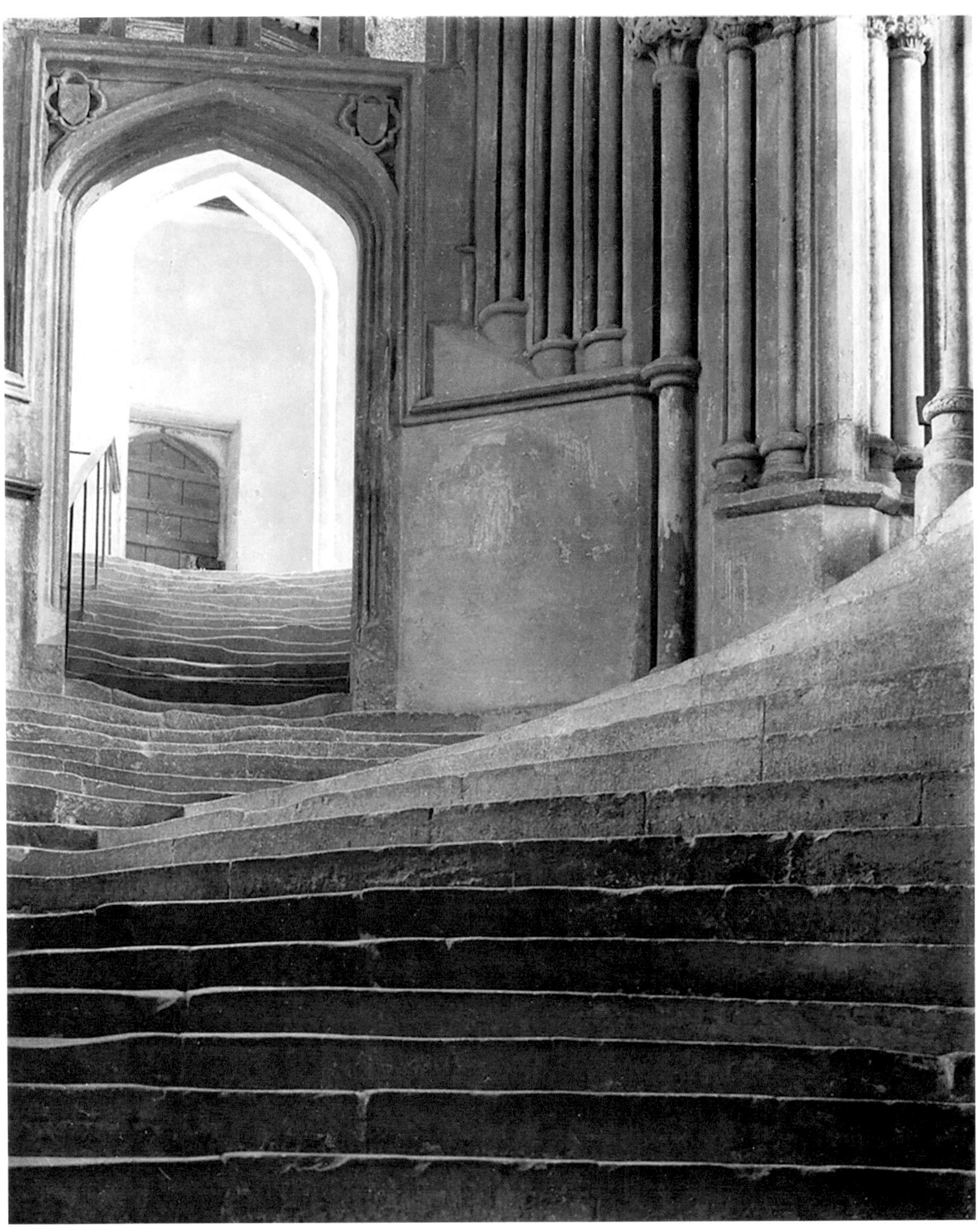

Figure 2.18. Frederick H. Evans, *A Sea of Steps*, stairs to the chapter house, Wells Cathedral, England, 1903. Platinum print, 22.86 × 18.44 cm. The Marjorie and Leonard Vernon Collection, gift of the Annenberg Foundation and Carol Vernon and Robert Turbin, Los Angeles County Museum of Art, accession number M.2008.40.736. http://collections.lacma.org/sites/default/files/remote_images/piction/ma-31332551-O3.jpg, Wikimedia Commons.

subject matter, which becomes more apparent when comparing it with his platinum print of the interior of Wells Cathedral of 1903 (Figure 2.18).

Using a tight cropping, which resembles Evans's, Brauchitsch might have aimed at expressing what Hoffmann explained in respect to the intentions of City Hall in his accompanying text. He wrote: "as leading work site of a city with more than two million inhabitants, City Hall had to communicate might and calm in its overall effect despite its liveliness in its details. Therefore, the intention for its architectural design and formation aimed at creating an energetic, calm, and simultaneously friendly atmosphere, while its individual parts were nevertheless vivid."[49] Brauchitsch's response was to employ the photographic means of cropping and staging with natural light, again joining the potentials of documentation and stagecraft in an unprecedented way.[50]

However, instead of enlivening the image space with human performers as he often did in Buch and Virchow, Brauchitsch relied on editorial and technical means of enhancement for the urban City Hall project. The strategies achieving a timeless beauty in Evans's "Sea of Steps" at Wells Cathedral translated into similar claims for "might and calm" in Berlin's modern civic architecture. In some ways, such bold abstractions are not far from what Claire Zimmerman described for the interrelation between Ludwig Mies van der Rohe's Barcelona Pavilion and its photographic representations of the 1930s. Unlike Hoffmann, however, Mies made sure that "visual experience at the Barcelona Pavilion was calibrated by bodily experience carefully choreographed in the building's design." For Mies, the architecture's plan already embodied "visual opportunities, or three-dimensional pictures."[51] While such careful consideration of the dynamic of the space as representation was not yet part of Hoffmann's style, his and Brauchitsch's collaborative work can be considered an important antecedent to such archi-photographic entanglements. Pursuing his course with his usual coherence, Brauchitsch's images refuted any potential concerns about historical context and mismatched dimensions by taking away the focus on the building's historic surroundings and by concentrating on the beauty of materials, surfaces, and craftsmanship.

City-Image Builders

City Hall was completed in 1911, after a long building period of eight years, and became the most explicitly and harshly criticized of Hoffmann's projects.

His detractors shared a sense that this building, while responding to the projection of the city's future development in relation to the competition for the Greater Berlin area in 1908–9, was oversized and designed without consideration for its historical environment. Unlike the work of his first decade in office, the City Hall was perceived as a "foreigner who, like Gulliver in Lilliput, was rising above the small surrounding buildings."[52] Its "untimely historicism," "eclecticism," and lack of modernity annoyed certain critics.[53] Planner and critic Hoffmann-Axthelm polemically summarized the criticism of this project, writing that "the 1900–1914 created Stadthaus . . . did without the historical masquerade and presented itself simply as a Wilhelminian administration building. In its ultra-sober bureaucratic posing it is still today not only an urban spatial catastrophe . . . but also as much a failure as Blankenstein's [Hoffmann's predecessor's] Police Headquarters."[54] Other critics have suggested that the addition of Stadthaus was deemed necessary by the city as an expansion of Berlin's historic City Hall ("the Red City Hall"); however, its enormous costs and the monumentality, which stood in pronounced contrast to the rest of Berlin's historic center until the 1920s, were deemed highly problematic and inappropriate.

Hoffmann-Axthelm called Ludwig Hoffmann a "city-image builder" (*Stadtbild-Baumeister*), avoiding the common term "city-builder" (*Stadtbaumeister*), which would have suggested command and control over an urban environment. Such control, if it had ever existed, had drifted into the hands of speculators and venture capitalists by the onset of Germany's "Foundation Era" after 1871. The joint Hoffmann/Brauchitsch city image that emerged from this collaboration was confronted by such contradictions of the modern city. Architectural historian Kenneth Frampton suggested that by 1925, the new generation of architects in Berlin spent most of their collective energy to overcoming Hoffmann's "reactionary politics,"[55] and it is not surprising then that both men's legacies were almost forgotten in the second half of the twentieth century. *Neubauten der Stadt Berlin* was never systematically concluded, as the slashing of city funds and looming outbreak of war put an abrupt halt to the project in 1912. Brauchitsch's entire studio, including his negatives, was likely destroyed during the 1939–45 war. Brauchitsch's allegiance to heliogravure beyond the medium's prime likely contributed to his vanishing from public consciousness. He created his portfolios at a time when this kind of technique and presentation had been overcome either by more explicitly artistic printing techniques or by mass-disseminated photography.[56]

Hoffmann and Brauchitsch's journey brings us back to the characterization of seeing in the city, which Yi-Fu Tuan described so aptly in the quote that opened this chapter.[57] Tuan's "patterns of reality" are effectively realized in Brauchitsch's photographs. Brauchitsch's take on Hoffmann's architecture responded to official purposes; he created a city image that conveyed a city of solid self-esteem on par with older European capitals. This image, and its particular narrative, was a cornerstone to Hoffmann's quest for a sincere and sensitive civic architecture and was tremendously important to the city administration as it attempted to rid the emerging metropolis of its image as an ahistorical climber among European capitals. The status of Berlin, and by extension, the newly formed German nation, was at stake. The city served as an ideal platform to play out and stage stately qualities such as progressive building, convincing engagement of architecture with its surroundings, a flexible attitude toward urban building tasks, the representational grandeur of civic architecture, and a command of modern photo-reproductive technologies. However, instead of employing a boosterist grand-style photography as some photographers in the service of city publicity and tourism did, Brauchitsch relied on a more serious and conscientious approach that kept grappling with its subject matter in an almost philosophical manner.

Official architects working for Berlin between 1871 and the 1920s had to overcome the paradox of modern city building—an achievement that, according to Hoffmann-Axthelm, was successfully achieved only in Berlin. In fact, such attempts might only have been possible in a city "which was so unsure of its architectural qualifications as Wilhelmine Berlin." Accordingly, the "city-image builder" attempted to "give back to the city that which it had lost during the Foundation Era, a dignified if not monumental public."[58]

But what image do we take away from this collaboration and what does it tell about both professions' roles in urban identity formation? While we find coherence in the unique collaboration between Brauchitsch and Hoffmann, the two mediums do not appear in sync if we look at architectural and photographic outputs of the turn of the century in Berlin more broadly. Brauchitsch's application of modern pictorial strategies such as cropping and staging, which were triggered in part by the circumstances and impetus of new reproductive possibilities and in part by aesthetic influences of Postimpressionism, met with Hoffmann's middle path between historicism and modernism.[59] Photography's applicability to reproduction and serial narratives did not demand any formal or aesthetic allegiances. Architecture, unlike photography, was under critical aesthetic scrutiny. Brauchitsch's city image breathed his medium's liberties, which the architect—confined by aesthetic and professional constrictions and expectations—could not have generated. Hoffmann's "city image" was one created out of limitations, of not being a city builder, but of being responsible to both the city and the state; Brauchitsch's city image was one thriving on Hoffmann's creation, but without its limitations.[60] The jointly generated city image of Berlin, "tested against the filtered perceptual input in a constant interacting process," would soon be fundamentally reconsidered as the 1914–18 war began and a younger generation of architects, who appropriated the camera for their own purposes, entered the arena.[61]

After World War I, the architect–photographer relationship and the relating of their different orders of representation shifted. Brauchitsch's and Hoffmann's close collaboration and understanding of the capabilities of architectural representation set the stage for more pronounced photo-architectural ventures as well as the development of architects' own photographic practices.[62] Le Corbusier, Erich Mendelsohn, and Walter Gropius used photographs of architecture as a means of note taking and reflection on the nature of architecture. The cocreated city image found in *Neubauten* marks a carefully calibrated tipping point in the city's self-reflection and self-assurance that would never be achieved again.

THREE

Tracing Transformation

Berlin's Urban Palimpsest in Photogrammetry and "Rubble Photography"

> Photography can be made most serviceable to Engineers and Architects, in illustrating—either for themselves or their employers—the progress of the works on which they may be engaged.
>
> —CUTHBERT M. BEDEM, "Photographic Pleasures 1855"

> Through photography, too, we can participate in new experiences of space, and in even greater measure through the film. With their help, and that of the new school of architects, we have attained an enlargement and sublimation of our appreciation of space, the comprehension of a new partial culture. Thanks to the photographer, humanity has acquired the power of perceiving its surroundings and its very existence, with new eyes.
>
> —LASZLO MOHOLY-NAGY, "From Pigment to Light"

The remarkable physical redefinition and expansion of Berlin stimulated a debate about historic preservation that evolved with growing urgency as the century came to a close. The late nineteenth century rekindled a historical and preservationist conscience, which was rooted in early nineteenth-century debates in Germany and throughout central Europe. Historic preservation in Germany originated during the Romantic movement at the beginning of the century, which was fed by the awakening of national pride after the Napoleonic Wars. This notion coincided with the preservationist activities of Eugène Emmanuel Viollet-le-Duc (1814–79) in France and John Ruskin (1819–1900) in England, who controversially debated the foundational principles of historic preservation. The cultural climate in the German-speaking states at the time provided the basis for a growing awareness for the existence and value of historical objects. Karl Friedrich Schinkel (1781–1841) and Ferdinand von Quast (1807–77) were two central voices in the field during the early and mid-nineteenth century. Georg Dehio's (1850–1932) and Cornelius Gurlitt's (1850–1938) work marked the second phase of the German preservation movement around 1900. The common focus of historic preservation had been the protection and preservation of historic monuments, buildings, and objects. France, England, Germany, and other European countries initially focused their architectural study and training—and their preservationist interest—on classical architecture. However, as the nineteenth century progressed, France, England, and, later, Germany began concentrating their interests on the country's medieval architectural heritage. Architects "declared an omnivorous interest in the monuments of all periods from the rise of the Etruscans to the Renaissance,"[1] and photography was part of it from its beginnings onward.

Bedem's and Moholy-Nagy's statements quoted above,[2] made almost fifty years apart, reveal a radical shift in the perception of photography's capabilities from the nineteenth to the twentieth centuries. With it they delineate the function and use of photography for different preservation and documentation efforts. While Bedem saw photography as narrowly dedicated to serving engineers and architects—very much in the spirit of François Arago and Charles Baudelaire in his report of the Salon of 1855—Moholy-Nagy articulated the enthusiasm of the inter–world wars era to experiment and employ photography and film as a creative medium. Spatial perception and experience, rather than reporting building progress, became Moholy-Nagy's central focus. The new notion of a modern, avant-garde perspective on the world was generated over the course of several decades and coincided with Berlin's most vigorous transformation and the epitomizing of its character of "forever becoming." This constant state of flux, its interfering with preservation initiatives, and the onset of novel and experimental photographic practices characterize this chapter's two core subjects: construction site photography that helped measure architectural and urban images and photographs of ruins and rubble.

What did measuring or "photogrammetric" images and rubble photographs say about the city, beyond the common narratives of taking stock and archiving a site? These images reveal the city's state of mind, the "mental life" of the metropolis, which Georg Simmel described as defined by the "attempt of the individual to maintain the independence and individuality of his existence against the sovereign powers of society, against the weight of the historical heritage and the external culture and technique of life."[3]

Metropolitan Transformations: Berlin and Paris

While Paris's radical transformations, initiated by Baron Haussmann, prompted the Parisian city government to commission photographers like Charles Marville (Figure 3.1) to document the buildings and city quarters that were determined for destruction and prompted Édouard Baldus (Figure 3.2) to "edit the urban scene in his Parisian views,"[4] Berlin's urban revamping did not trigger a similar reaction. What was termed "degagement" in Paris—a liberating move by city planners to rid the city of its old and unsanitary network of narrow alleys to make space for "grand avenues culminating in a series of key architectural monuments"[5]—was manifested in Berlin in more hectic fits and starts of uncoordinated development. This chaotic pace was shaped by power struggles between the city, private interests, and the state as embodied by the emperor. In contrast with the comprehensive and single-minded vision of Baron Haussmann in mid-nineteenth-century Paris, or the development of Vienna's Ringstraße, Berlin's urban transformations were piecemeal and stimulated by numerous voices. This unique situation was a reflection of Germany's cultural and political fragmentation despite the nation's official unification. While its neighbors started remodeling the urban fabric of their capitols, adjusting it to the flow of a growing populace and rail traffic in the 1850s, Berlin's city magistrate did not start its modernization effort until Berlin became the German capital in 1871 and did not hit its full stride until the 1880s.[6]

The rhetoric accompanying Berlin's modernization was remarkably different from the grandiloquence that was used to describe Haussmann's Paris. Berlin's answer to Parisian "degagement" was a kind of reckless demontage, which has been interpreted by contemporaries and more recent critics alike as guided by a "blatant disregard for the existing old city and promoted under the false claim of logistic improvements that required numerous breakthroughs for new roads and broadening of several historic streets in the historic city center."[7] Instead of embracing the city and its man-made and modern interventions, assessments of Berlin were dominated by dismay and frustration at the loss of the old.

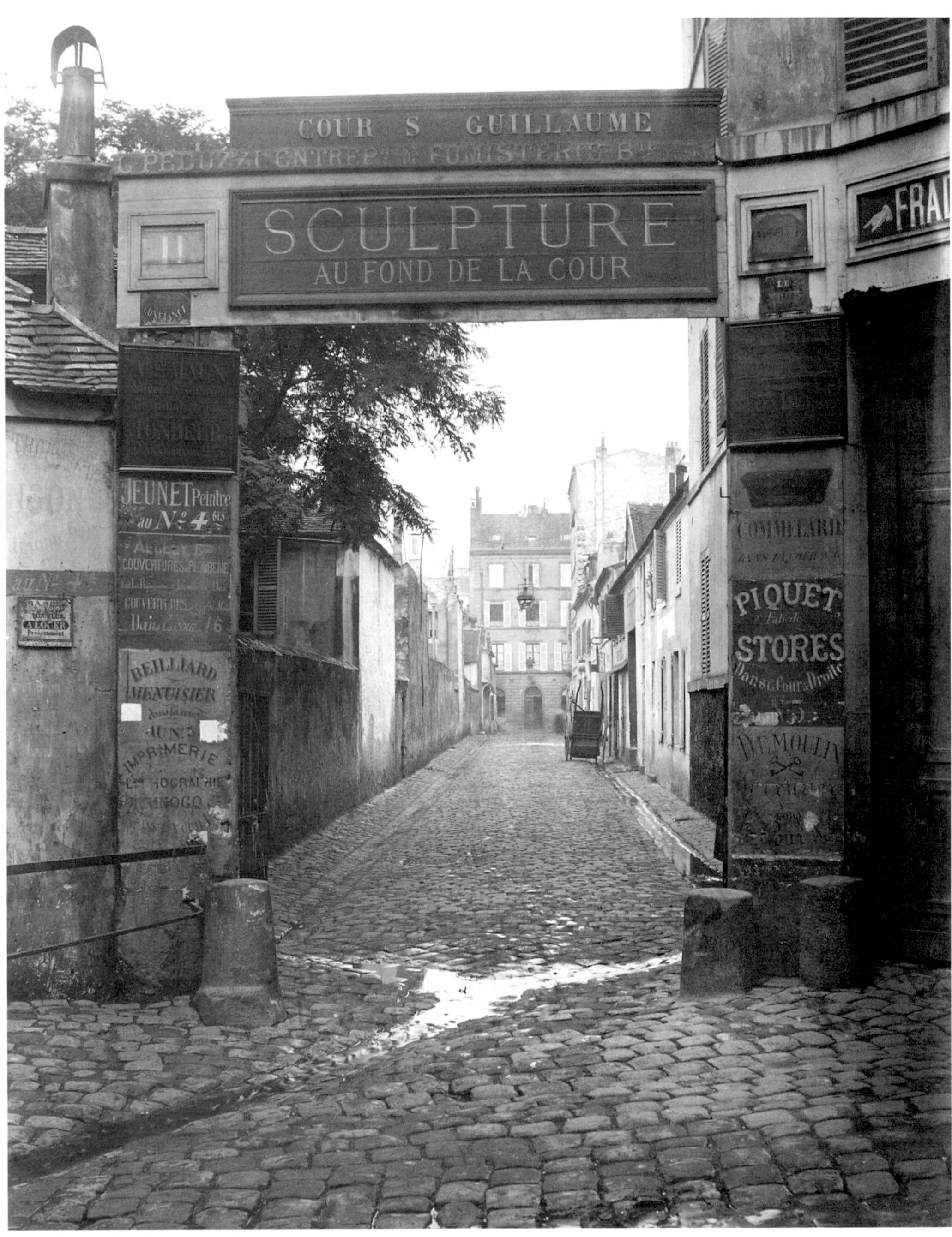

Figure 3.1. Charles Marville, *Cour Saint-Guillaume*, Paris, circa 1865. Albumen silver print from glass negative, 34.2 × 27.2 cm. Gilman Collection, Purchase, Alfred Stieglitz Society Gifts, 2005. Accession number 2005.100.378, Metropolitan Museum of Art, New York City. OASC.

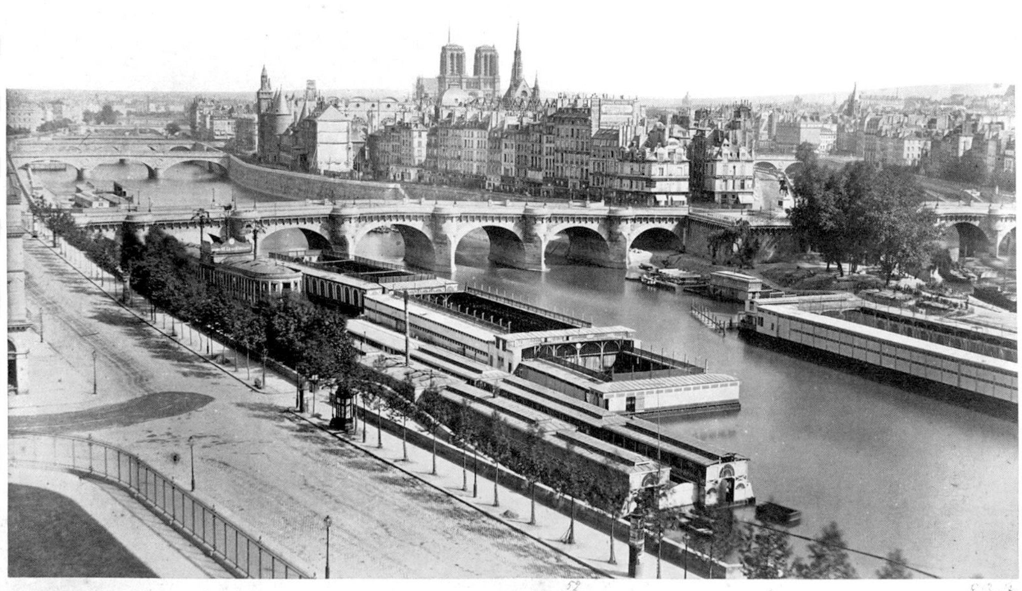

Figure 3.2. Édouard Baldus, *Panorama of la Cite*, circa 1860. Albumen silver print from glass negative, 20.3 × 28.3 cm. David Hunter McAlpin Fund, 1944. Accession number 44.55.1, Metropolitan Museum of Art, New York City. OASC.

Such sentiments persevere today, and Berlin's contemporary urban discourse is prominently manifested in the decades-long debates about the demolition of the socialist "Palace of the Republic" and the reconstruction of its predecessor on its site, the historic city castle.

On a local level, this ambiguity was in part due to Berlin city planner James Friedrich Hobrecht's (1825–1902) deliberately open 1862 grid and park system for Berlin's new residential areas in the north and east, and in part to public policy measures that granted developers significant freedom. In the city center, where representation mattered most, Emperor Wilhelm II took a personal interest in shaping the new metropolis. Soon after he succeeded his grandfather, Wilhelm I, and father, Friedrich III (who governed for only ninety-nine days), in 1888, he expressed a keen interest in the new capital's development, particularly with the projects of Ludwig Hoffmann. While new construction came to define the city, preserving historical structures and the memory of what defined old Berlin, Prussia, and the Holy Roman Empire of the German nation took center stage. Indeed, the unapologetic demolition of many historic buildings was a direct trigger for growing preservationist concern.

As a consequence, documentary city surveys in the French and German capitals of the 1860s through 1890s took on different perspectives and rhetorics. They represented either a publicly uttered and independently articulated sense of urgency, as exemplified in the works of Berlin's documentarians F. Albert Schwartz and Georg Bartels, or a more systematic, commission-driven exploration of the historic and new city, like Charles Marville's documentation of Parisian "upheaval of Haussmannism."[8] These studies are complex and vary in purpose and intention. Karen Rosenberg, for example, detects in Marville's oeuvre more than the work of a mere preservationist-minded technocrat; she notes ambitions "to give photography a permanent office in the modern city."[9] Similarly, in Berlin, at least for the early years of the Second Empire, photography was not simply a preservationist tool, but instead took an important role registering the experience of tabula rasa. Photographers, however, unlike critics and preservationists, kept a healthy distance from their subject matter. In a city that carried much less historical baggage and artistic reputation than other European metropolises, preservationist notions were often put into a different perspective by the spectacle of demolition and speculative development. Once people had started commenting on the disappearance of their city, many historic buildings and entire city quarters had already vanished, and demolition was both thrilling, sublime, and deeply concerning.

With his sympathetic descriptions of Berlin in *Bilder aus dem Berliner Leben*, Julius Rodenberg captured Berlin's unique situation between these contradictory forces.[10] Quoting the Melbourne-based newspaper *Imperial Review* of October 1883, he wrote in the late 1880s that "there is no gap between dead past and lively present, as in Rome and Paris. Life in this youthful city has been an uninterrupted one. It is the capital of a people on the rise and not about to depart."[11] Somewhere within the flow of life in this city, between past and present, lie the ruins and urban detritus of rubble images and the unfolding of the urban palimpsest of historic buildings being replaced by a new monument in measuring images. Before considering the photographs proper, however, it is important to gain a sense of the city of Berlin's urban development after 1871 and the role that historic preservation began to play in the Second German Empire.

Berlin's historic and urban development during the Wilhelmine Empire can be loosely grouped into two phases.[12] The first, which roughly encompasses the reign of Wilhelm I until 1888, was marked by severe economic fluctuations but a fairly stable political situation. The 1873 collapse of the Vienna stock exchange and the subsequent crash (*Gründerkrach*) marked the beginning of two decades of economic turbulence and urban demolition. This phase stretched into the 1890s and is thoroughly documented in photographs; parts of the old layer of the city were recorded, photographed, historically researched, and gradually and selectively overwritten. Otto von Bismarck, the chancellor of the German Empire from its inception and the driving force behind Germany's unification, was let go by Wilhelm II in 1890 due to political disagreements with the recently instated emperor. During the second phase, after 1900, demolition had become a familiar phenomenon in the city, and building activities slowed down.

Transformation was most palpable in Berlin's center, where prominent buildings like the old cathedral by Schinkel, the mint and the baroque prince's palace (Fürstenpalais), or the baroque residential and commercial complex of the Schloßfreiheit, which stood across the street from the city castle, had to yield to new construction. Building complexes along whole streets in the city center and bordering districts, including the historic Krögel district, had fallen into disrepair or were reconstructed, remodeled, or replaced by new buildings. The most prominent construction projects were the ones in Königstraße, the new construction of Mühlendammbrücke, Rosenstraße, and Kreuzbergstraße. During Wilhelm II's reign and, like Baron Haussmann's transformation of Paris under Napoleon III over two decades earlier—these changes were not merely pragmatic. The transformation or eradication of Berlin's built substance was a form of self-portrayal, even self-aggrandizement, which suited the emperor's own theatrical inclinations. In the words of curator Eberhard Roters, "The cityscape in the center surrounding the [Royal] palace was tidied up, ostentatiously beautified, and served to the world like a dynastic centerpiece."[13] As administrative buildings, businesses, and hotels spread throughout the inner city, its population dropped significantly. Around the turn of the century, similar concentrations took place in the rest of the older municipal area.[14]

Flatten, Expand, Animate: Photogrammetry in Berlin, 1894–1896

Photogrammetry, or measuring photography, would probably not exist without the institutionalization and professionalization of historic preservation in Germany, which started in the mid-nineteenth century. The series of seven measuring images discussed here was officially created to register progress on the construction site for a large equestrian monument in front of the castle's most prominent west façade. This endeavor granted the rare opportunity to capture the city castle's otherwise obstructed façade, which had been suddenly revealed by the demolition of the Schloßfreiheit. This complex consisted of ten buildings on the eastern side of Spreegraben between the Schloß and Schleusen Bridges (Figure 3.3). It was created after 1672 on prince-electorial grounds across from the castle and was inhabited—free of cost and taxes—by employees and favorites of the court. Later, when businesses moved into the ground floor, their owners moved in and the complex appeared as a row of buildings situated

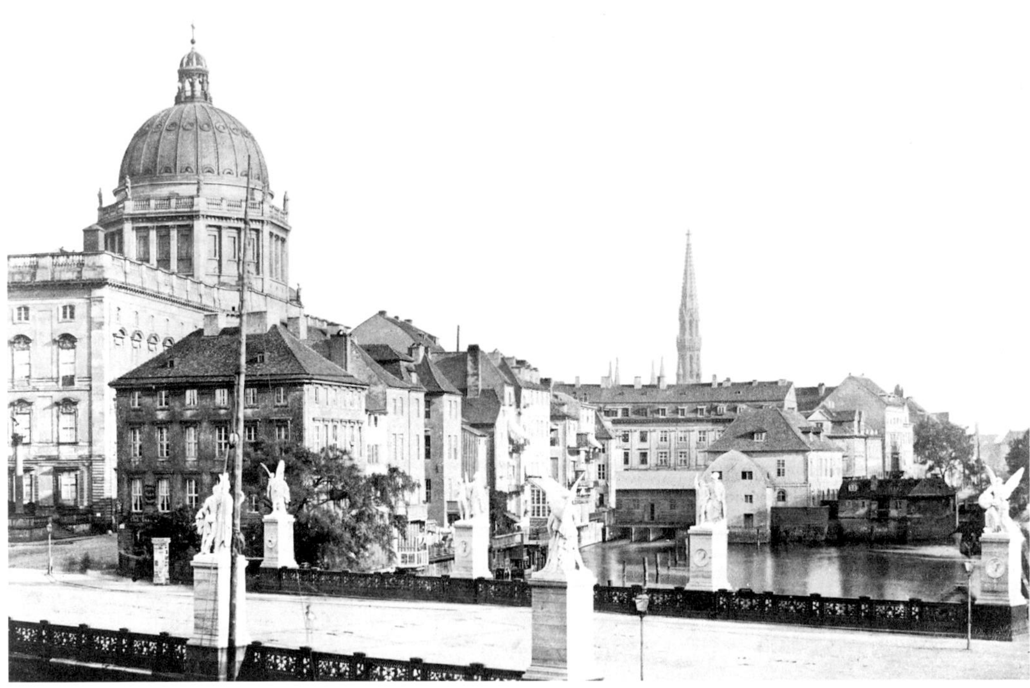

Figure 3.3. F. Albert Schwartz (photographic studio), *Das alte Berlin. Schloßbrücke und Werdersche Mühlen* (Old Berlin: Castle Bridge and Werder's Mills), Berlin, 1865. 12 × 17.60 cm. Inventory number GE 2006/104 VF. Copyright Stiftung Stadtmuseum Berlin.

before the castle like a quirky horizontal monolith.[15] Between 1892 and 1894, the buildings were demolished to make space for a monument to Wilhelm I, which was inaugurated in 1897.[16]

This set of photogrammetric images, like many such sets, were officially ordered to record progress; in this case, it documented the monument's construction on the site of the Schloßfreiheit. These images tell two parallel stories: one of a monument's construction, and one of Berlin's cultural heritage in the form of the castle's west façade. The implications of this awkward copresence of new construction and historical structure were far-ranging and highly impactful.

The Royal Prussian Photogrammetric Institute, which produced this image series, was headed from its foundation in 1885 by the inventor of this ingenious photographic technique, Albrecht Meydenbauer (1834–1921). As a young governmental building developer, Meydenbauer started to look for alternatives to the dangerous task of taking measurements of buildings, which he himself had to perform frequently in preparation for renovation work. In 1863, Meydenbauer developed the concepts of measuring photography, or photogrammetry, which would become a crucial means of documentation for architecture, art history, topography, and meteorology, and he publicly introduced the technology at the first international photographic exhibition in 1865. He generated these images in a photogrammetric camera, the Meßbildkammer (Figure 3.4), which had a special lens that corrected for perspective and adjusted distortions and vanishing lines. With a built-in instrument for measuring angles, it could enable the precise documentation and potential reconstruction of photographed buildings after they were demolished or destroyed, such as the capture of Berlin's French Cathedral (Figure 3.5). Based on the idea of mathematically generating absolute measurements of a building by reversing its perspective, it was, in essence, an architectural drawing technology: the photographic image as blueprint, without the usual measuring errors. As such, it lent itself to capturing not only buildings and historical monuments but also any three-dimensional object of cultural or historical significance for posterity. Here was a means to remake structures that might be lost to modernization and demolition, and without the mortal risk of climbing up monuments.[17]

With the help of written notes detailing the position from which the picture had been taken, it became possible to determine the measurements, to create

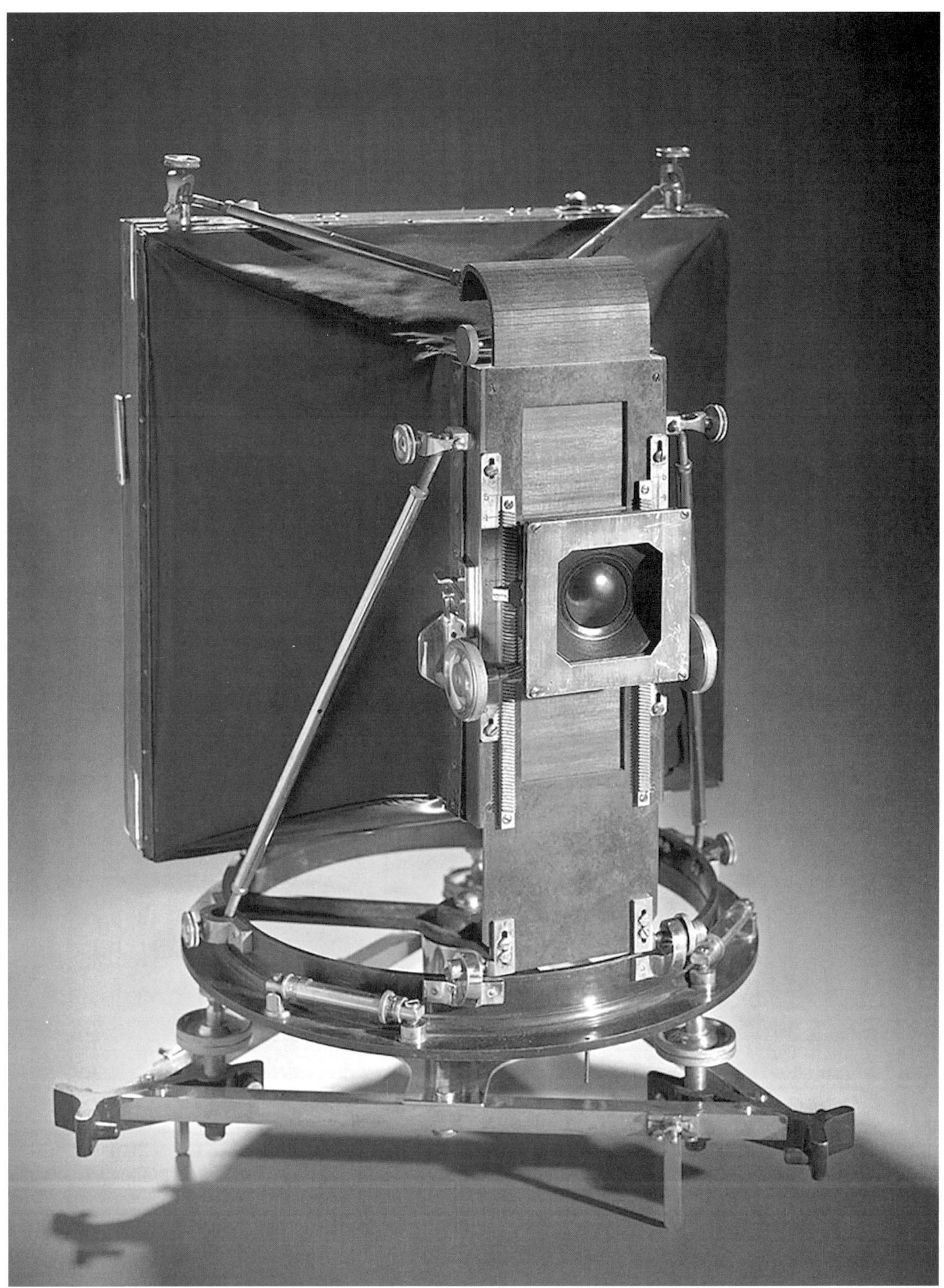

Figure 3.4. Measuring image/photogrammetric camera conceived and built by Albrecht Meydenbauer, German engineer, creator of architectural photogrammetry. Photograph by Simon Schmid, Swiss National Library. Wikimedia Commons.

scale drawings, or even to arrive at a precise reconstruction of that which had been represented two-dimensionally. With a photogrammetric image—usually the contact print or the enlargement of a 38.5 × 38.5 cm glass negative—it was possible to gather information not only about the dimensions and surface, but also about the location, the design, and the form of the photographed building.[18] The building became isolated, in a technically and aesthetically elegant way. However, the initial goal to follow the tenets of traditional perspective rendering by keeping vertical lines parallel was later abandoned by photogrammetrists. By the 1880s the Meßbild cameras "used extremely wide wide-angle lenses and their photographers allowed the consequent perspective lines to show" (Figure 3.5).[19]

Meydenbauer originally intended to erect a photogrammetric archive of Prussia's architectural and artistic monuments. Indeed, the Royal Prussian Photogrammetric Institute was the first organization of its kind that systematically archived buildings. In that regard, his goal was very much in line with survey initiatives such as the well-known Mission Héliographique in 1850s France. Resonating with the nineteenth century's fascination for Greek and Roman ruins, as well as for the remnants of the Gothic age, this plan expanded into the idea of creating an archive for the entire world's cultural heritage. Meydenbauer's vision was a forerunner to the German preservationist Georg Dehio's project for a comprehensive archive of monuments.

During Meydenbauer's directorship between 1885 and 1902, the institute produced 11,940 photogrammetric images in Prussia, on expeditions to Turkey and Greece, and of the ruins of Athens and Baalbek. However, the institute in Berlin did not compile a more systematic collection of Berlin monuments, as was done, for example, with the Romanesque churches in Cologne, until during and after the First World War, although numerous photographs were taken of the area around Museum Island and the castle.[20]

During 1896 and 1897, the Royal Prussian Photogrammetric Institute pursued a project in Berlin's city center, which comprised a series of eight photogrammetric images documenting the construction of an equestrian monument built to honor Wilhelm I (Figure 3.6). The series began with the documentation of the demolition site in front of the city castle. It continued with the laying of the foundation and ended with the presentation of the marble colonnades that served as a backdrop to the monument and of the equestrian statue.

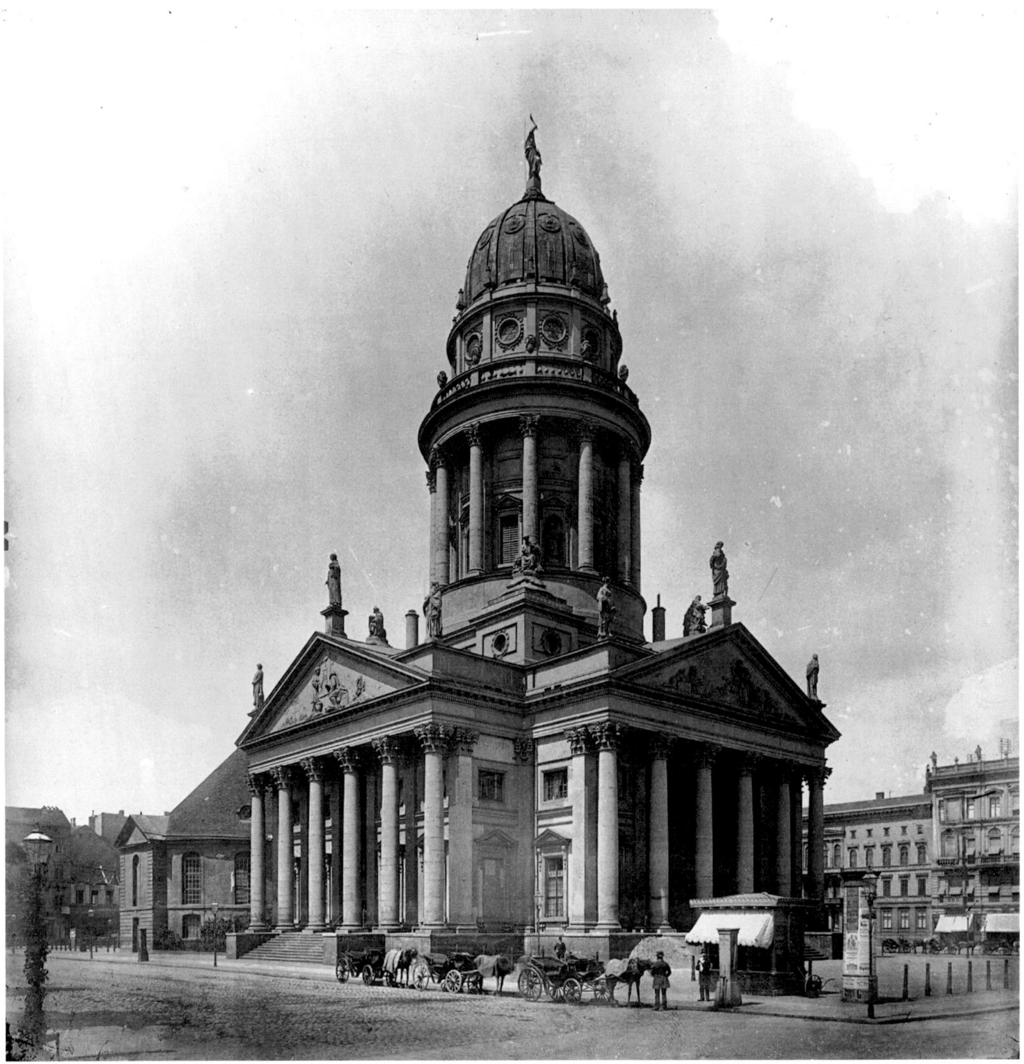

Figure 3.5. Albrecht Meydenbauer, *Französischer Dom* (French Cathedral), Berlin, 1882. Reproduced by Lindau & Borchart, Buchhandlung für Architektur und Kunstgewerbe. Photograph provided by Brandenburgisches Landesamt für Denkmalpflege.

The camera was pointed at the back of the growing monument, while the frame varied slightly from picture to picture, suggesting that the camera was set up anew for each photograph from approximately the same location. This sequential approach, which was rather unusual for photogrammetric images of historic buildings, created a peculiar contrast with the static consistency of the other central image motif besides the monument, the city castle's stately west façade.

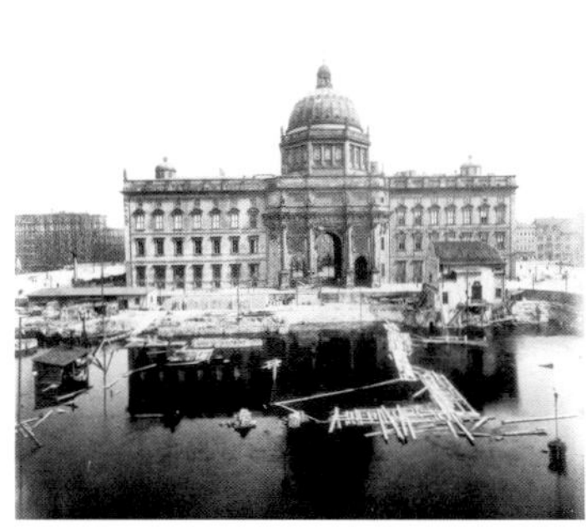
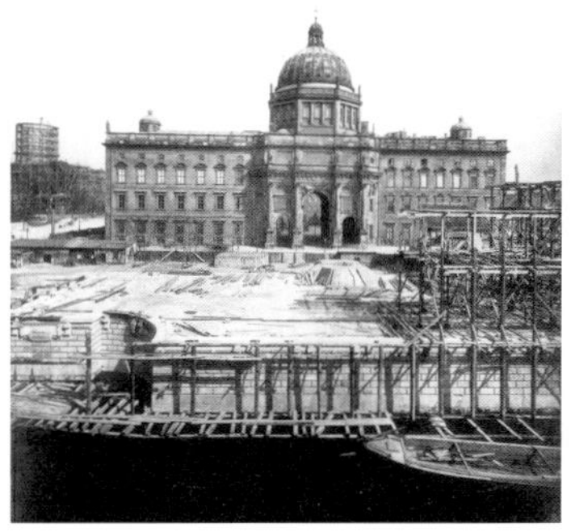
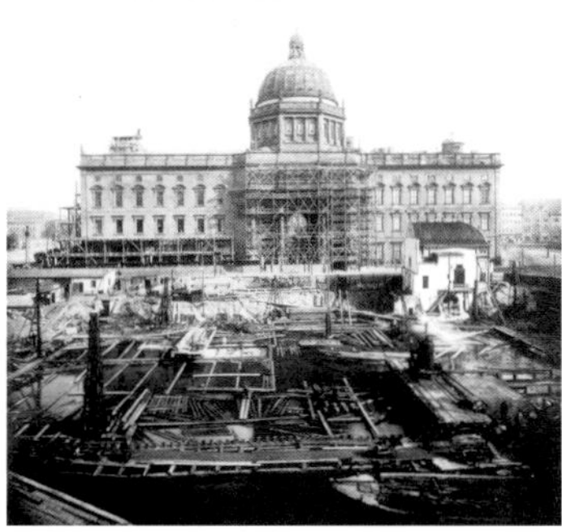
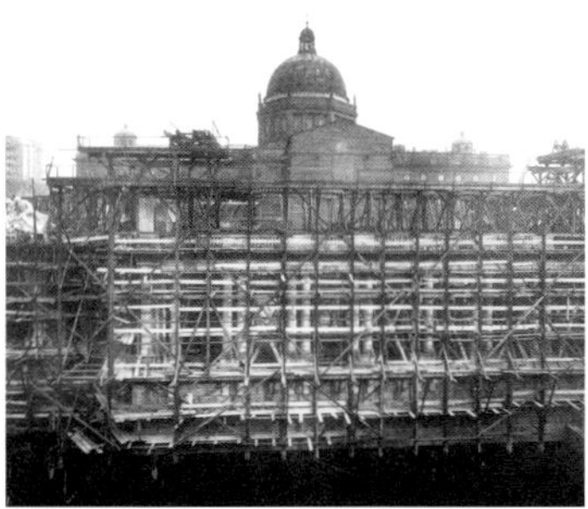
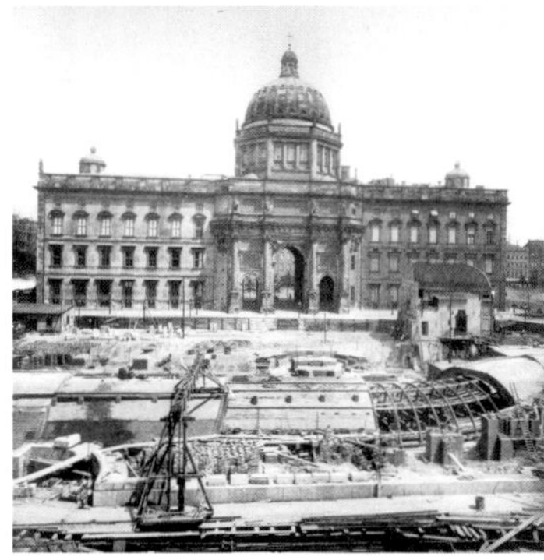
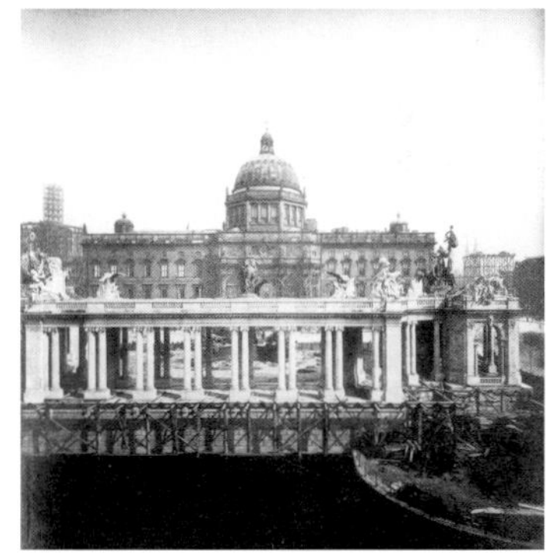
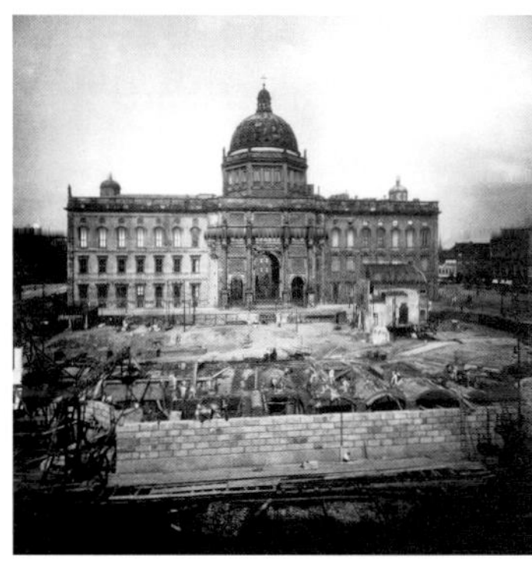
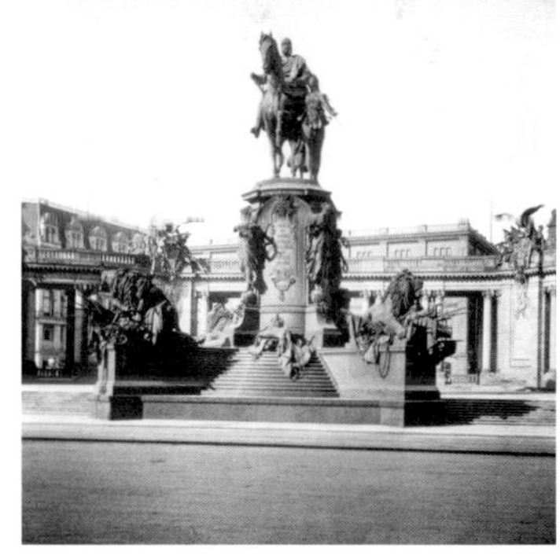

Figure 3.6. Staatliche Bildstelle/Royal Photogrammetric Institute, erection of the Wilhelm I monument. Kunstbibliothek, Staatliche Museen zu Berlin. Inventory numbers 240. 1475.2; 240. 1475.3; 240. 1475.3a; 240. 1475.4; 240. 1475.5; 240. 1475.6; 240. 1475.7; 240. 1475.8.

This disparity was underlined by what was visible on the left and right in the picture background: the new cathedral and the representative head-end buildings along Königstraße that were in the process of being erected. The individual images showed how the scaffolding took on ever-new configurations. In all likelihood, the photographs were taken directly from the window of the Photogrammetric Institute, which at the time was conveniently housed in Karl Friedrich Schinkel's Bauakademie (Building Academy), just opposite the castle's west wing. All these images were elevation-like, including a strictly frontal perspective and a high level of detail. But as a series, they actually presented the process of the monument's erection in an almost cinematic fashion—a style that was undoubtedly influenced by the first film screenings, which were taking place in Berlin and Paris around the same time.

The prime use of the series was to register and control the building activities on the construction site, which was a typical function of urban photography at the time. It was quite common to photographically document the progress on construction sites regularly as part of confirming the correct execution of a commission. The journal *Photographisches Wochenblatt* reports, for example, that measuring images were used to control the correct and timely execution of the erection of the London freight train station of the "Great Eastern Railway." The manufacturers of the massive iron parts were only paid after it was proven by a photograph of a respective day that they were mounted in place on the site.[21] The castle's west façade, which reappeared, elevation-like and unchanged, in each image like a reliable backdrop or stage set, was considered to be the castle's most sophisticated feature. It displayed both the Eosander Portal and the comparatively new castle's chapel dome, which had been concluded in 1853 and marked the end point of centuries of expansion work on the castle.

The Schloßfreiheit complex, which was replaced by the monument, had a unique story to tell. The complex's ownership granted "freedom from the castle" (*Schloß-Freiheit*), which meant that its inhabitants had administrative independence from the city and were direct subjects of the emperor.[22] Despite its age and centuries-long development, it was not regarded as noteworthy or historically and aesthetically relevant and would not have qualified as a monument, even under Dehio's broad understanding of the term. Even though it had certain picturesque qualities, which might have contributed to its rare depiction

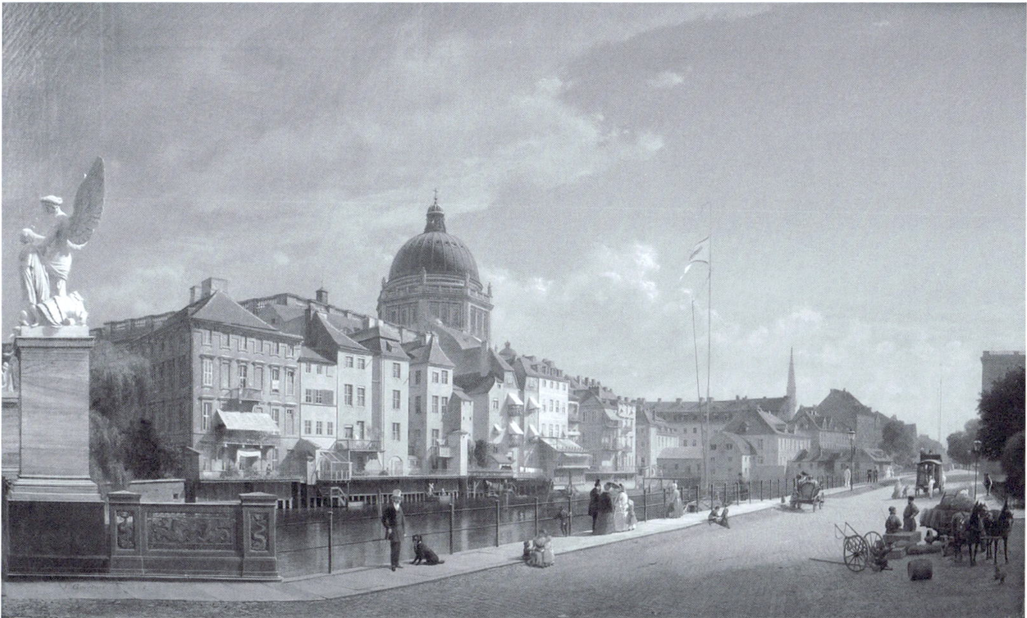

Figure 3.7. Eduard Gärtner, *Schlossfreiheit,* 1855. Oil on canvas. Alte Nationalgalerie Berlin. This building complex between the city castle's west wing and the Kupfergraben Channel was torn down in 1893–95 to make space for a monument for Emperor Wilhelm I. Wikimedia Commons.

in Eduard Gärtner's two paintings of the 1850s (Figure 3.7) and a number of photographs of the 1860s through 1890s, city officials and the emperor despised it and actively pursued its demolition. Its critics bemoaned it as an eyesore and considered it unsuitable for a truly modern capital.

The contrasting histories of both complexes, the Schloßfreiheit and the Wilhelm monument, set the stage for the complicated story of this image series—a story that emerges strikingly when one compares Eduard Gärtner's romantically enhanced cityscape of the Schloßfreiheit with the measuring image sequence of the monument. Gärtner presents the building complex from the northwest, revealing its irregularities and a romantic hotchpotch of buildings that had been added to the complex over several decades. The early afternoon sun and blue sky, textured and enhanced by some clouds that seem to be blowing over the city eastward, create a serene atmosphere. Berlin's Biedermeier bourgeoisie strolls along Kupfergraben Channel, which separates them from the ensemble of city castle and Schloßfreiheit.

The measuring image series approached its subject matter—demolition and monument construction—through strict frontality and seriality. Between Gärtner's midcentury idyll and the photogrammetrist's cinematic stills, significant formal, stylistic, and ideological changes in respect to urban representation and perception come to the fore. Both the painting and the set of photographs conveyed precise, detailed information, yet they eloquently put to use their fundamentally different means of articulating intentions. The painter dramatized through color and atmospheric elements and relied on his command of perspectival drawing and mastery of detail; the photogrammetrist used what was in front of him and worked with patience and technical finesse. By spacing his narrative and concentrating on the synchronicity of current building activities with historic buildings, he presented, in photographic black and white, a meaningful description of an ideologically combated site. While Gärtner, hoping to entice his midcentury clientele, used the painterly and interpretive means of his medium, the pictorial capacities of the photogrammetrists's image remained far more limited. However, the measuring image's great advantage was its potential to create sequential narratives. In the following years, both the expectations of and the style of measuring images changed. It became more tolerant to wide-angle distortions and more expressive. Robinson points out, "If pictures in the eighties had promised the viewer facts, the most extreme of the new pictures gave the viewer a selected view and a sense of atmosphere at the expense of providing any precise information about the specific building that was the subject of a picture."[23]

The design, choice of site, and erection of the monument for Wilhelm I was a widely and controversially debated issue in Berlin's cultural circles.[24] The inauguration had been announced with great fanfare but didn't seem to receive the response that the emperor had hoped for. Author and critic Alfred Kerr captured the ambivalence and awkward tension between demonstrative yet unfelt national pride and an inner numbness and indifference as he commented on the impending inauguration preparations in a letter on January 17, 1897:

> The new year ninety-seven doesn't seem to be off to a funny start. The German people, especially the Berliners, step up full of pride to the national celebrations, which brings the unveiling of the monarchic monument with omitted polling box at Schloßfreiheit; student fraternities also have already begun to get drunk in time

at gatherings called Kommers in honor of these festivities. But the general inner mood is depressed.[25]

This lack of excitement for the monument was shared among the city's intellectual and artistic avant-garde. It was echoed by Ludwig Hoffmann's comments about its weak and disappointing design by the emperor's favorite sculptor, Reinhold Begas. Begas's smaller sculptural work was appealing, but as Hoffmann wrote in his posthumously published memoirs, he "lacked the necessary sharp self-criticism and the caution that goes hand in hand with it."[26] Hoffmann, who passed the monument almost daily on his way to his studio, found the work unfortunately "uncoordinated and loose" and "resembling a theater decoration" rather than a serious memorial.[27] Max Osborn, in his 1909 history of Berlin's architectural and artistic highlights, focused on Begas's inability to handle large monument projects. Such a task was not only "against" the sculptor's "nature" but was also hopelessly outdated. This monument, Osborn bemoaned, was "uncharacteristic and without stronger expression."[28] The emperor, who had handpicked the sculptor, predictably disagreed, asserting that it "proved that Berlin's school of sculptors produces work that matches the beauty of work created in the Renaissance."[29] An unconventional take of the monument is Heinrich Zille's 1897 photograph (Figure 3.8).

The photogrammetric series captured a moment that embodied the ideological tensions that Berlin experienced at the time: the craving for national unity and identity through history and the desire to explicitly mark this identity through new urban developments. Wilhelm II's frame of reference in comparing Begas's work with artistic production and achievement in the (Italian) Renaissance revealed such tension in artistic discourse. While the emperor mused about past artistic achievements from which to reap meaning for contemporary design, artists like Max Liebermann, Lovis Corinth, and Max Slevogt challenged academic artistic traditions and were key protagonists of Berlin's art secession. The ambiguous message of these measuring images was in its sense of irony: the historical Schloßfreiheit ensemble had been replaced by a monument that claimed, through historicist design, a historicity that the original buildings had naturally possessed. However, the Schloßfreiheit, as the historically grown evidence of a bygone era's urban culture, did not seem to fit into the new image of modern urbanity.[30] A historicist monument was associated with

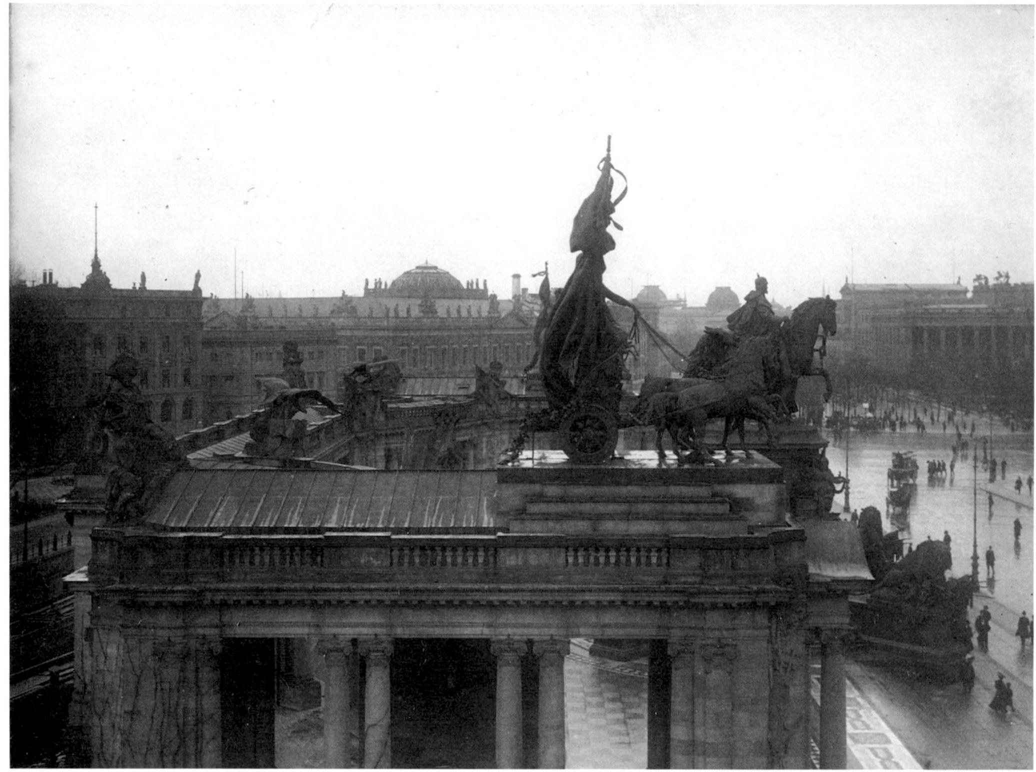

Figure 3.8. Heinrich Zille, *National-Denkmal Kaiser Wilhelms I. von Reinhold Begas* (National monument for Emperor Wilhelm I by Reinhold Begas), Spring 1897. Collodion print, matte. Inventory number WV41. Photograph provided by Berlinische Galerie.

greater symbolic power than the charisma of truly historical buildings—a way of thinking that does not seem too far removed from the current understanding of history in Berlin.

The cultural tension triggered by the replacement of a historic building with a historicist memorial is traceable within photography theory debates as well. Mid- to late nineteenth-century photography theory acknowledged photography as a medium that registered technically and without emotion. But it also alleged the emerging medium's almost magical qualities, which enabled photography to salvage buildings from their natural fate of demolition. To the mid-nineteenth-century viewer, fixing a site in a negative provided a means to separate form from matter. This insight was famously articulated by the American physician and author Oliver Wendell Holmes (1809–94) in his 1859 manuscript "The Stereoscope and the Stereograph." The consequence of this separation, he stated, was that

> matter as a visible object is of no great use any longer, except as the mould on which form is shaped. Give us a few negatives of a thing worth seeing, taken from different points of view, and that is all we want of it. Pull it down or burn it up, if you please. We must, perhaps, sacrifice some luxury in the loss of color; but form and light and shade are the great things, and even color can be added, and perhaps by and by may be got direct from Nature.[31]

Holmes, presaging Meydenbauer's and Dehio's preservationist views, suggested that what matters most about the material object was its "representative," its "skin." He wrote, "The consequence of this will soon be such an enormous collection of forms that they will have to be classified and arranged in vast libraries, as books are now." Holmes also invigorated later urges for comprehensive archives of culture, which Dehio would later approach with a more patriotic tone.

While Holmes considered the stereograph as the ideal medium to realize such a vision, Meydenbauer felt that it could best be achieved via photogrammetry. This was ironic. Photogrammetric technology visually flattened rather than expanded spatial perception, while the stereoscope's main feature as a 3-D viewer was that it simulated depth with two slightly misaligned images (Figure 3.9).[32] However, it was the former's measureable and systematizing qualities, rather than the stereograph's exquisite spatial illusion that provided adequate means for a comprehensive archive of the world's cultural heritage. Meydenbauer, the architect, had a keen and hands-on interest in saving crucial architectural data while the American polymath Holmes was curious about the popular qualities and potential for a wide dissemination of photography.

While the stereograph became a tremendously popular form of mass entertainment and spectacle from the 1850s through the early twentieth century, the photogrammetric image was used primarily for documentary purposes and had a much smaller audience. It did, however, possess a similarly strong aesthetic appeal and, like the daguerreotype, sparked a particular fascination among professional photographers. Both the stereograph and the photogrammetric image epitomized *truthfulness* to an extent that had not been realized in mechanized

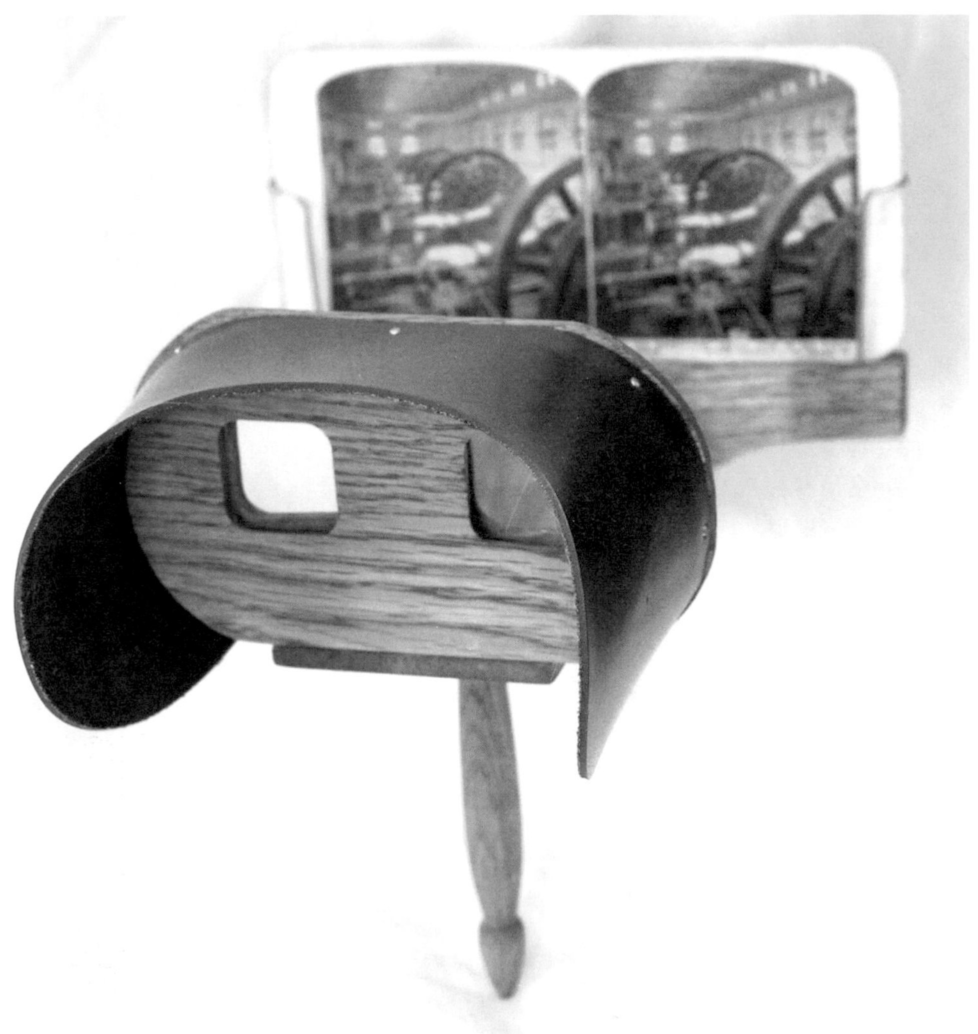

Figure 3.9. Reproduction of a Holmes stereoscope. Photo by Davepape, http://en.wikipedia.org.

image-making. Both possessed a degree of focus, clarity, and fine grain that left onlookers baffled. However, the photogrammetric image provided a mental space that far exceeded the idea of documenting, securing, and archiving.

Photogrammetry's technical particularities pushed it to the forefront of the Berlin makeover. Although the calotype of the French Mission Héliographique in the 1850s may have been able to finely depict buildings, its aesthetic effect, due to the paper negative and the quality of the tone, tended to a soft focus

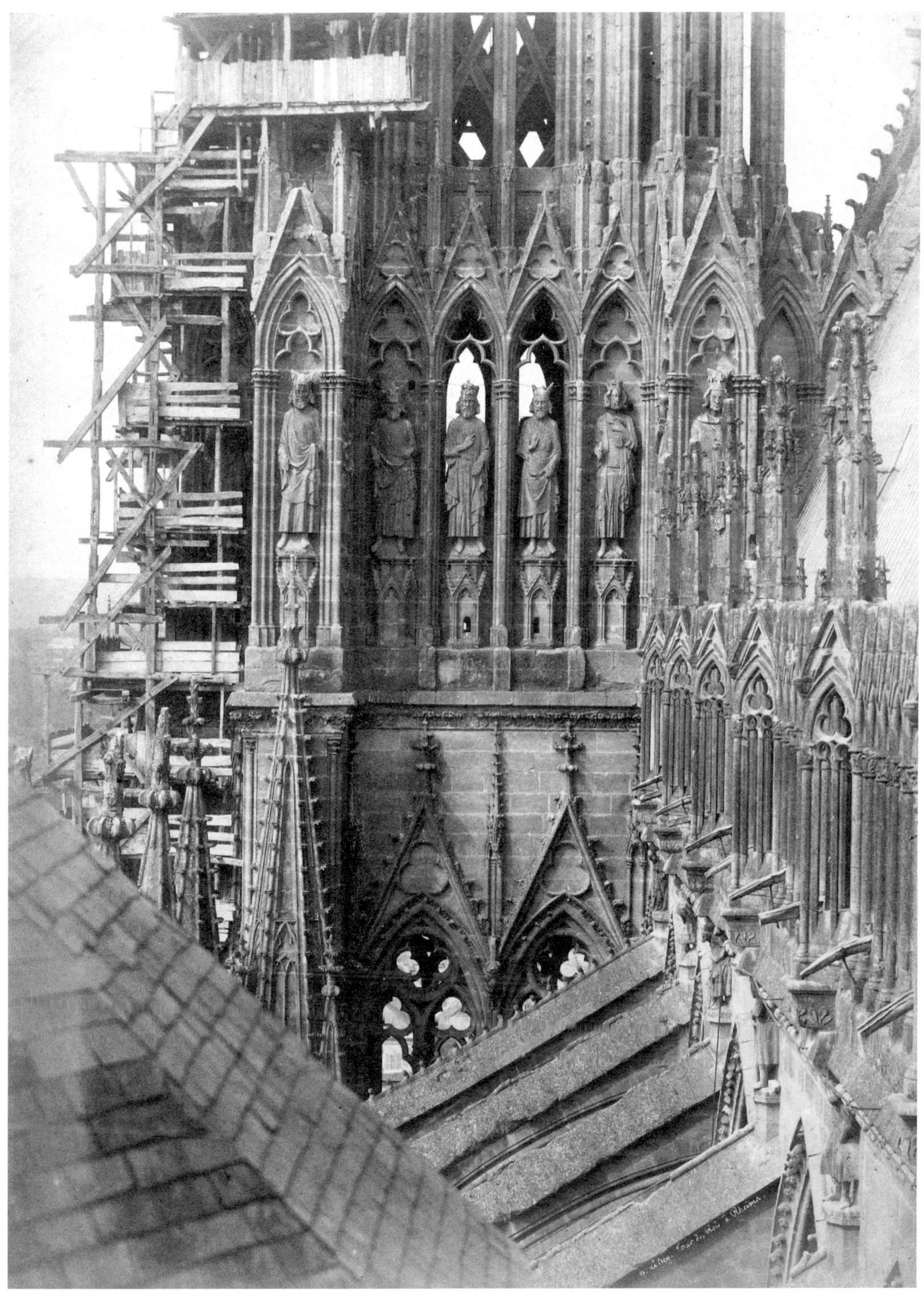

Figure 3.10. Henri Le Secq, Tower of Kings at Reims Cathedral, 1851. Salted paper, 3.51 × 2.59 cm. Wikimedia Commons.

and a coarse-grain image (see Figure 3.10).[33] The photogrammetric image, by contrast, was carried out at first with the very fine-grained and exact wet collodion process, then with the dry plate. This produced an image that was sharp, true to detail, authentic, and immediate.

Meydenbauer was, from the beginning, keenly aware of the pictorial form of the photogrammetric image, and over time he became increasingly adept at negotiating both the technical and the aesthetic aspects of his images. It is not surprising, then, that his photographs gained recognition at trade exhibitions and art venues for both their technical finesse and their aesthetic qualities.[34] Eduard Doležal, a surveyor of monuments, stated that "whoever had the opportunity to see the enlargements of the Photogrammetric Institute in Berlin has to admit that they constitute true works of art."[35] Meydenbauer, however, never understood photogrammetry as an artistic medium;[36] he always considered it to be a technical form.

The technical and aesthetic qualities of the Whilhelm I monument images, in tandem with their parallel narratives, revealed the broad range of challenges in the urban transformation process: between preservation and longing for a historical rooting on the one hand and a modern affirmation of such historical foundations on the other. This systematic photographic capture focused on the castle and on "fixing" the gaze.[37] This move was supposed to curtail the faster pace of the modern metropolis embodied in the new monument and represented by the moving image. The individual photogrammetric image, with its relentless lack of any motion, revealed a desire to slow down what was happening in the city if not bring it to a halt. Yet this project's seriality also hinted at new visual coping strategies and at what Jonathan Crary identified as the "fundamentally distinct" nature of the cinematic compared to "previous historical forms of simulation."[38]

The series' subject matter was officially the site of transformation in Berlin's center, but it was actually about the city's history. The monument's erection created a spatiotemporal contrast to the static castle face not because it stood for innovation but rather because it represented a piece of invented history that awkwardly clashed with the castle's authentic historicity. The image series ended up being an illustrative statement about Wilhelm II's understanding of rulership and the era's desire to favorably interpret and reframe history.

High-Speed Ruins: Rubble Photography in Berlin

In 1907, Georg Simmel published a short essay about "The Ruin." In it, he pointed out that "the fact that life, with its wealth and its changes, once dwelled here [within the ruin] constitutes an immediately perceived presence. The ruin creates the present form of a past life, not according to the contents or remnants of that life, but according to its past as such."[39] Similarly vivid thoughts about the meaning of the ruin as a "present form of the past," a manifestation of architecture's ephemerality, might have busied author Friedrich Fuchs's mind when he claimed, a few years earlier in 1901, the victimhood of historic buildings. He wrote:

> Again one of Berlin's oldest buildings is about to fall victim to the pickax—a phenomenon that is reported almost daily in Berlin's newspapers. With that, one of the last remnants of the good old days disappears to make space for one of those monstrous tenement buildings or office buildings, which pop up from the ground like mushrooms.[40]

These thoughts expressed the palpable sense among many Berliners that their city was being dramatically revamped: old was exchanged for new, turning large parts of it into sites of ruin and rubble. But was demolition merely destructive? Or might demolition and photography have catalyzed one another, creating a new genre of visual documentation for an emergent urban spectacle? Photographs of demolition sites during this era, which represent a significant part of Berlin urban photographic collections, complicate our understanding both of the classic ruin image and of disaster or demolition documentation. Given local photographers' great interest in buildings under demolition in late nineteenth- and early twentieth-century Berlin, we might even speak of an independent genre of rubble photography, which, while inspired by preservationist intentions, merged with their audience's craving for spectacle and entertainment.

Considering the time of its emergence, however, rubble photography has to be discussed less as an artistic genre and more as a subcategory of both "event photography"—a form of documentary photography that was enabled by faster photographic technology and by the development of cheaper cameras in the 1880s—and photojournalism, which developed hand in hand with the growing culture of illustrated magazines and the invention of the handheld Leica camera in the 1920s.

The notion of "rubble photography" helps to rethink received images of preservation and suggests novel ways that this moment in the city yielded new physical and temporal relationships to image-making. While nominally similar, rubble photography is distinct in its context and its agency from rubble films (*Trümmerfilme*), a series of post–World War II works set in bombed-out German cities that captured moral themes and physical realities of that era (Figure 3.11). Robert Shandley defines these as "films that take the *mise en scène* of destroyed Germany as a background and metaphor of the destruction of German's [*sic*] own sense of themselves."[41] Produced between roughly 1946 and 1949, these films "confront postwar realities" (Rentschler); but while they stemmed from a period of "physical, political and moral chaos," they "are topical forms from a time often regarded as devoid of topics" (Shandley).[42]

Rubble photography emerged earlier, amid urban restructuring rather than urban warfare. However, neither Berlin's post–world war ruins nor those of the Wilhelmine Empire have qualities that travel writer Rose Macaulay calls

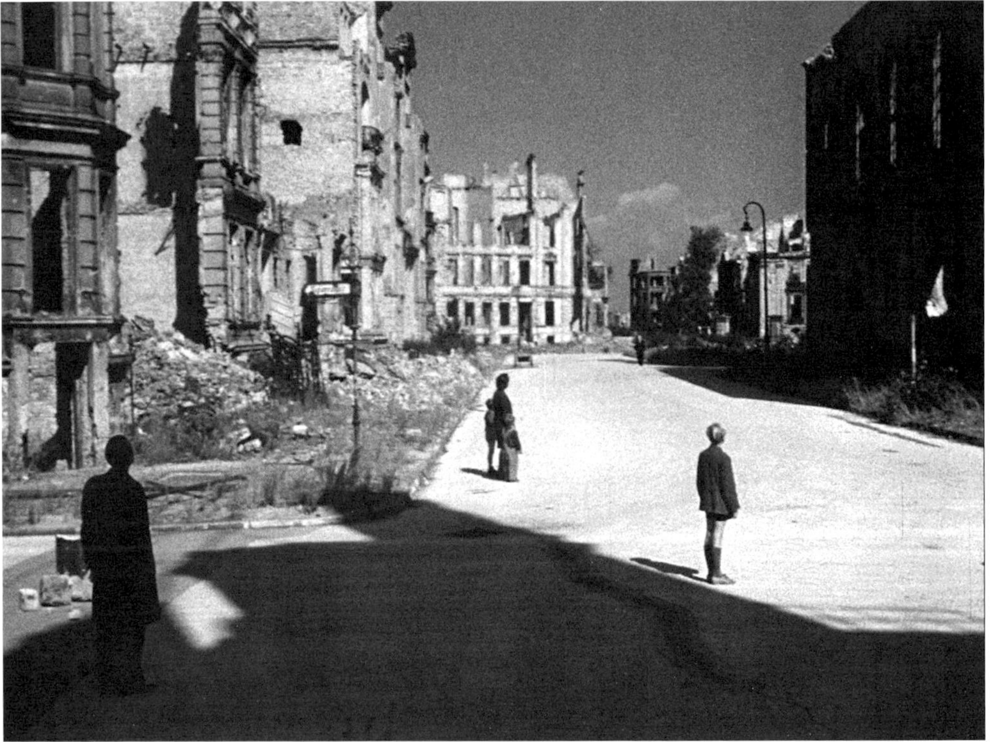

Figure 3.11. Still from Roberto Rosselini, *Germania anno zero* (*Germany Year Zero*), 1948.

"pleasing decay." Neither are they ruins that are a kind of "fantasy, veiled by the mind's dark imaginings," but rather signifiers of a stark urban reality and presence. They are rubble images.[43] Unlike earlier paintings of ruins, rubble photography was characterized by instantaneously depicting different stages of demolition, in single images or in sequences, and were disseminated rapidly. It included street views, individual residential and public buildings, infrastructural works such as bridges, and, sometimes, parts of city quarters. Photographers focused on capturing ruinous structures like piles of rubble, empty window openings, newly exposed interior walls, stairwells, and rooms, and construction sites with scaffolding or fences. The photographers were either independent professionals, members of the Royal Photogrammetric Institute, or, increasingly, as photo equipment became more affordable and easier to handle, bystanders who happened to own a camera.

Rubble as matter and ruins as their composition have been both medium and muse for architects, artists, and poets since the Renaissance.[44] The ruin (from Latin *ruere*, "to fall") here is understood as a building that is falling apart (due to natural disassembling, neglect, or forceful impact) or a building's leftovers. Brian Dillon, in his survey of the function of ruins and their pictorial representation, begins his analysis in the Renaissance, where he finds that the ruin was "first of all a legible remnant, a repository of written knowledge."[45] Rome's ruins in the fifteenth century, Dillon asserts, had already been figured as "a sort of scattered cipher: a text that was alternately readable and utterly mysterious."[46] This dichotomy between the literal and the symbolic, the pragmatic and the emotional, would remain a characteristic of the ruin throughout the eighteenth, nineteenth, and twentieth centuries. What changed was the reading of the ruin. While it was regarded as an "image both of natural disasters and of the catastrophes of human history" and found articulation in the sublime during the eighteenth century, the nineteenth century saw a departure from such a dark reading of the ruin, according to Dillon, to embrace its fragmentary character as inherently artistic. Artists didn't simply aspire to resolution in depicting already existing ruins,[47] but rather reimagined finished, intact buildings as ruins, ironically constructing the latter pictorially. With the onset of urbanization in England, France, and, later, Germany, ruins appeared as the result not only of war or neglect but also of planned demolition. Thus, it is understandable that toward the end of the nineteenth century the ruin was considered to be a phenomenon that occurred naturally as part of the tension between culture and nature. The ruin turned into the intermediary between "persistence and decay."[48] The fragmentary ruin or rubble image found its place between holding on and letting go of the historic urban fabric, and the systematic destruction occurring in Berlin. The ruin image in Berlin gave birth to new methods and tactics for urban image-making, including proto-photojournalistic habits of quick response to current events and skillful moves in order to position oneself effectively for the photograph.

Two photogrammetric images, likely taken around 1900, serve as prime examples of the genre. One image, commissioned by the Royal Prussian Photogrammetric Institute, showed demolition work on a small, classicist city house on Blücherstraße 22, which was probably built in the mid-nineteenth century and was then ready to be replaced by larger developments. Another image captured the front façade of a house at Oberwallstraße 3 during demolition.

The Blücherstraße image is typical of architecture and demolition photographs of the time. The photographer stood across the street and at a slight angle to the building to capture both the front elevation and parts of the side of the building. The perspectival view of the building gives a sense of its size and spatial dimensions. The image also captured the temporary wooden fence, which was erected to shield the construction site from passersby. The photographer purposefully avoided including people, focusing solely on the structure and its voided window openings. Apparently, demolition of the building was imminent, and its replacement was already indicated in the neighboring four-story Foundation Era building on the right side of the picture. This large building's bare firewall reaches deep into the background, making the small house appear even meeker—a remnant of a bygone era. In comparison to the larger and newer building, Blücherstraße 22 (Figure 3.12) comes across as a cottage or countryside retreat. In fact, the name "Blücherstraße" appears in Berlin's nineteenth-century Kreuzberg district, a part of which was heavily used by the military for barracks and parade grounds and only developed systematically during the 1880s. By the turn of the century, this formerly rural area had been completely urbanized. Oberwallstraße (Figure 3.13), on the other hand, is a street in the city center, not far from both the city castle and the famous Boulevard Unter den Linden. The Royal Prussian Photogrammetric Institute's image of a lonesome façade and its empty window frames in this central location

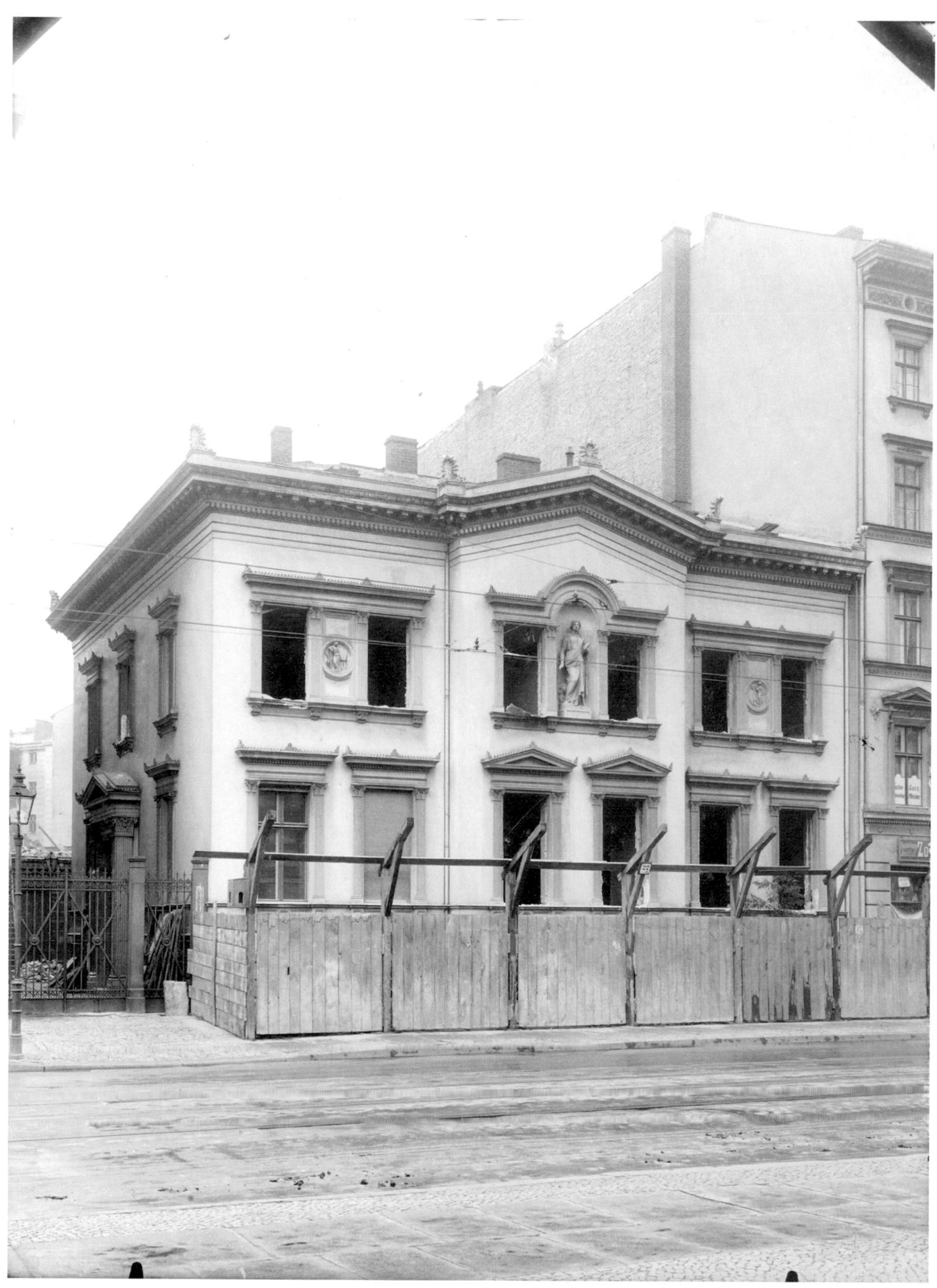

Figure 3.12. Royal Photogrammetric Institute (Königliche Messbildanstalt/Staatliche Bildstelle), Blücherstraße 22 at an angle from the left, no year. The building was originally built in 1865 and has been demolished. Photograph, 18 × 24 cm. Kunstbibliothek, Staatliche Museen zu Berlin, Album 263, inventory number 2469.1.

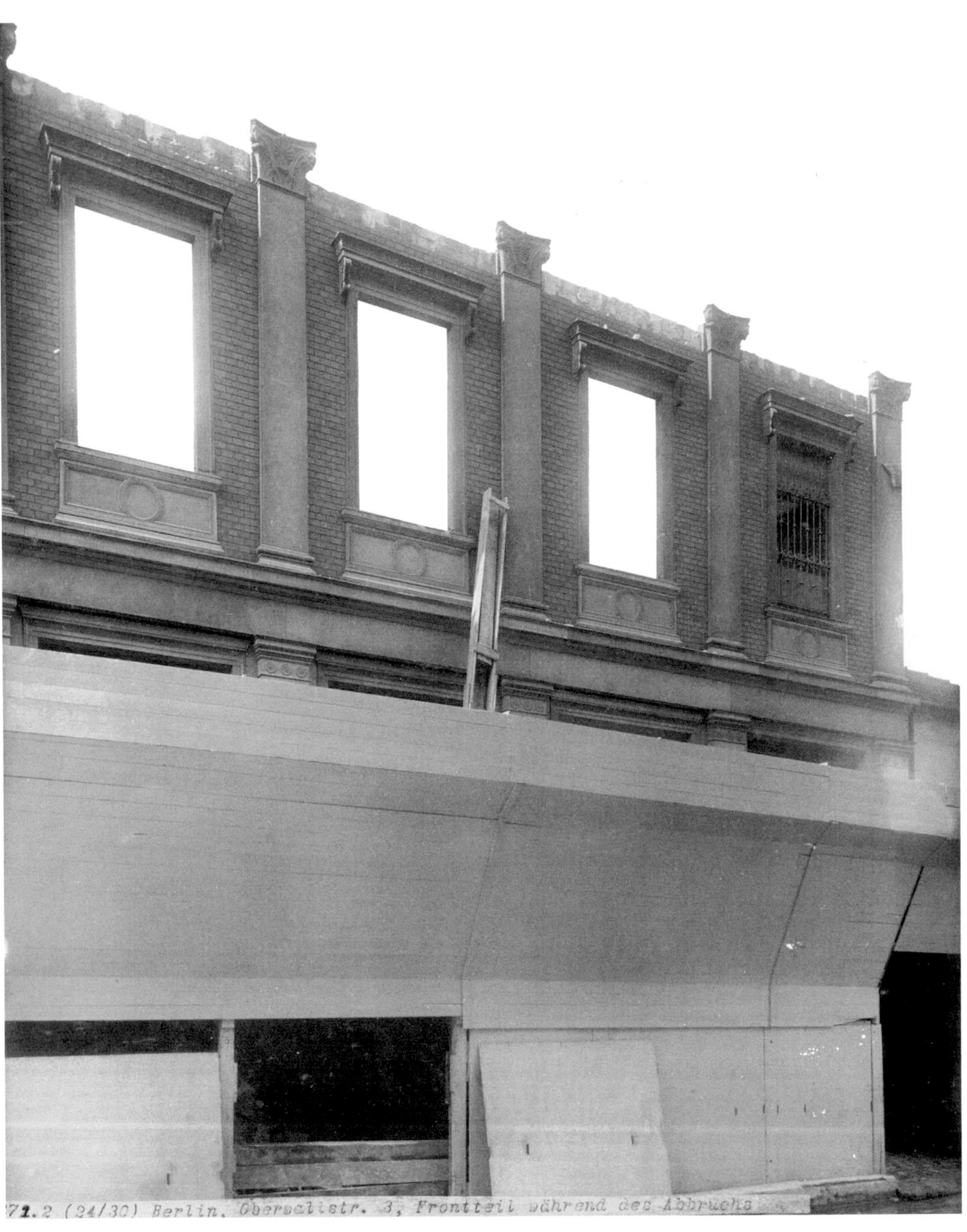

Figure 3.13. Royal Photogrammetric Institute (Königliche Messbildanstalt/Staatliche Bildstelle), Oberwallstraße 3, front during demolition, no year. Photograph, 24 × 30 cm. Kunstbibliothek, Staatliche Museen zu Berlin, Album 263, inventory number 2471.2.

underlines the fleeting and time-sensitive nature of urban transformation in Berlin. We may deduce from these images that demolition was not only a phenomenon of the urban periphery, but that it was undertaken with equal fervor in the city center.

Today, a number of Wilhelmine photographers who explored the city are well known, notably F. Albert Schwartz and Georg Bartels. Both photographed in the city center as well as in the new districts and outskirts of town.[49] As soon as the daily press gave word that a house or street demolition was imminent, they packed their large-format cameras (18 × 24 cm and 24 × 30 cm, respectively) and rushed off to capture the site before the wrecking crew arrived. Even though demolition initiatives were never comprehensive or systematic, they were usually successful in arriving in time to photograph the structures that were scheduled for destruction.

In 1887, Schwartz photographed a house in the midst of demolition in the central intersection of Spandauerstraße and Kaiser-Wilhelm-Straße (Karl-Liebknecht-Straße today) (Figure 3.14). There he captured the interior features of the house, as it had only been partially destroyed, and revealed several ripped-open stories. The image shows the exposed interior of an apartment room of the half-demolished house with remnants of wallpaper, ceilings, and wood flooring, doors leading into voids, and zigzag patterns indicating the former location of stairwells. Only the left side of a large building was removed, while the right side, in order to preserve and sustain it, was supported with massive wood planks. Here, too, the photographer had to deal with a view obstructed by a fence, which he circumvented by photographing from an elevated point, most likely from a house across the street. Such a panoramic perspective was common for more prominent and historically significant motifs. The effort that went into gaining access to an elevated viewpoint suggests the photographer's keen interest in capturing demolition that went far beyond a casual snapshot attitude.

Another photographer who documented the demolition of a building in a similar fashion was Hugo Rudolphy (1855–1919), who, starting in 1896, appears in Berlin's address books as "photographer and painter." His photograph of a house on Berlin's Jagowstraße 30 (Figure 3.15),[50] while similar to Schwartz's in terms of motif, puts the structure into a different light: either the photographer or someone who mounted the photograph onto a matting board handwrote in pencil

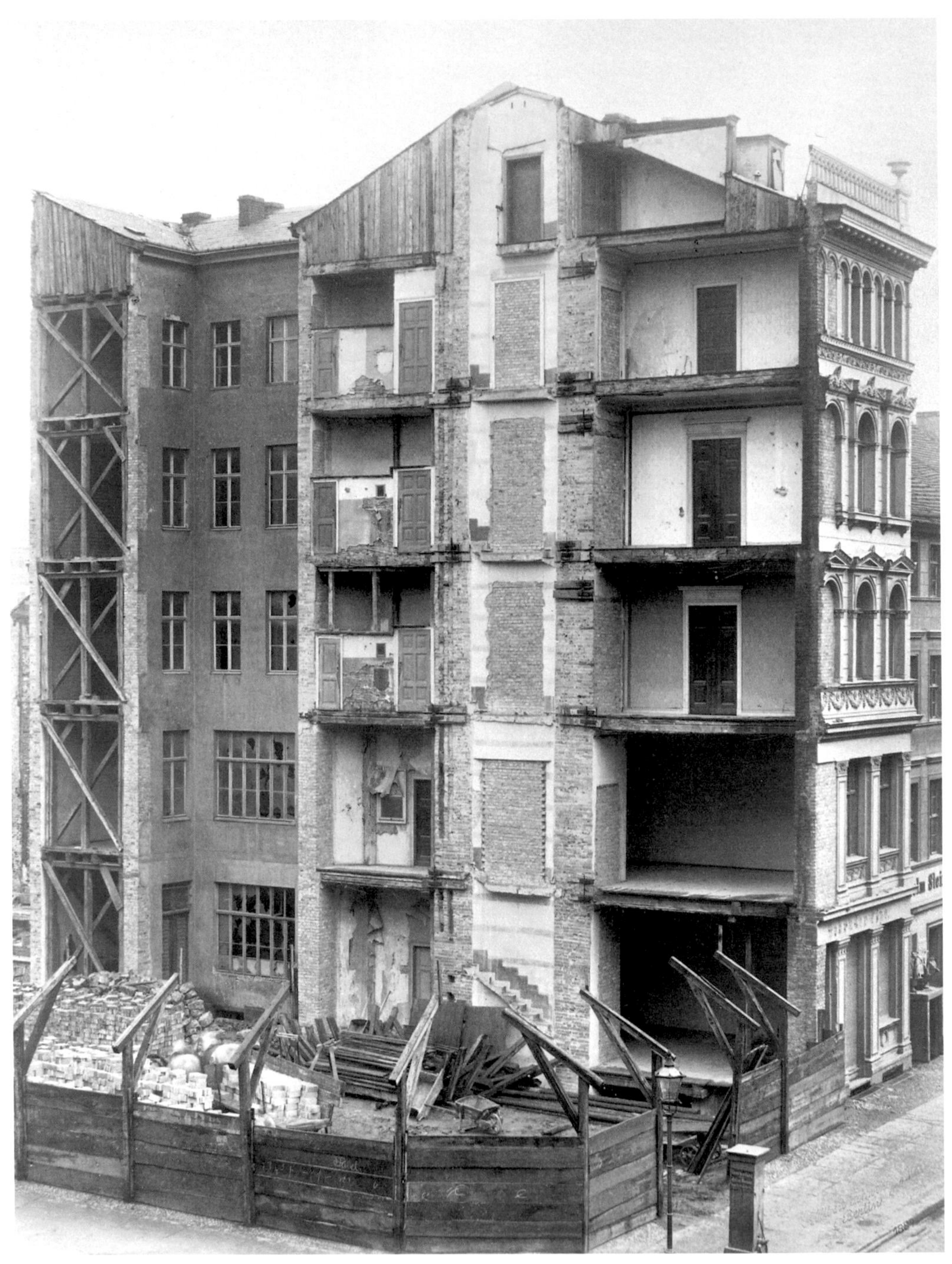

Figure 3.14. F. Albert Schwartz, Spandauerstraße corner of Kaiser-Wilhelm-Straße, 1887. Photograph, 35 × 25 cm. Landesarchiv Berlin, F Rep. 290-01-01 number 477.

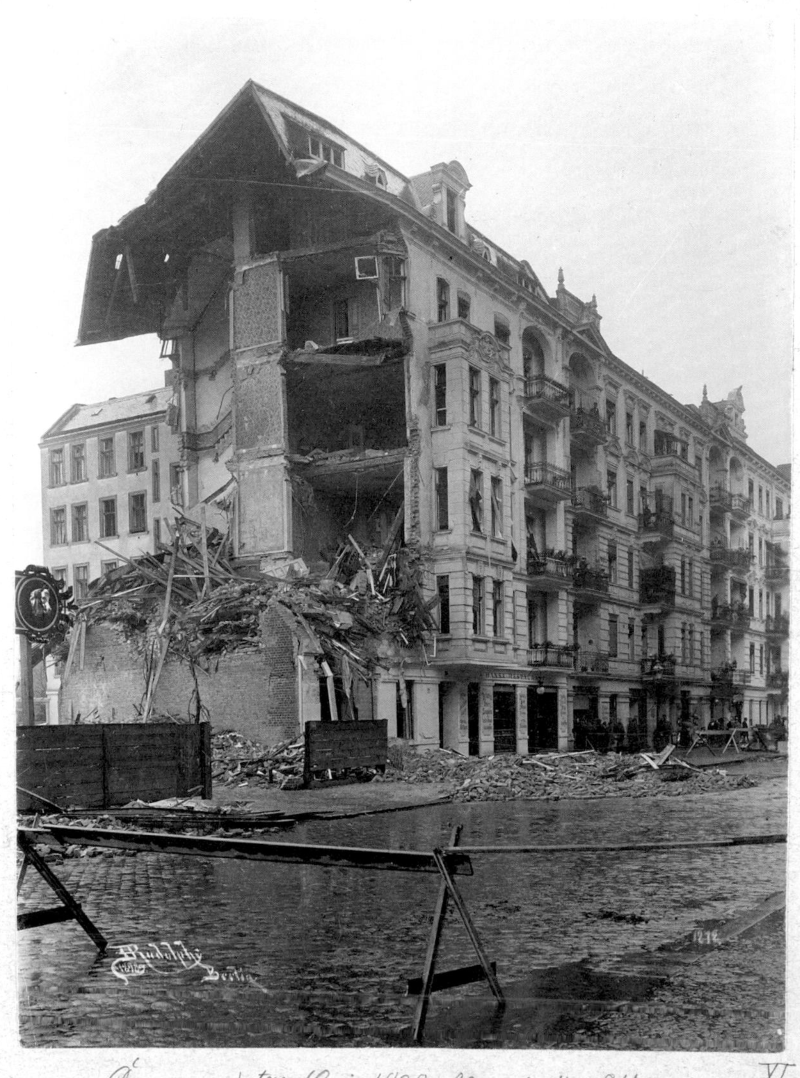

Figure 3.15. Hugo Rudolphy, Jagowstraße 30, 1898. "Das am 4ten Mai 1898 Abends 11,50 Uhr gesprengte Haus, Jagow Straße No.30" (May 4th, 1898, in the evening at 11:50, detonated house, Jagow Street No. 30). Photograph. Inventory number IV. 65/791V. Copyright Stiftung Stadtmuseum Berlin. Photograph by Oliver Ziebe, Berlin.

underneath the image: "House Jagow Straße No.30 which was demolished on May 4th, 1898, in the evening at 11.50h." Adding this text suggests that this photograph was likely not taken at a demolition but rather at the site of an accidental explosion, as demolition work around midnight was unlikely. More than any of the other images discussed here, this image exudes the immediacy of reportage photography, which would become the medium's most common and widely used function in the 1920s.

A final pair of photographic examples by Georg Bartels capture the city center's Rosenstraße (Figures 3.16 and 3.17) and attempted something more comprehensive than the work of Schwartz, Rudolphy, or the Photogrammetric Institute. In a sweeping panorama, Bartels captured an entire block after partial demolition and then returned to the site once its new development was completed for a second photograph. The first image was labeled "Rosenstraße,

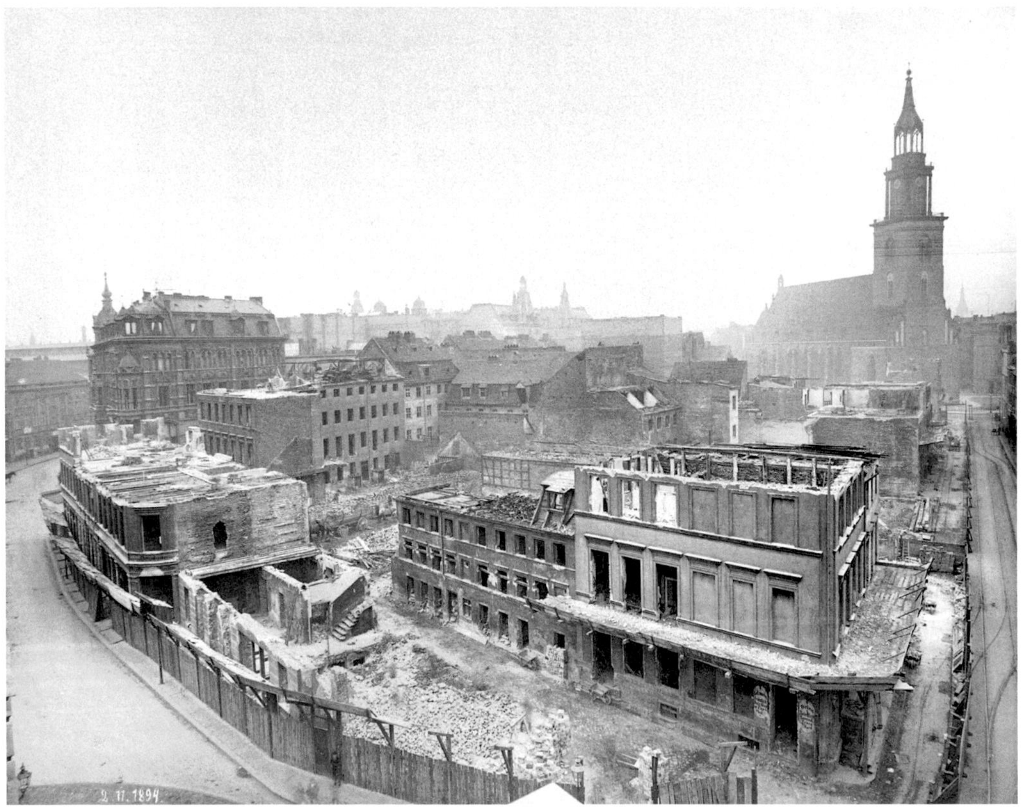

Figure 3.16. Georg Bartels, Rosenstraße, east side, November 2, 1894. Photograph Landesarchiv Berlin, F Rep. 290-01-02 number 74.

eastern side during demolition, overview of the entire territory. 1894";[51] the second image was taken from a point of view slightly moved to the west, emphasizing the finished construction on the east side of Rosenstraße.

Throughout his career, Bartels seems to have particularly enjoyed photographing chaotic urban situations and construction sites. He displayed a proclivity for the fragmented, the detonated, and the ripped open. These included single images and series on subjects from the building activities around Berlin's Kreuzberg (a mountain of rubble crowned by Schinkel's Kreuzberg monument to the Napoleonic Wars) to the mounting of the new Fischerbrücke (Fisher Bridge), and the removal and new construction of the Mühlendammbrücke (Mühlendamm Bridge). In Rosenstraße, his before-and-after approach tellingly communicated the drastic material process of the city's transformation and laid bare its palimpsest-like character.

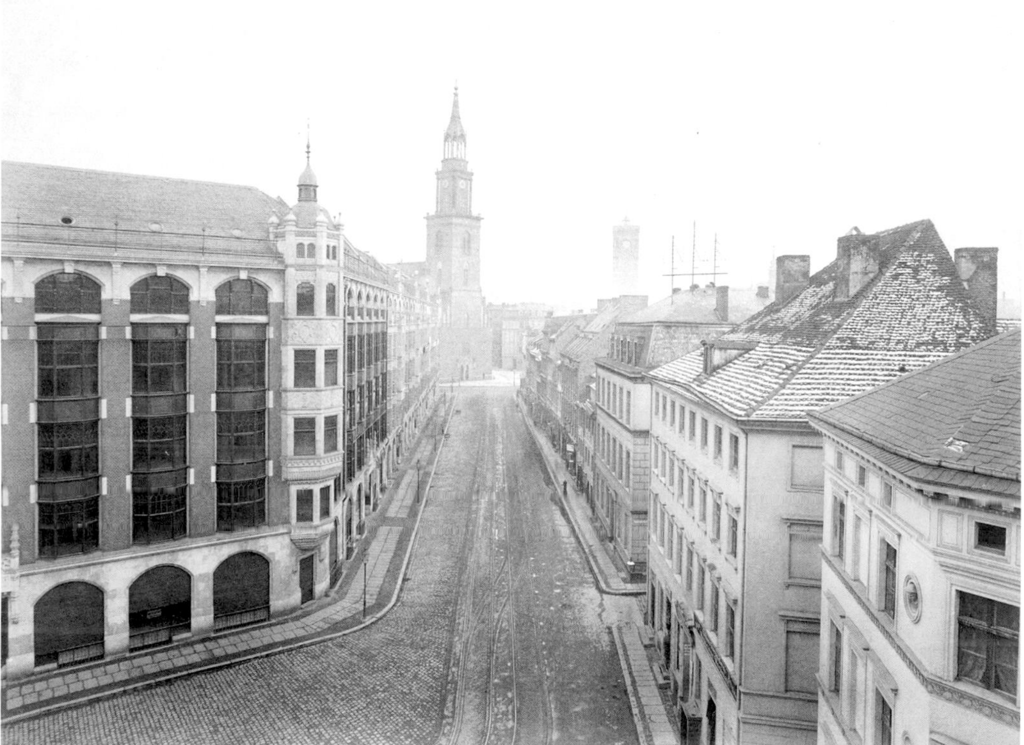

Figure 3.17. Georg Bartels, Rosenstraße, with a view of Marienkirche, 1896. Photograph. Inventory number IV 68/479 V. Copyright Stiftung Stadtmuseum Berlin. Photograph by Michael Setzpfandt, Berlin.

A distinction between ruin and rubble photography emerges in the latter's emphasis on material process and detail, as its images often focused on the raw stuff of urban buildings and their demolition. Like two sequences from a movie, the terrain seemed to become animate as empty or demolished lots were seen closed and replaced with new, taller structures. Rubble photography captured spontaneous methods but also a gesture toward the filmic, as speed drove the need for, but also the method of, making images in this context. Unlike the static composition of ruins, rubble photography lived in fleeting, transformative moments. Preservation through such photography became part of the process of suspended animation in the city.

In addition to drawings, watercolors, gouaches, and oil sketches by artists such as Adolph von Menzel (Figure 3.18)[52] and Friedrich Wilhelm Klose (Figure 3.19), or a rare painting by Fritz Gehrke (Figure 3.20) depicting the detonation of the Berlin Old Cathedral in 1893, by the second half of the nineteenth century the image of the ruin had become a predominantly photographic genre in Berlin. Ruin photographs took aesthetic inspiration from their predecessors and technical hints from photogrammetry and street photography. However, paintings of the era such as Gehrke's reveal in their "photographic" instantaneous appearance the cross-pollination of photographic and painterly aesthetics. In this moment, the painting achieved greater liveliness while photographs with the identical subject matter, such as those by Schwartz, were more constrained and often served a purely operational function as a legal tool for reporting construction or demolition progress (Figure 3.21).[53]

In order to understand the logics of rubble photography, it is helpful to look more closely into the iconographic and ideological implications of ruin paintings of the late eighteenth and early nineteenth century. Caspar David Friedrich and some of his contemporaries depicted ruins, but they often went beyond mere representation by painting completely intact buildings in a state of destruction. Examples of this are Friedrich's Jacobi Church in Greifswald and the cathedral in Meissen (Figure 3.22), as well as Hubert Robert's depiction of the Grand Gallery of the Louvre in ruins (Figure 3.23); Joseph Michael Gandy's image of the ruinous remnants of Sir John Soane's Bank of England (Figure 3.24); and Gustave Flaubert's fantasizing about a post-earthquake Paris. Ruin-images have often been understood as expressions of *vanitas,* of the inevitability

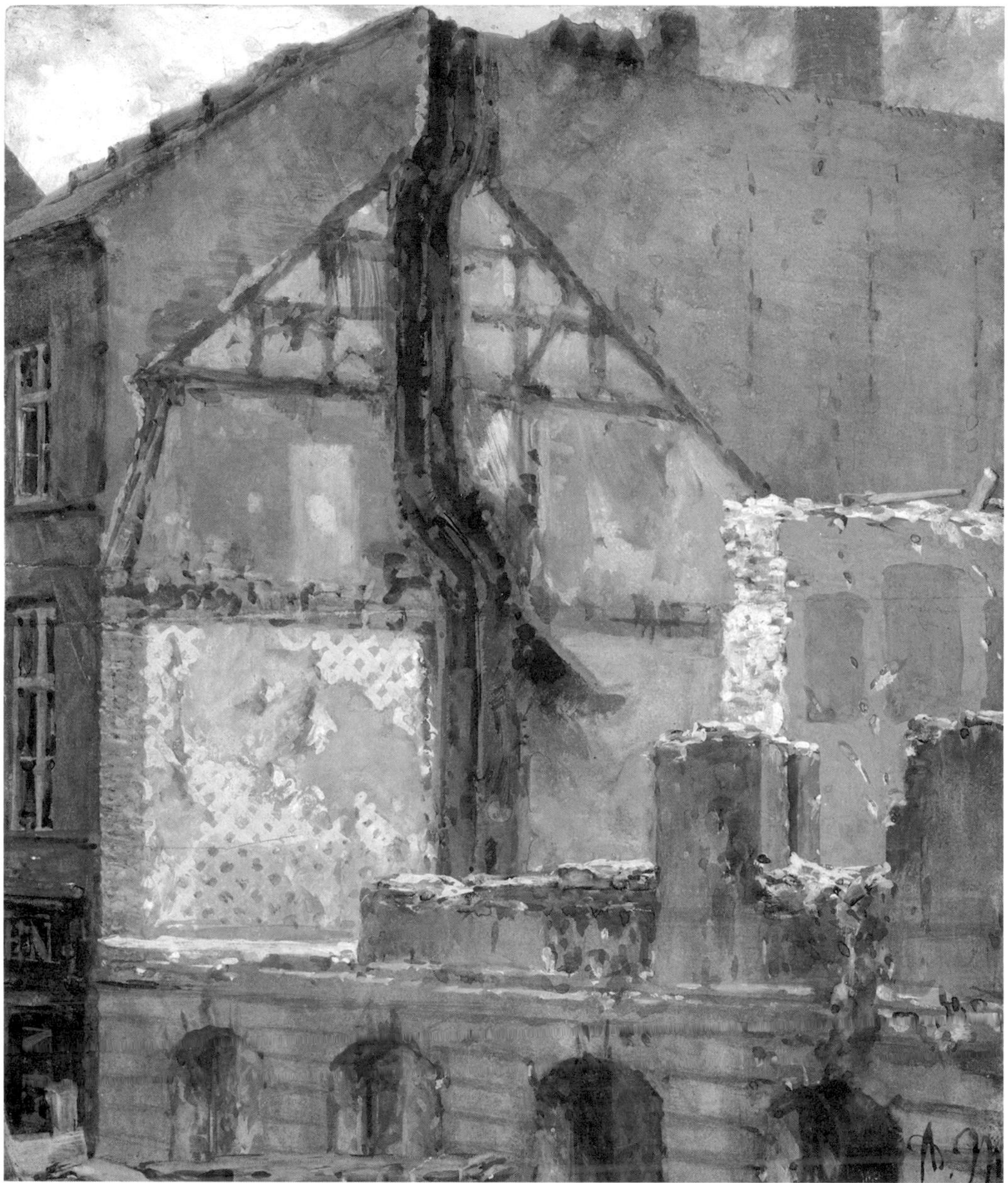

Figure 3.18. Adolph von Menzel, *House in the Process of Demolition*, 1863–83. Gouache on paper, 21.4 × 18.4 cm. From Kinderalbum. Inventory number KdZ 28752 (SZ Menzel Kat. 1017), Kupferstichkabinett Preußischer Kulturbesitz, Berlin. Photograph by Art Resource, NYC.

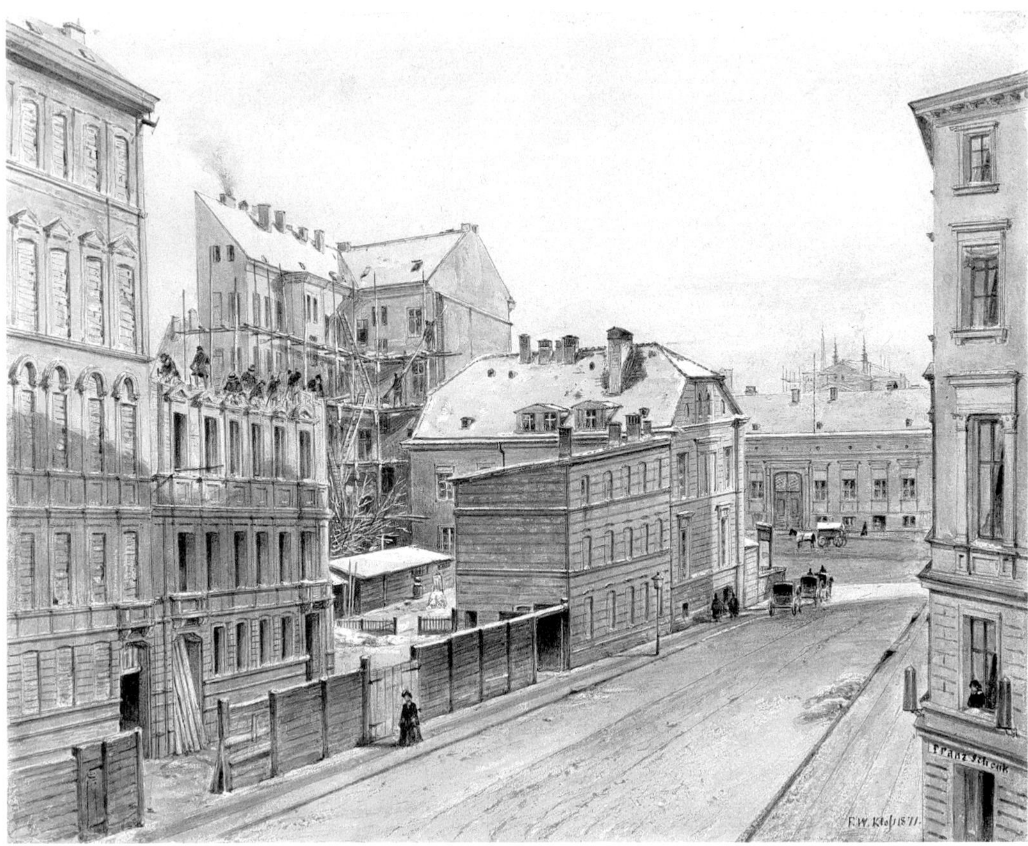

Figure 3.19. Friedrich Wilhelm Klose, *View from Lottumstrasse toward Schönhauser Allee*, 1871. Watercolor, 22.7 × 28.7 cm. Inventory number VII 60/883 w. Copyright Stiftung Stadtmuseum Berlin.

of death.[54] The gloom in this kind of interpretation, which also suggests an understanding of all human action as threatened by destruction, reveals a tragic understanding of history. The German art historian Werner Hofmann, who convincingly unfolds this era's array of existential pessimism, sums it up by stating that "the threatened, in his self-assurance wavering individual was captured by nature's destructive violence."[55]

The existential anxiety of the early nineteenth century contrasts greatly with the sobriety that would emerge in Berlin in its later decades. Drawings, oil sketches, and photographs of building demolition were meant primarily to capture an urban reality and were neither able to nor interested in inventing such destruction as an existential statement. The radically different function of the

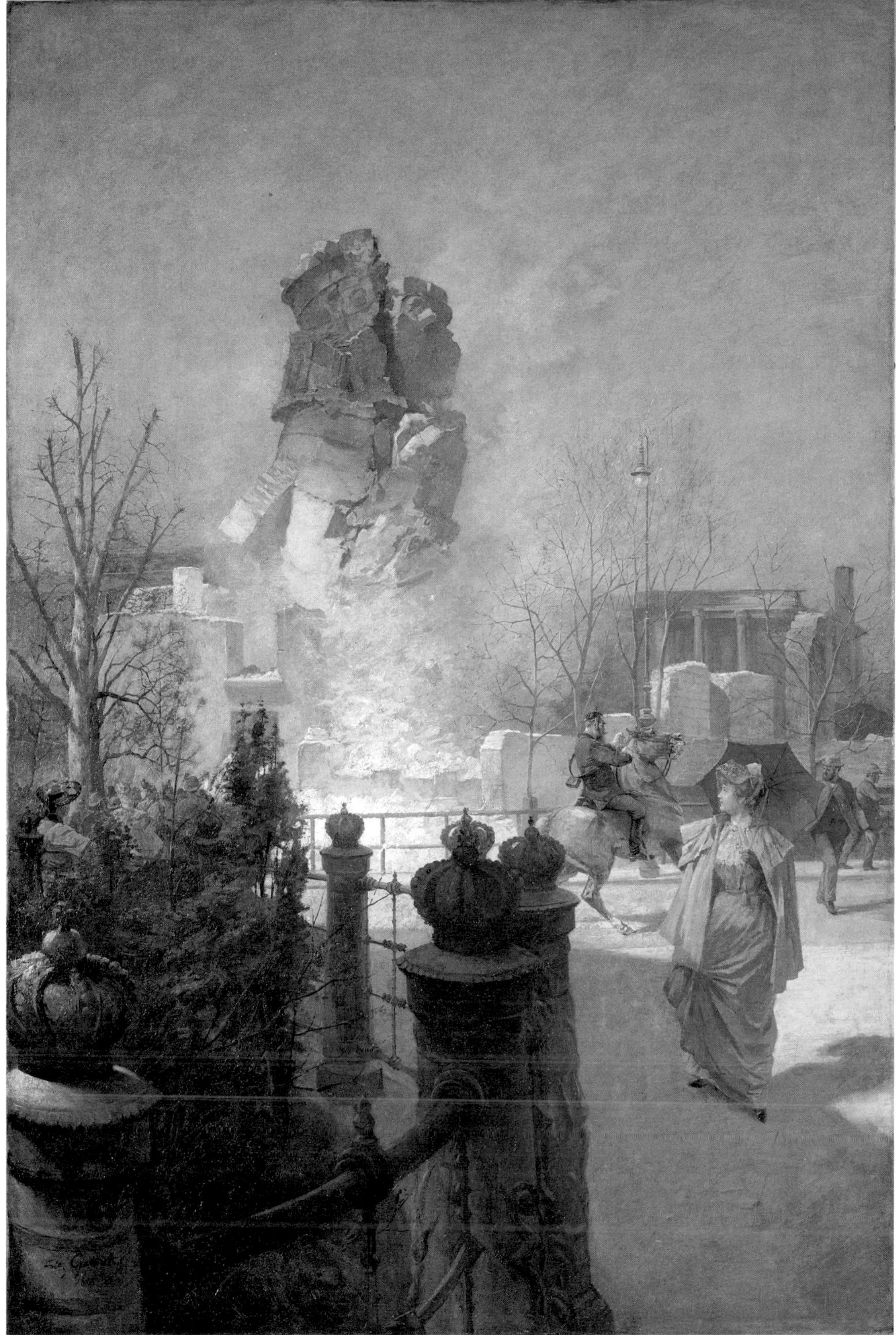

Figure 3.20. Fritz Gehrke, *Die Sprengung des Berliner Doms* (The detonation of Berlin's cathedral), 1893. Oil on canvas, 123 × 84 cm. Inventory number GEM 84/9. Copyright Stiftung Stadtmuseum Berlin. Photograph by Hans-Joachim Bartsch, Berlin.

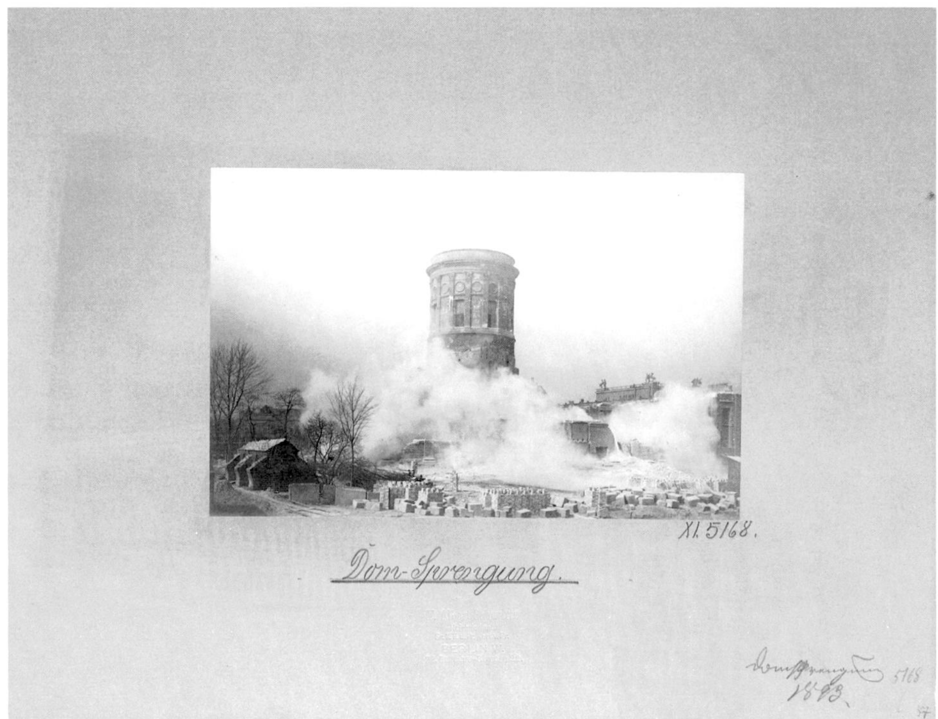

Figure 3.21 F. Albert Schwartz (photographic studio), *Die Sprengung des alten Doms* (The detonation of the old cathedral), 1893. Paper on carton, 11.8 × 18.4 cm. Inventory number XI 5168. Copyright Stiftung Stadtmuseum Berlin. Photograph by Oliver Ziebe, Berlin.

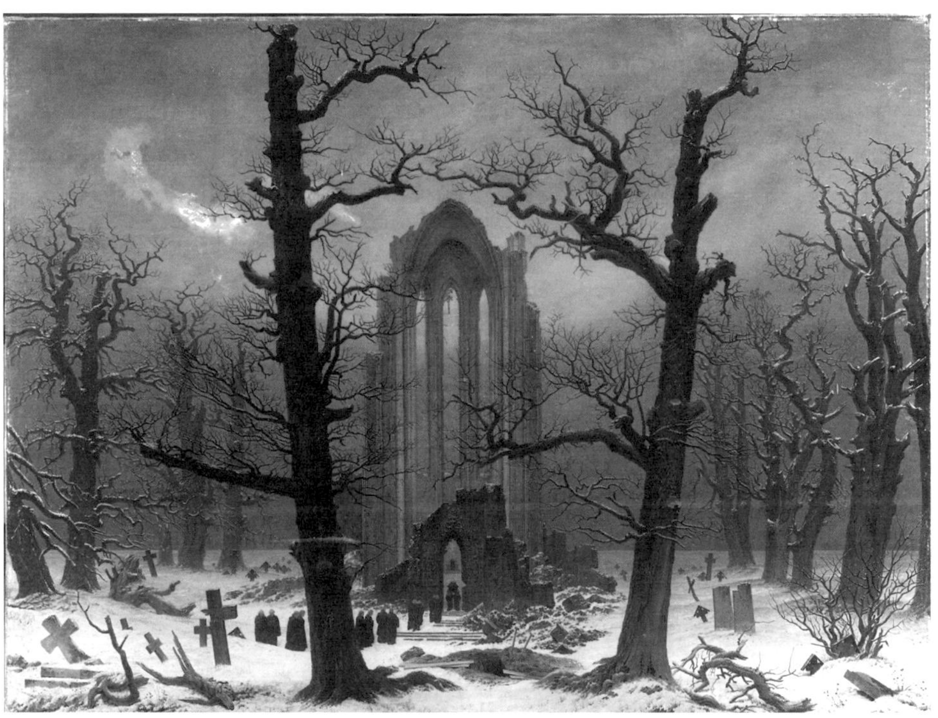

Figure 3.22. Caspar David Friedrich, *Klosterfriedhof im Schnee* (A monastery's cemetery in the snow), 1817–18. Formerly Nationalgalerie, Berlin. Bpk Berlin/ Nationalgalerie, Berlin/ Art Resource, NYC.

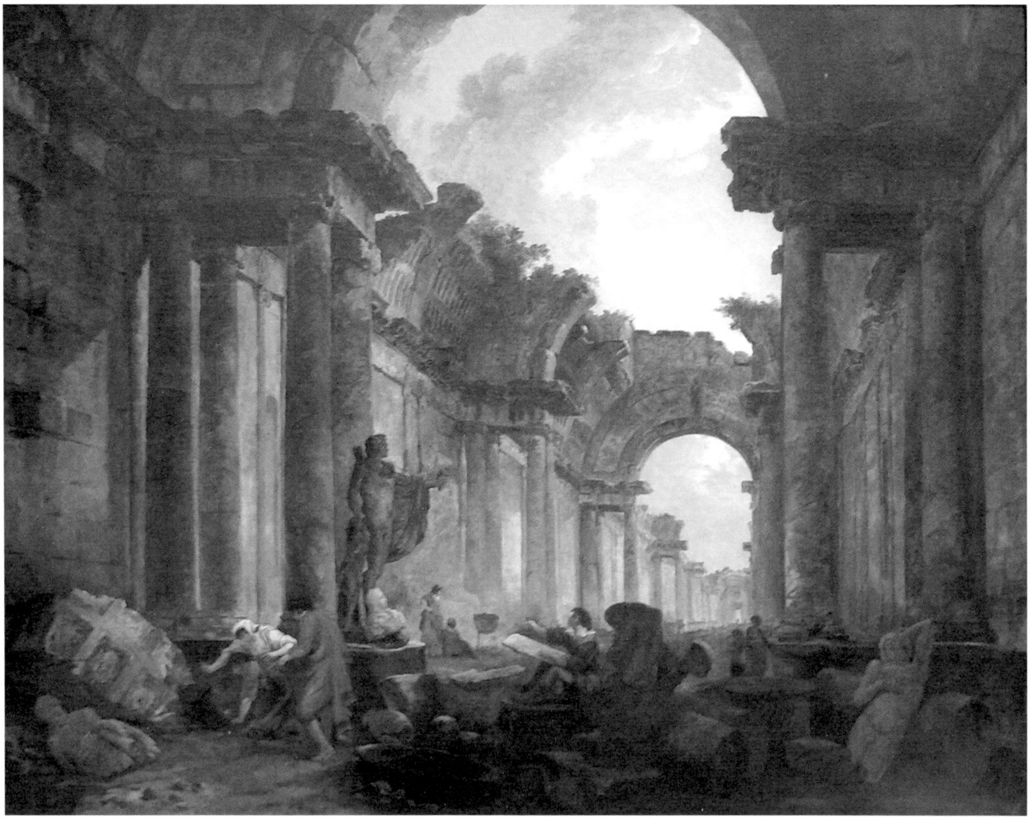

Figure 3.23. Hubert Robert, imaginary view of the Grand Gallery of the Louvre in ruins, Salon of 1796. Oil on canvas. Louvre. Wikimedia Commons.

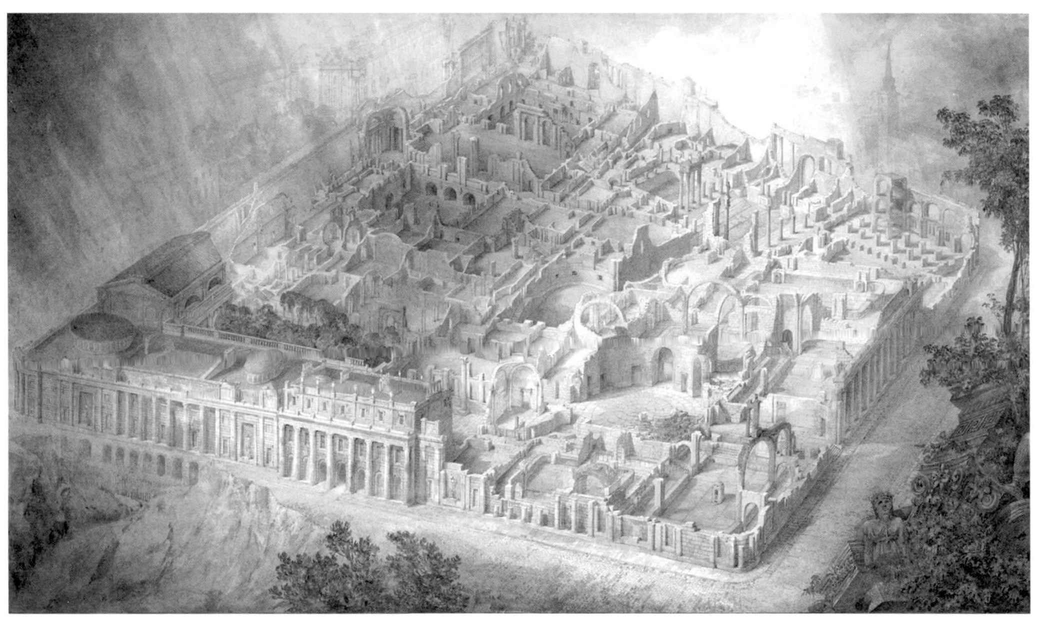

Figure 3.24. Joseph Michael Gandy, cutaway perspective drawing of the Bank of England as a ruin, 1830. Copyright Sir John Soane's Museum, London.

iconographically similar ruin painting and rubble photograph is indicated by their form and distribution. Initially used as sketch, photographs replaced drawings and oil sketches, which were never intended as creative interpretations of the world but rather—in quasi-anticipation of photography—as instantaneous registrations of processes in flux. Here, photography complied with Baudelaire's classification of it as mere servant (to the sciences) with no claim to artistry.[56] As if anticipating methods that were later made famous by police photographer Arthur Felling (popularly known as Weegee),[57] Berlin photographers tried to keep track of buildings that were projected for demolition and to photograph them before they disappeared into a pile of rubble. In the rubble photograph, the early nineteenth-century painting's tragic outlook onto history was replaced by a matter-of-fact scene aesthetic. The past, embodied not merely in the ruin but in the transitional status of rubble itself, was being explored with novel methods and in response to new demands as dictated by changing attitudes to history and identity.

However, the rubble photograph has gained enduring agency over time: in a Simmelian vein, it traced the past once again. The reexamination of empty window openings and skeletal leftovers of buildings affects our own engagement with the stuff of the city in transition. In considering the Parisian Eugene Atget, Walter Benjamin cast the city as a crime scene and photographs as forensic, a nimble practice in action.[58] While Weegee's work was more literally engaged with murder and the matter at hand was human flesh, the rubble photographers who preceded him appear to have engaged with a more metaphorical violence in their images of "the murdered city."[59] The independent genre of rubble photography that emerged in this moment broadens any notion that photography was innocently bound up with mere spontaneity, technical prowess, or as a forerunner to more advanced forms of snapshot and digital photography; rather, rubble photography was tactical, dynamic, and materially and ideologically rooted in its urban historical moment.

Such shifting notions of a modern, avant-garde perspective on the world did not occur suddenly; it was generated over a period of several decades and coincided with Berlin's most vigorous transformation and the epitomizing of its character of "forever becoming." Measuring images and photographs of ruins and rubble both pointed at and embodied the tension between stasis and motion, between shifting media cultures of romantic invention, elevation, and moving pictures. As media forms that had evolved over centuries, they can be read as pictorial comments and reflections on an era's lack of preparedness to, and courageous attempt at, emotionally and viscerally grasping the city's physical and material changes.

The city image that emerged from both photogrammetry and rubble photography was, on the surface, a portrait of transformation. But it was also an image of resolve, acknowledgment, and acceptance of the uncoordinated and messy flow of urban change. Both processes and image forms presented a kind of paradox: rooted in long-established conventions of architectural representation and romantic pictorial expression, they morphed into powerful articulations of collective anxiety and became a means to overcome it. The measuring image turned into a form of resistance, of silent protest; it dutifully depicted monument construction while actually engaging with the castle's façade and the construction sites surrounding it. Meanwhile, the rubble photograph was a clever embrace of a romantic iconography disguised in a modern snapshot aesthetic. Photographers were not just capturing the city; they were creatively and productively interacting with massive psychosocial challenges.

FOUR

Inventing Tradition

The Märkische Museum and *Picturesque Berlin*

> [This project] will be eager to capture in images for today and the future . . . that which as the witnesses of an unjustly almost forgotten, yet barely recovered past deserves with our love to be preserved permanently; that which, familiar to all of us, is able to trigger new impulses by taking a new vantage point; at times also that which, mostly unnoticed, here or there, still in the midst of the metropolis, lives its quiet and picturesque life—everything ultimately to bring closer to Berliners their own city and to reacquaint them with it.
>
> —GEORG REICKE, *Picturesque Berlin: Images and Views*

In his introduction to the three-volume photo publication *Das malerische Berlin: Bilder und Blicke* (*Picturesque Berlin: Images and Views*), Dr. Georg Reicke, the director of Berlin's city museum, captured the core sentiments regarding the city at the turn of the century.[1] Emphasizing the "unjustly almost forgotten" and "mostly unnoticed" aspects of the city, he suggested an antagonism between old and new that had built momentum during the nineteenth century's last decade. During this time, Berlin's cultural and political elite became aware of, and more explicitly involved in, ongoing discourses concerning historic preservation and the reevaluation of the historic as both an aesthetic and an emotional phenomenon. Reicke deeply related to these old parts of Berlin, describing them as "liv[ing] quiet and picturesque li[ves]" and suggesting that Berliners treat them as acquaintances that needed reconnection and love.

As Berlin became "newer," more attention was being paid to its "old" character and roots, and this interest grew after the turn of the century. Berlin's city museum, the Märkische Provinzial Museum, which had been founded in 1874 and moved into its new Ludwig Hoffmann–designed building in 1908, developed a powerful presence in the city's collective civic identity and commissioned the city-funded publication *Picturesque Berlin: Images and Views*, which intended to capture the painterly and charming aspects of Berlin (Figure 4.1). Between 1911 and 1914, under the editorial guidance of Max Osborn, the museum published three volumes of artistic photographs depicting sites of historic interest in the city. (The original plan included seven volumes but was scuttled after the outbreak of World War I.) Originally conceptualized as a comprehensive endeavor showing old and new Berlin, this publication ended up only featuring the old or extraurban parts of the city. Because of a change in preferences in regard to photographic documentation, funding for this project was never reestablished after the war.

The three completed volumes' photographic interpretation of historical structures showed historic buildings, streetscapes, and courtyards in the city's old Krögel and Fischer–Kietz areas, both part of Berlin's historic city center. These images captured the city's long-standing areas, but they were about more than mere historical documentation. Depicting and eternalizing built structures that were about to disappear or be demolished assumed a role that was not obvious at first sight. These images of crumbling, picturesque structures became reminders and emblems of a presumably wholesome past, which mitigated the uncertainty of national identity in the present and for the future. These images' association with home (local and national identity, known as *Heimat*) links them to the problematic concept of German populace (*Volk*) and the notion of "Old Berlin." The latter was a popular fiction that was displayed and disseminated through different media such as photo postcards, albums of drawings and photographs, and a popular special exhibition named "Old Berlin" at Berlin's trade exposition of 1896 at Treptow Park. The Berlin of the Märkische Museum's *Picturesque Berlin* project constructed a kind of embodied experience and bore a stronger resemblance to the almost exotic "Old Berlin" fantasy at the exposition in Treptow than to the diligently researched and narrated illustrated architecture histories of Berlin that were created during the 1870s through 1890s (Figure 4.2).

Through its particular photographic imaginary, Berlin grew beyond its significance as marker of an urban state of being and became a unifying generator of a national identity. The image of "Old Berlin" that this project invoked distinguished itself significantly from the "New Berlin" that had been constructed in *Berlin Life*. Unlike in the Berlin panoramas, "Old Berlin" was the product of careful, mostly vertically framed glimpses of historic alleys and picturesque

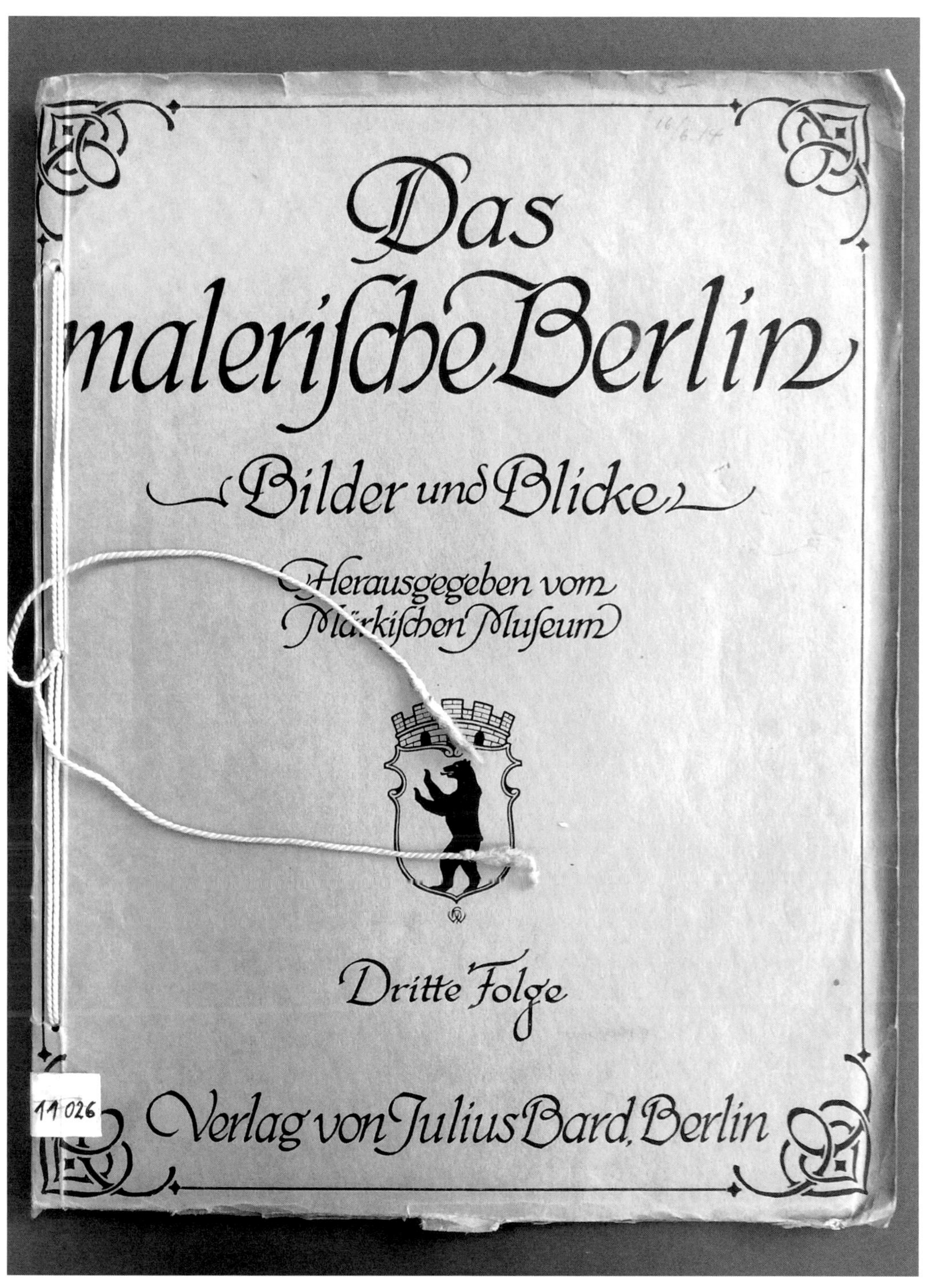

Das
maleriſche Berlin
Bilder und Blicke
Herausgegeben vom
Märkiſchen Muſeum
Dritte Folge
Verlag von Julius Bard, Berlin

Figure 4.1. Title page for Märkische Museum, editor, *Das malerische Berlin: Bilder und Blicke*, vol. 3 (Berlin: Verlag von Julius Bard, 1914). Copyright Stiftung Stadtmuseum Berlin.

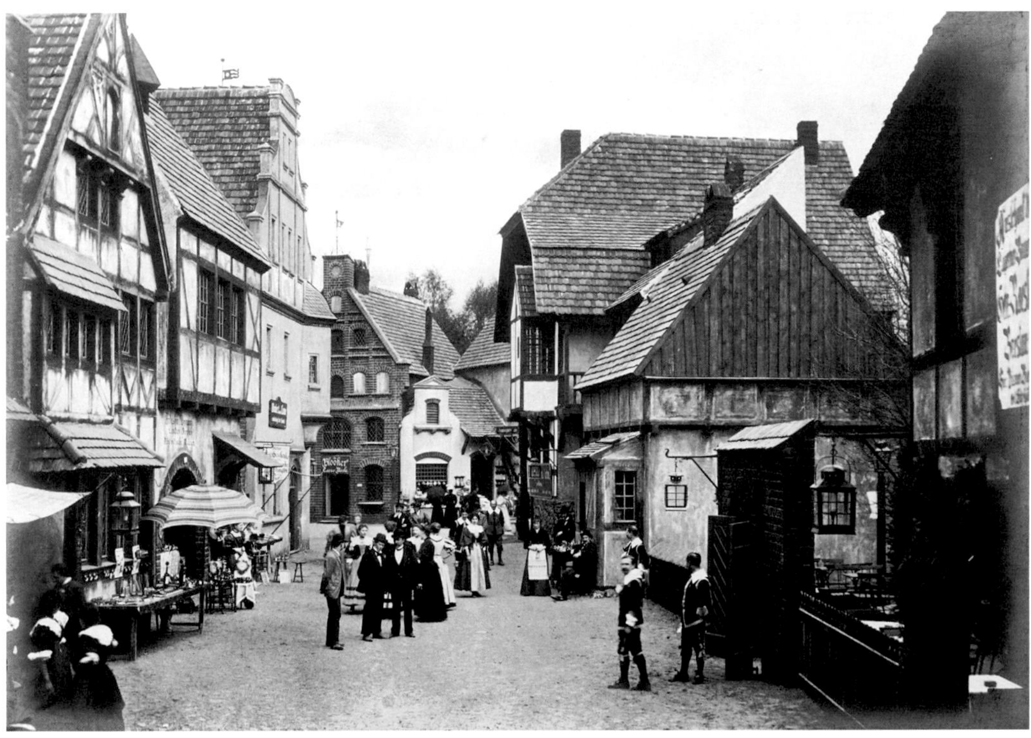

Figure 4.2. Ottomar Anschütz, *Alt-Berlin* (Old Berlin), Treptow, 1896. 48 × 64 cm. Inventory number SM 2010-0191.2. Copyright Stiftung Stadtmuseum Berlin.

courtyards. Whereas Brauchitsch used selective composition and scenography to capture Berlin's new architecture, "Old Berlin" sought out and brought to light many places in Berlin that were considered crime-ridden slums. Through engaging with and reconsidering the city's oldest buildings and sites, *Picturesque Berlin* relied on history and its traces to achieve a sense of unity that political and planning forces were not able to create. The project's effectiveness sprang from its seemingly innocuous claim of presenting "painterly images and views." As an aesthetic endeavor, it was more likely to engage the viewer through an immediate experience of beauty than would a didactic or academic project.

These representations were described by the term *malerisch*, which can be translated literally as *painterly* or, more metaphorically, as *picturesque*. This term was invoked not only by the three-volume set of *Picturesque Berlin* but also by the 1902 special Christmas issue of *Berlin Life*,[2] the popular journal that was discussed in chapter 1, with the same title "Picturesque Berlin." *Berlin Life* and the Märkische's *Picturesque Berlin* bore different definitions and assumptions about what constitutes "picturesqueness." This difference is telling in respect to the Märkische Museum's distinct trajectory. *Berlin Life* took a discussion of well-known Berlin painters' city depictions as opportunity to define "picturesque" as "that which the painters have discovered" in the city (Figures 4.3–4.5). While museums such as the Märkische Provinzial Museum secured an image of "Old Berlin" by collecting drawings and paintings of the city's historic sections and by amassing ancient objects of the region, the paintings of *Berlin Life*, according to Fuchs, focused on the *modern* city. They depicted a "condensed life" fed by sentiments like a strong sense of being alive (*Lebensgefühl*) and love of home (*Heimatliebe*).[3] This distinction between the capabilities of photographs

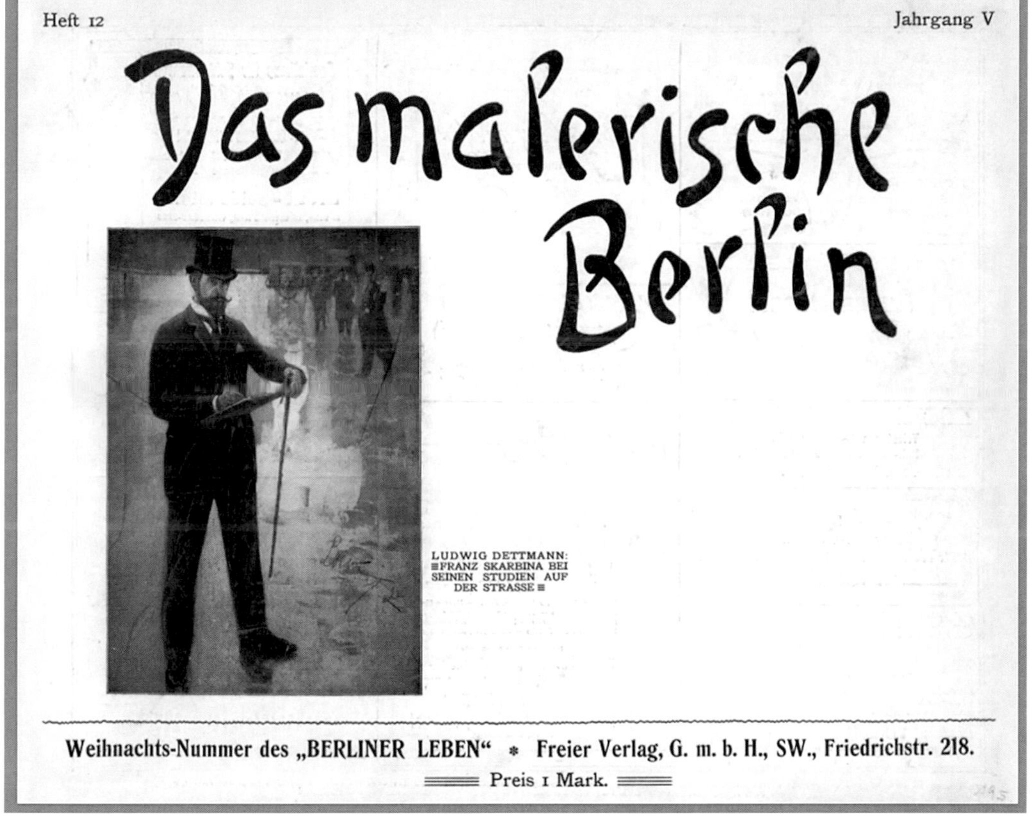
Heft 12

Jahrgang V

Das malerische Berlin

LUDWIG DETTMANN: FRANZ SKARBINA BEI SEINEN STUDIEN AUF DER STRASSE

Weihnachts-Nummer des „BERLINER LEBEN" * Freier Verlag, G. m. b. H., SW., Friedrichstr. 218.

Preis 1 Mark.

Figure 4.3. Title page of Friedrich Fuchs, "Das malerische Berlin," special Christmas issue, *Berliner Leben* 5 (1902), Freier Verlag, G.m.b.H., Staatsbibliothek Berlin. Digitized by the Zentral- und Landesbibliothek Berlin, 2016. https://digital.zlb.de.

Das malerische Berlin.

Von Friedrich Fuchs.

Viele Stimmen höre ich, die fragen: Berlin und malerisch? Denn für eine Mehrzahl der Gemüter verquickt sich dies Eigenschaftswort mit Vorstellungen von Burgruinen, die finster träumerisch ein friedliches Flussthal überragen oder von altertümlichen Städtchen, die mit ihren roten Dächern aus dem Waldgrün lugen. Der Rhein, Alt-Heidelberg, Rothenburg! Doch dass Berlin „direkt" malerisch wäre, davon hat man denn doch noch nichts gehört. Amusieren thut man sich dort ja grossartig: dieser Trubel überall und die vielen

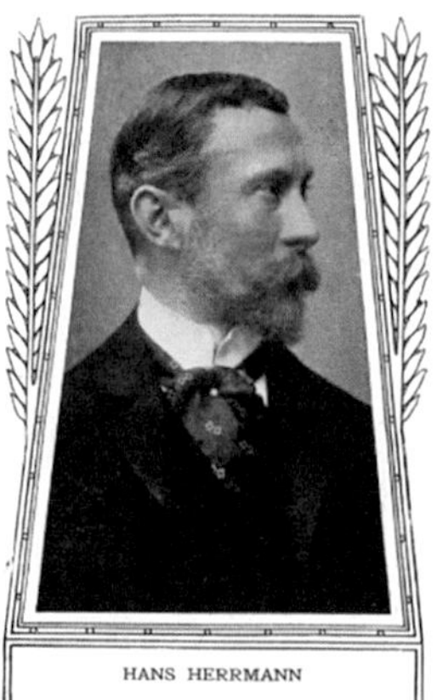
HANS HERRMANN

eleganten Läden! Aber alles ist doch noch so neu, — die neuen Häuser, die langen geraden Strassen!

Freilich lassen sich im heutigen Berlin die Bauten, die älter als fünfzig Jahre sind, an den zehn Fingern herzählen, und die ältesten sind auch noch nicht alt. Was der erste und der zweite Friedrich erbauen liessen: Schloss und Zeughaus von Schlüter, die „Gensdarmentürme" und die „Kolonnaden" von Gontard sind dafür aber Dinge, die es schöner und charaktervoller nirgendwo auf der Welt giebt. Und dann Schinkel, der mit seinen feingebildeten Neigungen einem merkwürdigen Zeitalter den einzig eigentümlichen Ausdruck erfand: Neue Wache, Altes

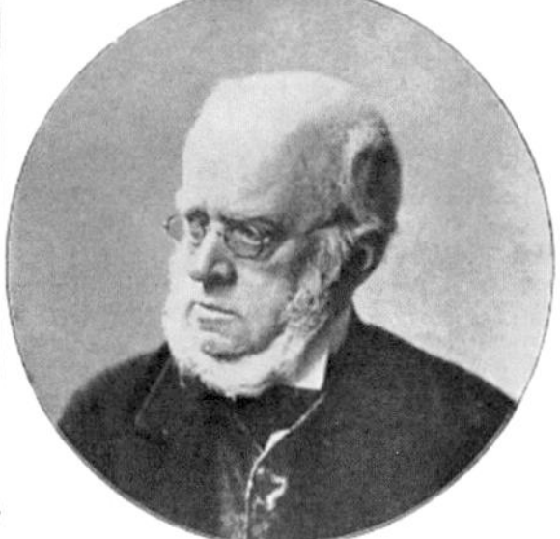
ADOLF MENZEL

Museum, Schauspielhaus, ja auch der Backsteinkasten der Bauakademie sind Schöpfungsbauten. Diese vereinzelten Gebäude können nun nicht wohl den Charakter des grossen neuen Berlins bestimmen, kaum mehr beherrschen sie die Plätze, für die sie gedacht waren. Aber was will es zur Not besagen? Ein Bau, der schön ist und stilrecht, braucht an sich noch nicht durchaus malerisch zu sein. Für die Maler wird er erst durch allerhand Zuständlichkeiten zum interessanten Objekt. Und übrigens ist die Species „Architekturmaler", welche bauliche Schönheiten mit liebevoller, sachlicher Genauigkeit konterfeite, am Aussterben. Was es aber an malerischen „Parthien" und „Motiven" aus dem alten Berlin während der letzten Jahrzehnte noch gab, das hat vor allen Dingen Julius Jacob mit seinem treu verliebten Spürsinn aufgepürscht und in zahlreichen Bildern und Blättern einer Nachwelt, die dafür viel dankbarer sein sollte, überliefert. Auch Georg Schöbel hat wunderliche Winkel der Altstadt, pietätvoll abgebildet; und der Malerradierer Bernhard Mannfeld, der, in Romantik schwelgend, durch alle deutschen Gaue gezogen ist, hat in dem für seine Technik respektablen Blatte „Schillerplatz" vom historischen Berlin einen Ausschnitt voll starken Stimmungsreizes gegeben. Aber schon zeigt sich in manchen Darstellungen Jacobs nicht mehr nur der Hang zum Idyllischen und Altromantischen, nicht mehr nur das Befangene vom Zauber der Vergangenheit, sondern das Magnetische einer neuen Sphäre, die frische Freude am intensiven Leben, an der Gegenwart. [illegible] klingt in manches Bild das Brausen vom Werktag der grossen Stadt.

Denn wenn es auch an altem Gemäuer und imposanten Strassendurchblicken in Berlin mangelt, so ist doch eine Schar, eine Schule von Berliner Malern erstanden, die es sich von Goethe nicht zweimal hat

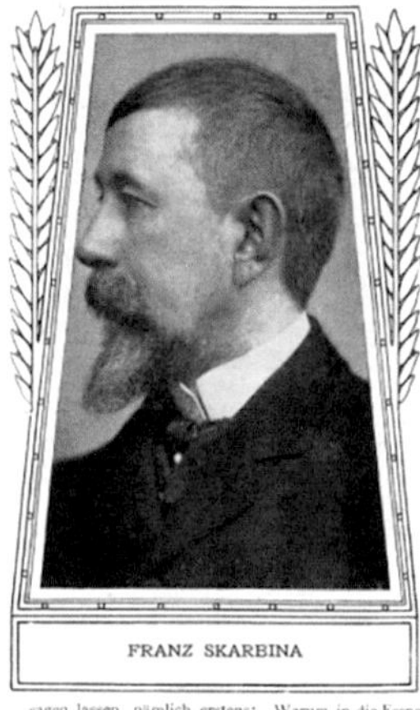
FRANZ SKARBINA

sagen lassen, nämlich erstens: „Warum in die Ferne schweifen . . . ." und zweitens: „Greift nur hinein ins volle Menschenleben . . . ." Es versteht sich von selbst, dass künstlerische Arbeitsnaturen, wie Adolf Menzel und Max Liebermann solches malten, das sie am Orte ihres Weilens, auf ihren Spaziergängen, von ihren Fenstern aus wahrnahmen. Ihrer schnell und kräftig zupackenden Art und unfehlbaren Beobachtung verdanken wir darum verschiedene

Figure 4.4. Image depicting three Berlin-based and well-known painters (Hans Herrmann, Adolf Menzel, and Franz Skarbina), from Friedrich Fuchs's article in "Das malerische Berlin," special Christmas issue, *Berliner Leben* 5 (1902), no pagination, Staatsbibliothek Berlin. Digitized by the Zentral- und Landesbibliothek Berlin, 2016. https://digital.zlb.de.

and paintings and their respective ability to address and represent the picturesque city suggests that photographs eternalize while paintings interpret and infuse images with sentiments of love and affection.

As discussions of Berlin's newness and ugliness persisted, the city's image and its adaptability to aesthetic standards of beauty became a central subject matter for journalists, travelers, art critics, and urban reformers. Berlin increasingly defined itself through its persistent states of change,[4] and found itself compared negatively to its peer cities by planners, architects, artists, and tourists who associated historicity with beauty. Three German critics help to frame this dilemma and to contextualize urban photography in Berlin: architect and theorist August Endell, educator and author Willi Warstat, and photo critic Anton Mayer, all

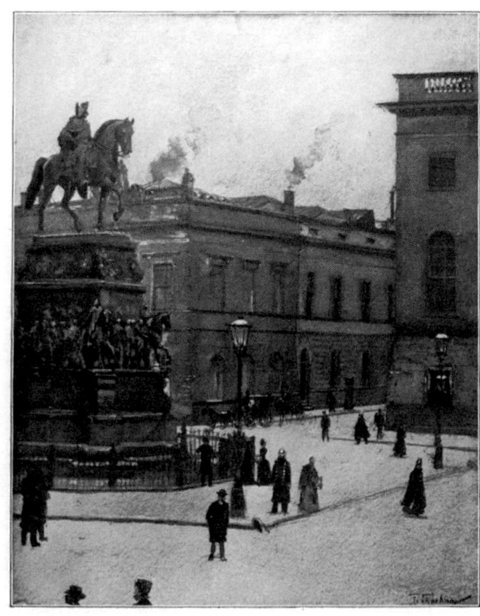

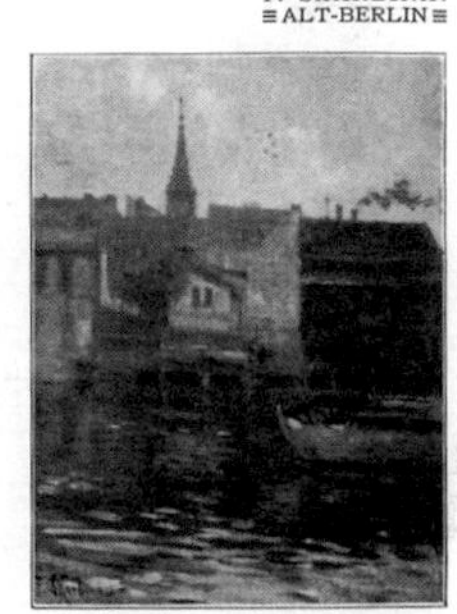

Figure 4.5. Image depicting two city paintings by Franz Skarbina from Friedrich Fuchs's article in "Das malerische Berlin," special Christmas issue, *Berliner Leben* 5 (1902), no pagination, Staatsbibliothek Berlin. Digitized by the Zentral- und Landesbibliothek Berlin, 2016. https://digital.zlb.de.

of whom wrote about the interlinking forces of the city, standards of beauty, art, and photography. Endell was a prominent voice in the urban reform debate at the turn of the century,[5] and emphatically suggested in his 1908 volume *Die Schönheit der großen Stadt* (*The Beauty of the Metropolis*) that one should embrace the city in terms of immediate experience and question conventional and long-established notions of beauty. This phenomenological approach was shaped by Endell's background in philosophy and psychology. He encouraged his contemporaries to embrace the modern city, its ordinary details, and even its ugliness, to recognize the beauty in everyday phenomena. He writes, "One can roam Berlin's new parts for hours and still has the feeling to not move at all. Everything seems so monotonous despite the desire to attract attention, to distinguish oneself from one's neighbor. But here too, in this gruesome pile of stones, lives beauty."[6]

One year later, in a six-page article for the photographic yearbook of 1909, Willi Warstat also raised the issue of urban representation and beauty. In "Die

Schönheit der grossen Stadt als künstlerisches Problem für den Photographen" ("The Beauty of the Metropolis as Artistic Problem for the Photographer"), Warstat bemoaned the lack of interest in "modern metropolitan life" (*modernes Großstadtleben*) on the part of "the photographic arts" and argued that the city, this "restless, yet strong and lively creature," deserved recognition for its aesthetic value. While the city had developed such great significance for modern life and the "pursuit of universal aesthetic artistic culture," "the conquest of such aesthetic new territory," the metropolis, was opposed by "problems deeply rooted in the nature of the photographic arts."[7] This nature of photography became the central subject of his 1913 publication *Die künstlerische Photographie* (*Artistic Photography*), in which he came to the conclusion that "the entire history of artistic photography is basically nothing else but a history of the wrestling with an unartistic technology for possibilities to achieve artistic personal expression." Each period of art photo history was "marked by technical progress, the use of new technological means in the struggle against photography's categorical representational truthfulness."[8] How could such an unartistic medium operate in and capture a city that was considered by most as unworthy of artistic attention? Most photographers resolved this conflict by picking out what they deemed Berlin's "painterly" qualities, which, in their minds, qualified the city as beautiful. These sites included the city's few historic spots and the parks, but rarely its modern corners and neighborhoods. In that respect, photographs reiterated assumptions that formed the basis of the Märkische Museum's project.

However, in the spirit of Endell, photographers began to engage with the modern and everyday aspects of the city. This shifting understanding of urban beauty became apparent in a text titled "Bilder des Großstadtlebens" ("Images of Metropolitan Life") by the amateur photographer and writer Anton Mayer, which was published in the amateur photography journal *Photographische Mitteilungen* (*Photographic Reports*) in 1909.[9] Mayer, like Endell, pointed out that amateur photographers needed to change the misconception of their city by taking the time and leisure to discover its inherent beauty and painterly qualities in ordinary and typical situations such as street work, rainy days in the city, horses, and traffic.[10] This openness to the everyday distinguished Mayer from those who preferred, in the words of Warstat, "painterly" and historic spots.[11] According to Mayer, and with the increasingly common amateur snapshooter in mind, it was crucial to avoid any staging or catching the attention of pedestrians. He suggested the use of a modern handheld reflex camera and a range of strategies to avoid public awareness.[12]

In Endell and Mayer we find an architect and a practicing photographer who are ready to engage with the modern urban environment, no matter how stark or even ugly it might be. In that respect they followed in the footsteps of painters like Edouard Manet and Gustave Caillebotte, who one generation earlier had pioneered the artistic consideration of Parisian everyday life and who were championed by Charles Baudelaire. Warstat, however, cautiously attempted to marry photographers with the historic remnants in the modern city, a perspective that placed photographers in artistic limbo due to Berlin's aesthetic and experiential "American-ness." The nineteenth-century industrial city was a universal target for cultural critics, and, as noted in previous chapters, Berlin had been singled out as matching the negatively associated characteristics of modernity and likeness to North America. Speaking of the American city, William Sharpe and Leonard Wallock point out that the modern city "is scorned, this time not for being too unnatural, but because it is not civilized enough, compared with its European counterparts." At the same time, "in many countries, after the industrial revolution the city [as such] acquired a negative image unequalled in the history of its representation."[13] Without "historic value" and therefore lacking creative potential, modern Berlin would remain an unlikely motif and less attractive to artistic photographers.

By the late 1890s, other European metropolises such as Hamburg, Dresden, Vienna, London, and Paris were considered to be much more photogenic than Berlin and had also developed a reputation as photo-artistic centers. Berlin came to be known as a scientific and technological center for photography, but its creative photographic achievements (which were often developed by amateurs) remained scarce in comparison. Endell, Warstat, and Mayer all echo an understanding and reading of the city as an organic, naturally grown, and natural whole, which was to be recognized as beautiful only through careful artistic engagement. This natural body, however, was overwritten by the forces of industrial capitalism and speculation. The classic late eighteenth- and nineteenth-century urban metaphor of city as organism was, by the time these authors wrote about the city, about to be replaced by the diagrammatically defined and described atomic city. The normative model of the city as organism formed with the development of biology in the eighteenth and nineteenth centuries and rested on assumptions about the nature of organisms such as their autonomous qualities, existence of boundaries, and specific size. Today, Sharpe and Wallock explain in their seminal publication on visions of the modern city that the definition of the city relies on the

> atom—a nuclear city and "orbiting" electron-suburbs—thereby combining connotations of both space and energy. The shift from the organism to the atomic particle, from biology to physics, from something familiar and instantly apprehendable to a structure that we have probably seen only in diagram and that represents lines of force—all this is indicative of our increasingly complex and insecure sense of the contemporary city.[14]

The three realized volumes of *Picturesque Berlin: Images and Views*, which will be discussed in depth on the following pages, permit a glimpse into an era, the first decade of the twentieth century, that while exposed to this "increasingly complex and insecure sense of the contemporary city," was fascinated with historic structures and convinced of the importance of history and the past for its own sake.[15] This conviction was most significantly manifested in the institutionalization of historic preservation.

European Cultures of Historic Preservation

Claims, assumptions, and expectations of urban historical survey projects were closely linked to European and German historic preservation debates. Two main arguments dominated debates of the German preservationist movement of the turn of the century, derived from a disagreement on whether a historic building that showed signs of decay was to be preserved or restored to some kind of completeness. Those who favored preservation understood heritage protection as a form of maintenance and of securing with great consciousness what remained of a historic building or object; the other side aimed at reconstructing, even potentially improving, a historic building, which always implied editing—removal and addition—of substance. This dichotomy was already established and hotly debated midcentury when the Frenchman Eugène Emmanuel Viollet-le-Duc (1814–79) and the Brit John Ruskin (1819–1900) fundamentally disagreed whether to *preserve* (Ruskin) or *restore* (Viollet-le-Duc) historic buildings.[16] Fifty years later, Germany's foremost preservationist, Georg Dehio (1850–1932), articulated a strong opposition to any creative or reinterpretive intervention by architects that claimed to improve historic buildings by inventing and adding parts that tried to imitate historic styles.[17]

Dehio also understood that historic preservation was a phenomenon that when embraced by the entire populace, was an effective means to bolster a sense of shared national identity, explaining that "the feeling that a people who possess many and old monuments is a noble people has to seep into all its social strata."[18] For Dehio, preservation "without sentimentality, pedantism, or romantic arbitrariness" was meant to be a "self-evident and natural utterance of self-respect, as recognition of the right of the dead to the best of those alive."[19] Dehio and two Hamburg-based photography promoters, the art historian, art educator, and museum director Alfred Lichtwark (1852–1914)[20] and the merchant, art collector, curator, and exhibition organizer Ernst Wilhelm Juhl (1850–1915),[21] emphasized the crucial function of local organizations and schools for instilling into Germans a sensibility about their historic roots and sense of homeland, especially in "our restless times."[22] Both Lichtwark and Juhl suggested the use of photography as a "school for the gaze" and regarded it as the "ideal tool for the aesthetic education of large parts of the population."[23] Catering to and corresponding with the same affirmative notion were the era's museum-mania and the aspirations to "selectively organize" the past in order to provide a coherent base for "the construction of the future,"[24] the excessive tendency to erect monuments to the memory of national leaders, and the urge to assemble objects and different forms of representations in collections and archives.

Preservation versus restoration was not a uniquely German issue; other European nation-states shared concerns about the "pursuit of one's present identity from the past."[25] Eric Hobsbawm coined the phrase of "tradition invention" by nation-states in order to retroactively legitimize their claim for coherent identity and, as Andreas Huyssen put it, "to give cultural coherence to conflictive societies in the throes of the Industrial Revolution and colonial expansion."[26]

Around 1900, in response to the challenges of establishing a sense of national identity, a distinctly German cultural and preservationist movement called homeland preservation or homeland protection (*Heimatschutz*) emerged. The term *Heimatschutz* was the brainchild of Ernst Rudorff, who founded the Deutsche

Heimatschutzbewegung (German Homeland Preservation) movement in 1904. This essentially bourgeois movement was manifested both in the visual arts and in German literature, through various periodical publications and educational initiatives. The ideological motivations of *Heimatschutz*'s proponents ranged from national pride and nationalistic chauvinism to antiurban and antimodern leanings. This heterogeneous cultural movement aspired, through literature, journalistic efforts, educational measures, and the visual arts, to reconnect to the "homeland." The movement promoted photography as a medium to capture the newly discovered and positively beset idea of the "Heimat."[27] One of its central purposes was, in the words of its founding charter, the preservation of historic monuments and of "traditional rural and civic building techniques and existing buildings and building complexes."[28] The urge to cement a framework of tradition through mechanisms of cultural invention or to "restore" historic buildings was paralleled by *Heimatschutz*'s goal to preserve, secure, and perpetuate traditions and memories of a village, city, or region. Visual media was assumed to be an effective means to educate the public about historic objects, buildings, sites, and traditions, and amateur photography was to play a central role in this effort.

The interplay of a newly awakening national consciousness with an interest in "the history of the fatherland and the monuments of the past"[29] triggered great interest in capturing historical evidence of the city as well. During a city council meeting in 1886, Berlin's magistrate discussed the public financing of urban and architectural photographs of the city and decided to allocate at least 1,500 marks per year for the acquisition of photographs by city institutions. The magistrate asserted that "the institutes, magistrate-library, city archive, Märkische Museum, state archive, and the Berlin historical society and the local architects' association strongly supported the creation of a large amount of images of individual buildings as well as vistas of Berlin." The magistrate also proudly announced that "part of this image pool, which had traditionally only consisted of drawings, etchings, lithographs, and water colors, was of late *also photographs*" (emphasis added).[30] In the archive of the Märkische Museum, a memo of a directorial meeting on January 19, 1910—by Otto Siegfried Pniower (1859–1932), then assistant to the museum's custodian, Rudolph Buchholz, who was in charge of the graphic collection—confirmed that the museum had received a specially dedicated photography fund of 1,000–1,500 marks every year from 1885 to 1905. These photographs were initially produced by F. Albert Schwartz, Hermann Rückwardt, and other studios; later, other photographers, such as Georg Bartels and Hugo Rudolphy, were also consulted. The most prominent photographers, Schwartz and Rückwardt, received 20 marks for "main images," and for additional images of the same location, 10 marks. Bartels, who took over in 1892, only received 12 marks for such a "main image" and 6 marks for each additional image.[31]

The Märkische Museum's publication *Picturesque Berlin: Images and Views* was an important manifestation of such notions. Its form derived from the concept of the photographic survey, a systematic and detailed method of registry that had become internationally employed to document cultural heritage.[32] The photo survey came to reflect a complex set of overarching historiographical questions about national and cultural identity, modernity, and memory. By 1910, according to Pniower, a total of about 3,500 photographs had been amassed, half of which "satisfied artistic demands."[33] Pniower further explained that these photographs were not exhibited; they were stored in portfolios instead.[34] The city's goal was very much in line with the original understanding of a survey: to "convey the memory of remarkable Berlin buildings, of characteristic prospects of entire city quarters." With the decision to build up a photographic inventory for Berlin, the city administration also determined precisely which building types qualified and how they should be documented. The original and primary measure was to "depict the outer parts" of memorable buildings that should be collected in a publication of a "unique pictorial work about the history of Berlin after creating an inventory of Berlin's monuments."[35] Unlike such inventorial indexes, but based on their comprehensive capture of the city's monuments, the city-financed *Picturesque Berlin* was to be understood as a creative and deliberately inventive body of work.

Previous national documentary efforts served as models for the project but were also distinct in their documentary nature. In 1874, the Verband Deutscher Architekten- und Ingenieurvereine (Alliance of German Architects' and Engineers' Associations) initiated research on and strategies for the preservation of German historic monuments. A memorandum about the exploration and preservation of German monuments, published as a response to this debate, prompted "the governments of [Germany's] individual states, larger cities, and notably the province-administrations in Prussia, often supported by History and

Antiquity societies" to research their artistic monuments and to publish monument catalogs.[36]

The alliance's research kicked off a series of urban survey photography projects, which became evident in a number of publications and projects in Berlin. Some of the surveys investigated and systematically assessed certain aspects of Berlin's architecture and its history, such as *Die Bau- und Kunstdenkmäler von Berlin* (*Berlin's Architectural and Artistic Monuments*) (1893) (Figure 4.6), *Berlin und seine Bauten* (*Berlin and Its Buildings*) (1877 and 1896) (Figure 4.7), and Ludwig Hoffmann's *Neubauten der Stadt Berlin* (*New Buildings of the City of Berlin*) (1902–12). Other photographs and projects focused on living conditions in tenement buildings, such as the Housing Inquest report ("Wohnungs-Enquête der Berliner Ortskrankenkasse") (1903–20), or simply collected and archived individual photographs.

Berlin and Its Buildings, published by Berlin Architects' Association, was first released in 1877, with a much extended follow-up in 1896; it is recognized today as one of the most comprehensive documentations of Berlin's architecture.[37] This opus aimed to make "Berlin and its buildings/architectural monuments the subject of a comprehensive, well-rounded presentation" and became an all-encompassing reference book for Berlin's buildings, urban development, architectural education, building materials, and methods. This publication also brought together an impressive collection of differently mediated images and sources. It combined commissioned photographs by Alex Krajewski and Georg Bartels with heliogravures by Hermann Rückwardt, images provided by Wasmuth Publishers,[38] and a number of Germany's most important architectural periodicals, including *Centralblatt der Bauverwaltung*, *Zeitschrift für Bauwesen*, and *Deutsche Bauzeitung*.[39]

Richard Borrmann's 1893 publication *Berlin's Architectural and Artistic Monuments* was also inspired by the 1874 initiative.[40] In 1887, Berlin's city magistrate asked Richard Borrmann to publish the Berlin inventory. In his foreword, Borrmann explained that he understood his work as an "art-topographical inventory" ("kunsttophographisches Verzeichnis"), which followed the model of other such projects in other Prussian provinces and states of the German Empire. Borrmann's decidedly art-historical approach was modelled after, and took as a measure of quality, earlier publications by Georg Gottfried Küster and Friedrich Nicolai. More explicitly patriotic and focused on a dichotomy of old and

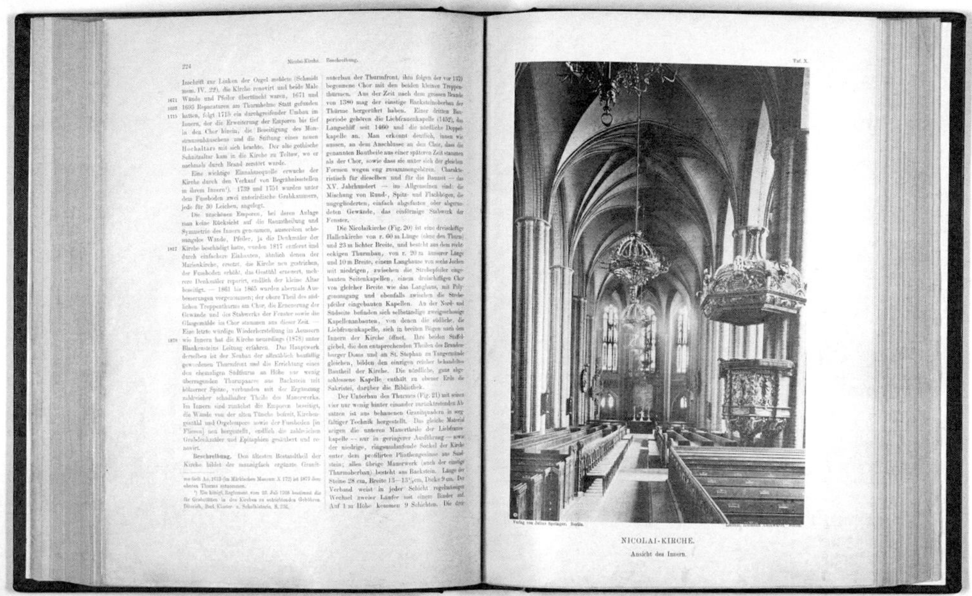

Figure 4.6. Double page from Richard Borrmann, *Die Bau- und Kunstdenkmäler von Berlin* (Berlin: Springer, 1893), 224–25. Copyright Stiftung Stadtmuseum Berlin. Photograph by Michael Setzpfandt, Berlin.

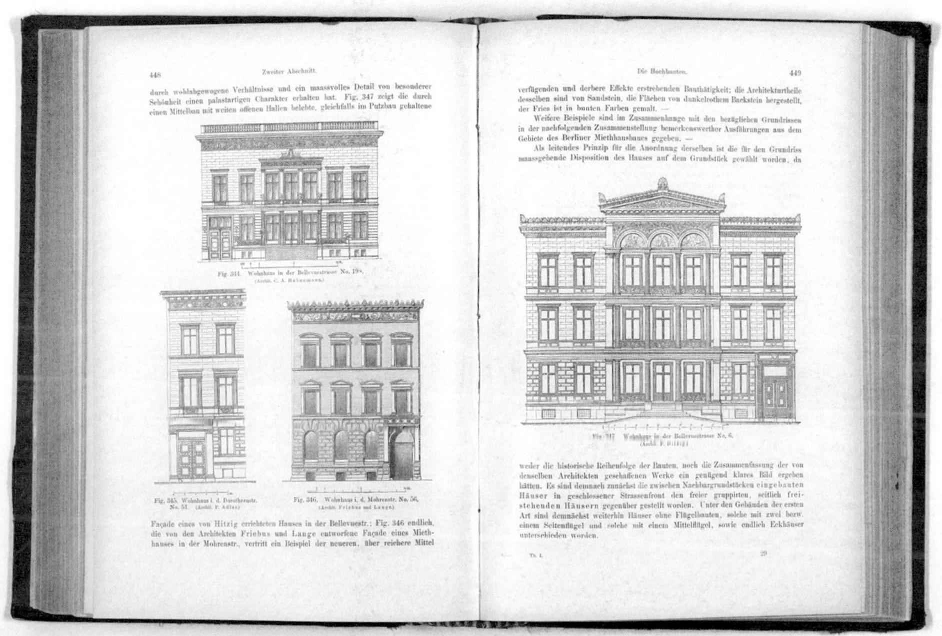

Figure 4.7. Double page from Architekten-Verein zu Berlin und Vereinigung Berliner Architekten, *Berlin und seine Bauten*, 3 vols. (Berlin: Ernst, 1896), 448–49. Copyright Stiftung Stadtmuseum Berlin. Photograph by Michael Setzpfandt, Berlin.

new Berlin than was *Berlin and Its Buildings*, Borrmann introduced its spirit as inspired by an "increased national consciousness" and a "raised interest in the history of the homeland and monuments of the past." The volume was organized according to building types and was intended to "demonstrate how and for what reasons the living conditions and institutions of the original urban community has been transformed over time into today's conditions." Borrmann relied on drawings, etchings, heliogravure illustrations by Hermann Rückwardt, and zinc etchings by Heinrich Riffarth's reproduction company.[41]

The Housing Inquest ("Wohnungs-Enquête") of a local health insurer "for tradespeople and businesspeople as well as pharmacists in Berlin" ("Ortskrankenkasse für den Gewerbebetrieb der Kaufläute, Handelsleute und Apotheker in Berlin") was the only social-reformist study of living conditions in tenements in Berlin that is documented as having been created and that was supported by photographs of apartment interiors and exteriors. This study was triggered by a growing understanding of the connections between poor living conditions and illness and involved both a statistical evaluation of living conditions and the publication of photographs (Figures 4.8–4.11).[42]

Historic Preservation and the Märkische Museum

The Märkische Museum was founded in 1874 by Berlin's citizenry as a cultural-historical museum for the city and region, and its stated mission was the preservation of cultural objects, vernacular paraphernalia, and memories of the history of the city and its surroundings. By the 1890s, the museum administration proposed the construction of a new building, which Ludwig Hoffmann planned and finished by 1908. Hoffmann's reimagination of Brandenburg's historic architectural styles and choreography of room sequences exemplified an empathetic approach to the history of the region. Kurt Winkler, who directed the museum from 2003 through 2006, explained that the new museum building aimed at achieving something very much in line with the educational and experiential efforts by the *Heimatschutz* movement in providing for its visitors "a counter experience to the one of the metropolis in the process of formation and determined by the acceleration of all its life aspects." Hoffmann intended for visitors to "experience instead the slowing down, the delving into a sequence of

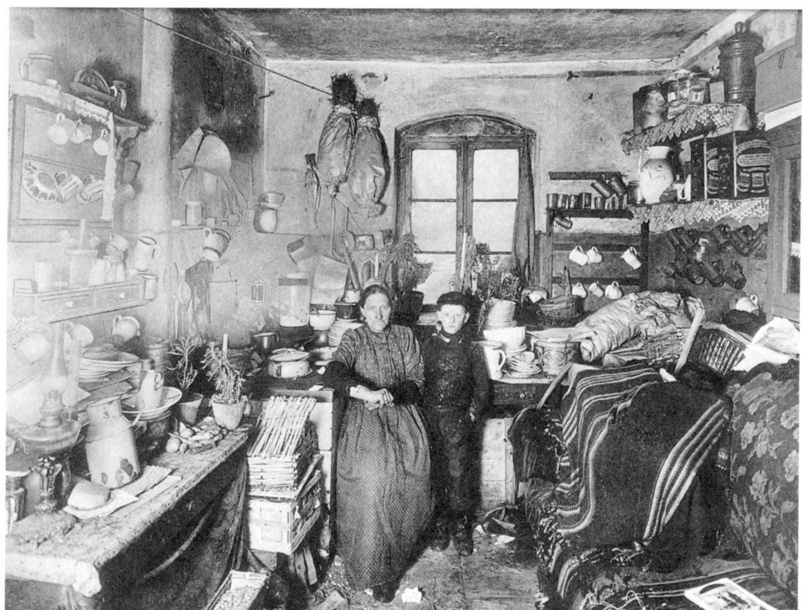

Figure 4.8. "Unsere erste Wohnungs-Enquête. Im Auftrag des Vorstands der Ortskrankenkasse Berlin" ("Our first Housing Inquest. At the commission of the board of the local health insurance of Berlin"). Photographic documentation of a couple with two sons in kitchen in dwelling Berlin-N, Seestraße 27. Photograph by an unknown photographer of Heinrich Lichte and Company, 1909. Inventory number AKG61902. Image provided by akg-images.

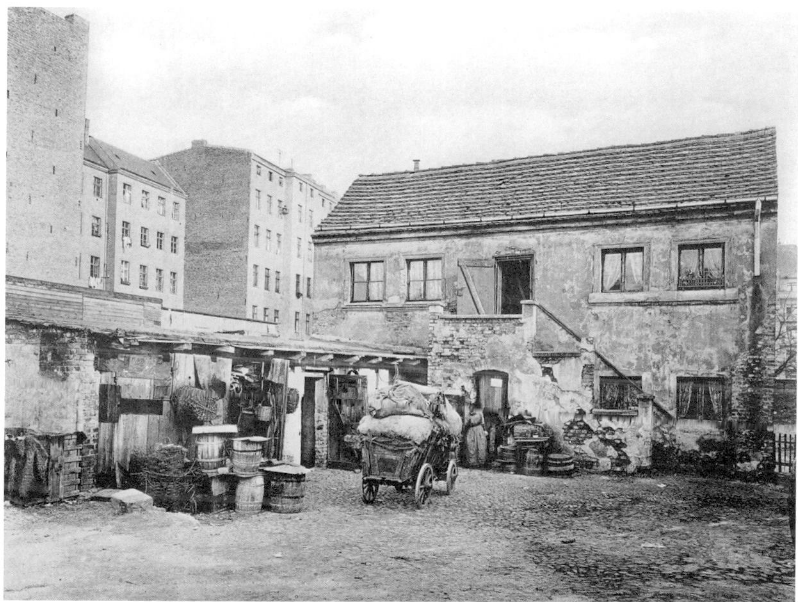

Figure 4.9. "Unsere erste Wohnungs-Enquête. Im Auftrag des Vorstands der Ortskrankenkasse Berlin." View of a backyard, Seestraße 27, Berlin. Photograph by an unknown photographer of Heinrich Lichte and Company, 1909. Inventory number AKG61900. Image provided by akg-images.

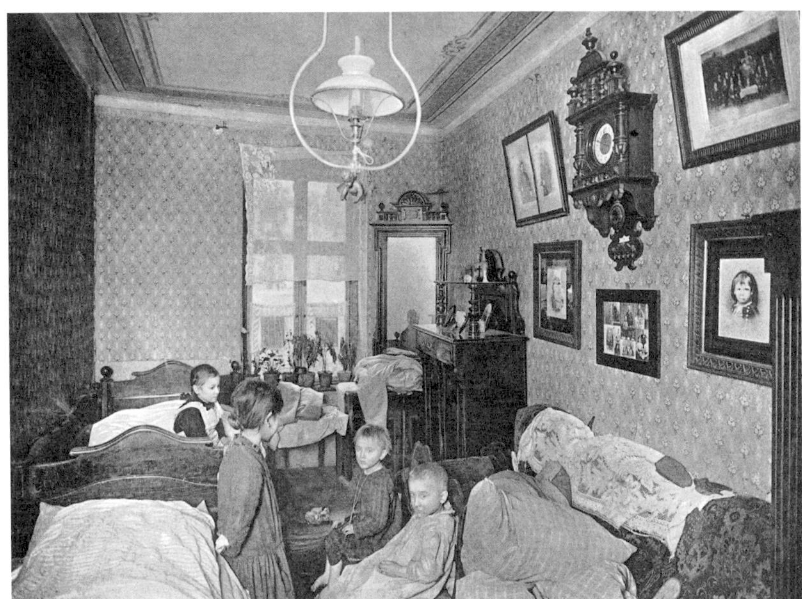

Figure 4.10. "Unsere erste Wohnungs-Enquête. Im Auftrag des Vorstands der Ortskrankenkasse Berlin." Photographic documentation of Berlin-N, Grünthaler Straße 6, second wing, first stairway, living room for three adults and six children. Photograph, 1919–20. Inventory number AKG62012. Image provided by akg-images.

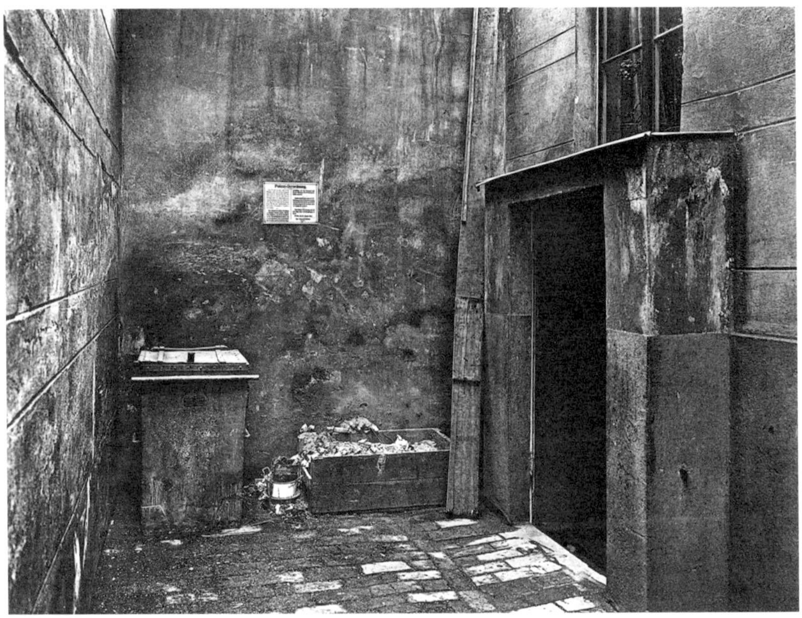

Figure 4.11. "Unsere erste Wohnungs-Enquête. Im Auftrag des Vorstands der Ortskrankenkasse Berlin." Photographic documentation of the entry to a basement dwelling, Berlin-SO, Manteuffelstraße 27. Photograph by an unknown photographer of Heinrich Lichte and Company, 1906. Inventory number AKG62046. Image provided by akg-images.

'tableaus' and to become themselves part of the very narrative that 'Berliners and Märkers' had constituted through thousands of gifts to their museum."[43]

In 1909, the Märkische Museum began focusing its efforts in the photographic survey project *Picturesque Berlin: Images and Views*, whose character was remarkably different from that of predecessors such as the Berlin Architects' Association's and Bormann's publications as well as the Wohnungs-Enquête project and the differently interpreted "picturesque Berlin" in *Berlin Life*. This explicitly image-focused endeavor was supposed to depict the unique aspects of the city, as defined by the residents of the era, and what presumably made it beautiful: its historic remnants (Figure 4.12).

The changing focus of *Picturesque Berlin* away from creating an inventory of Berlin's monuments toward the subject of beauty reflected a growing awareness and concern about how the city was perceived, by both its inhabitants and its potential visitors. It recalls Endell's, Warstat's, and Mayer's considerations for the city as well. Max Osborn, a member of the acquisitions committee of the National Gallery in Berlin and of the Art Commission of the City of Berlin, was commissioned in 1910 to establish the archive that would be assembled in *Picturesque Berlin*. Osborn, whose many published works included a 1909 book about Berlin's monuments and history, hinted at the shifted claims for urban photography in his emotive words in 1910:

> Slowly and mostly unnoticed, a new love for Berlin has prospered. It was fashionable for years to aesthetically ignore the capital; more than it ever deserved. And then, the great historical wave came upon us and we were reminded that even this "American" city in Europe had a very appealing artistic past. . . . "Old Berlin" became a positive code word and, on top of that, people developed an unheard-of fondness for the past's scarce witnesses and monuments.[44]

This rhetorical linking of the historic with the beautiful shifted the photographic discourse away from registering the city as subject of systematic study and toward a more artistic interpretation. The image of Berlin that emerged from this description was intended to uncover an authentic history in an otherwise challengingly new city—one that had neglected and erased most of its historical architecture and quarters without a trace. Such rediscovery and representation of certain overlooked aspects of the city as a promotional measure was echoed in the introductory words of Berlin's deputy mayor, Dr. Georg

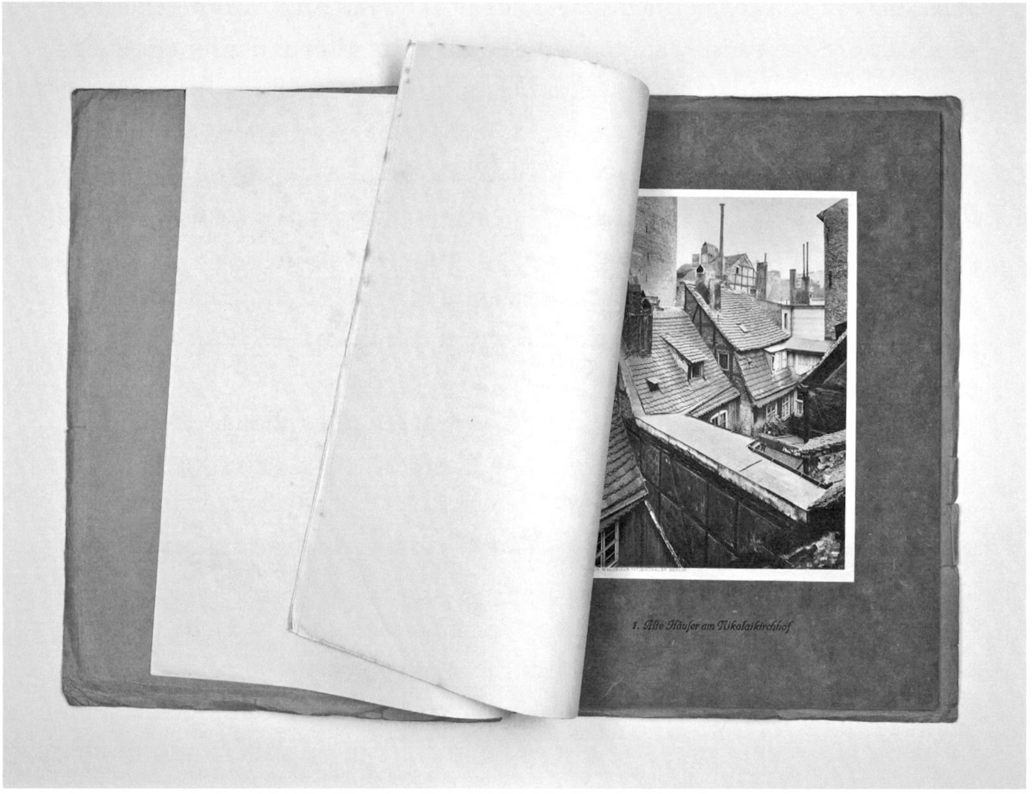

Figure 4.12. Portfolio Cover, *Das malerische Berlin: Bilder und Blicke,* vol. 3 (Berlin: Verlag von Julius Bard, 1914). Heliogravure, 36.5 × 28.5 cm. Inventory number IV. Copyright Stiftung Stadtmuseum Berlin. Photograph by Oliver Ziebe, Berlin. Image by Waldemar Titzenthaler, *Alte Häuser am Nikolaikirchhof* (Old Houses at Nikolai Churchyard).

Reicke,[45] for volume 1 of *Picturesque Berlin*. Highlighting that "Berlin is not loved enough either by foreigners or by Berliners," Reicke suggested "a finer, quieter, and very consoling kind of discovery, which sees the past within the contemporary, which recognizes with gratitude traditional values, and which also knows to halt at the sight of intimate corners of a passed era, which have been left aside by the growing metropolis." As Berlin "has not had any moment to think of its past" during the last generation, the Märkische Museum's and these publications' task and function were "to remind it constantly of its origin and to point the viewer with it to the plentitude of possibilities of further progress."[46]

Osborn, who recently had published a more conventional illustrated architectural history of Berlin,[47] seems to have approached this opportunity with great enthusiasm. Originally planned as a comprehensive exploration, it was to result in a set of large-format photographic portfolios of different aspects of the city. The well-connected Osborn managed to bring on board three highly regarded photographers: the Hamburg-based artistic photographer Rudolf Dührkoop (1848–1918), the documentarian Waldemar Titzenthaler (1869–1937), and the architectural photographer Ernst von Brauchitsch (1856–1932), as well as the Royal Prussian Photogrammetric Institute. Most of the photographs in the publication were taken by Dührkoop, and it displayed Brauchitsch's photographs of Hoffmann's museum building. Waldemar Titzenthaler took the majority of the images that were printed in volume 3.

The series' three realized issues focused exclusively on historic structures, the old parts of town, and suburban sites: The first group of images was called "Old Berlin" (1911) and focused on the historic Krögel district, castles, churches, and monuments. The second captured singularly famous buildings and squares (1912) such as various parts of the city castle, both Altes Museum and the new Märkische Museum building (in one of Ernst von Brauchitsch's depictions of its grown-over Renaissance wing), and various palaces ("palais" of the city's nobility) and tourist sites. The last one assembled views of "old corners and courtyards" (1914) and depicted historic residential buildings both in Berlin's impoverished center and in its wealthy western suburban Tiergarten district. Osborn addressed the history of their subjects in introductory texts for both the 1912 and 1914 volumes. The envisioned topics for the other portfolios were parks and squares, bridges and canals, street life and types of populace (*Volkstypen*), and traffic and industrial complexes.

Despite the hope expressed by the museum's director to reacquaint the city to its inhabitants and to visitors, their audience seems to have been highly selective. Copies of either single issues or the entire set of three volumes were sent out to city officials such as Berlin's president of police and the Royal Art Academy, publishers like Rudolf Mosse, and museum directors across the country, like the Germanic National Museum's in Nuremberg.[48] Given the broad spectrum of systematic precursors of this survey project, *Picturesque Berlin* can be understood as an exquisite collection of images that were treated as sentimental rather than educational or preservationist projects. Their intended audiences did not include the architects, planners, and students of architecture who had been targeted by earlier publications.

Each portfolio contained twelve rotogravures (*Kupfertiefdrucke*), which were produced via a printing drum. The rotogravures were generated by gridded halftones—a technique that was much cheaper than the older and nongridded halftone-printing method that created heliogravures. Starting in 1895, rotogravures had been published in mass editions by Karl Klič, the inventor of both heliogravure and rotogravure. This new technique's beautiful and soft tonal transitions were widely admired for their subtlety and accuracy. While originally only known to a small circle of industrialists because of the high costs for the machine equipment, the rotogravure soon became the predominant printing process for picture postcards and illustrated magazines that boasted high subscription numbers.[49] The rotogravure is still used for high-quality color printing in industrial processes. Inscriptions and annotations of images varied from edition to edition. In some editions, image reproductions were solidly glued onto their matting board, and sometimes they were only loosely attached and could be lifted. At times, a white frame distinguished the reproductions, and the photographers' name was mentioned. In other cases, the image was displayed without further information.

The first volume of *Picturesque Berlin* depicts scenes from the old Krögel section of Berlin's historic city. Krögel was comprised of a narrow system of courtyards and street corners, which were grouped around the Krögel alley (Krögelgasse) and located directly above a former arm of the Spree. The economic situation of the Krögel's original population of small handicraft enterprise-operators and their families grew increasingly dire in the late nineteenth century, which caused social decline. By the 1930s, the neighborhood was considered a slum and demolished. However, its painterly appeal led to its romanticization during the turn of the century and rendered it a popular destination for Berlin's photographers.[50]

As aestheticized object, Berlin's Krögel provided a welcome filter for anxieties of alienation and the sense of detachment from an increasingly unfamiliar city. It didn't matter that the past that these images were constructing was neither more agreeable nor coherent than the present appeared to be. A presentation of historical consciousness was at risk—both through the museum's vision and in photography—of becoming nothing but a construct of national ideology or utopia. Almost all of the better-known Berlin photographers, as well as many whose names are forgotten today, worked in the Krögel area. Max Missmann created a series of Krögel images between 1903 and 1907, and Waldemar Titzenthaler made many trips to the old town as did other fellow members of local history and homeland associations such as photographers Heinrich Zille, F. Albert Schwartz, and Georg Bartels.

A photograph for the first portfolio by Dührkoop shows a group of children in the Am Krögel alley (Figure 4.13). The photographer positioned them in a spot where the street adjacent to Am Krögel lets a ray of sun through. This cobblestoned alley is narrow and shadowy and winds slightly rightward, bending into the background. The alley is drained through a slight central depression of the street level. Two-storied, pitched-roofed houses tightly enclose the pathway. The house façade in the foreground on the left is crumbling away, exposing its masonry on the ground floor. The children are the only protagonists, and their presence is clearly intentional. They are neatly dressed in starched, bright outfits, starkly contrasting with the neglect of their urban environment. The children seem to have been transplanted from a different, friendlier world into this unforgiving milieu.

Dührkoop was not focused on rendering the architecture alone, and his unabashed romanticization of the Krögel is strikingly different from well-known earlier photographic surveys of slums such as those by Jacob Riis (Figure 4.14), Lewis Hine (in New York City), or Thomas Annan (in Glasgow) (Figure 4.15)—or from the Berlin Enquête survey. Dührkoop's works contrasted strongly with those of Heinrich Zille (Figures 4.16 and 4.17), who often included spontaneous gatherings of Krögel inhabitants or focused on particular details. Zille, a painter, cartoonist, and skilled amateur photographer, took photographs frequently in the Krögel district during the turn of the century, and according to his biographer, Winfried Ranke, the district was his favorite subject.[51] Zille, well known for his sensitive photographs of working-class Berliners and a member of Berlin's historical society, which was promoting *Heimatschutz* strategies for photographers, focused on building details and captured inhabitants of the Krögel more naturally than his pictorialist contemporaries.[52]

Dührkoop selectively emphasizes the romantic, even idyllic appearance of Krögel. His approach was not uncommon among artistic photographers of this era, as demonstrated by other photographs of urban sites published in a 1909 issue of the German amateur photography journal *Photographische Mitteilungen*

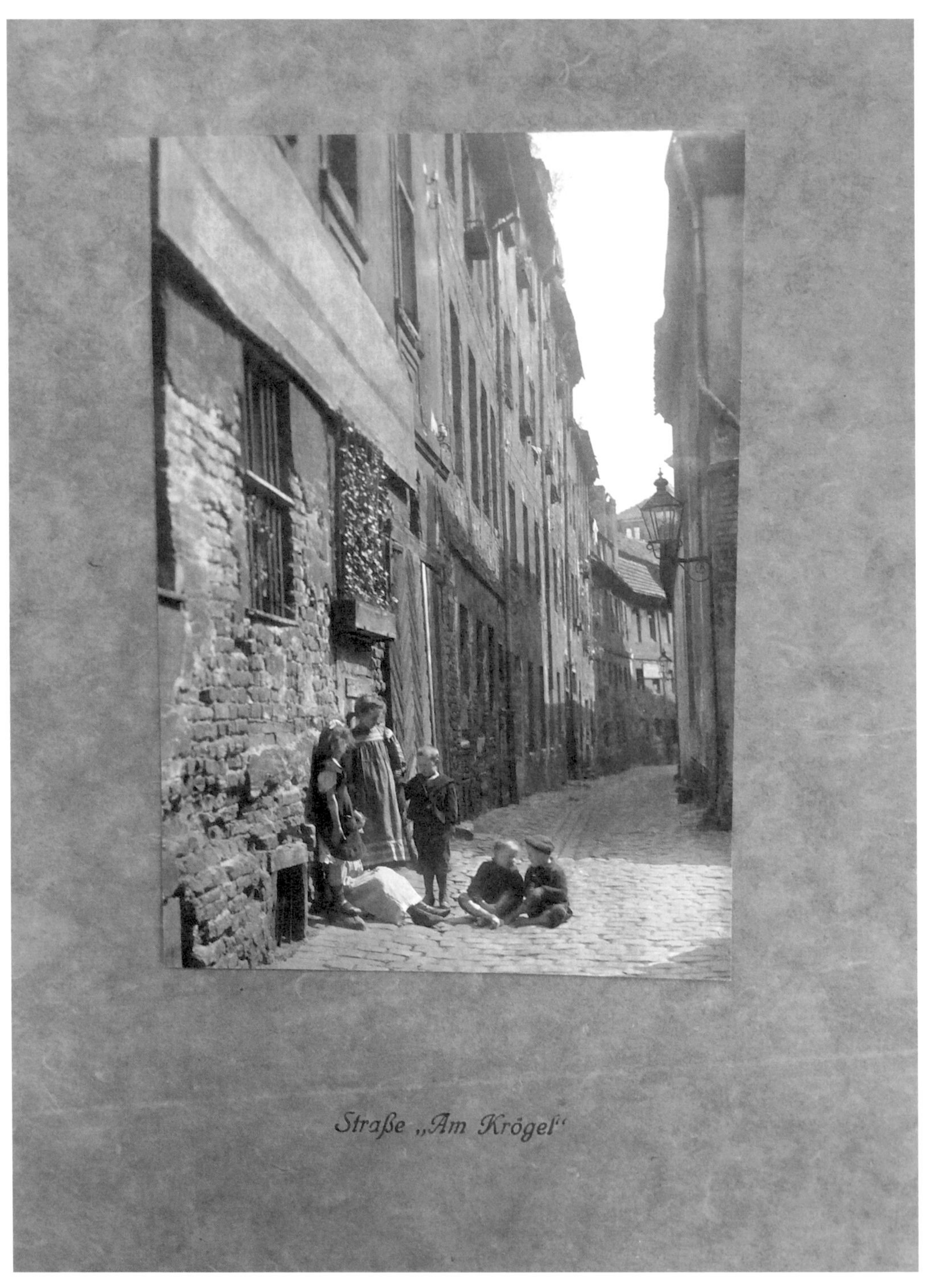

Figure 4.13. Rudolf Dührkoop, *Straße, "Am Krögel"* ("Am Krögel" Street). From the portfolio *Das malerische Berlin: Bilder und Blicke,* vol. 1 (Berlin: Verlag von Julius Bard, 1911), image no. 6. Rotogravure, 21.5 × 15.6 cm. Copyright Stiftung Stadtmuseum Berlin.

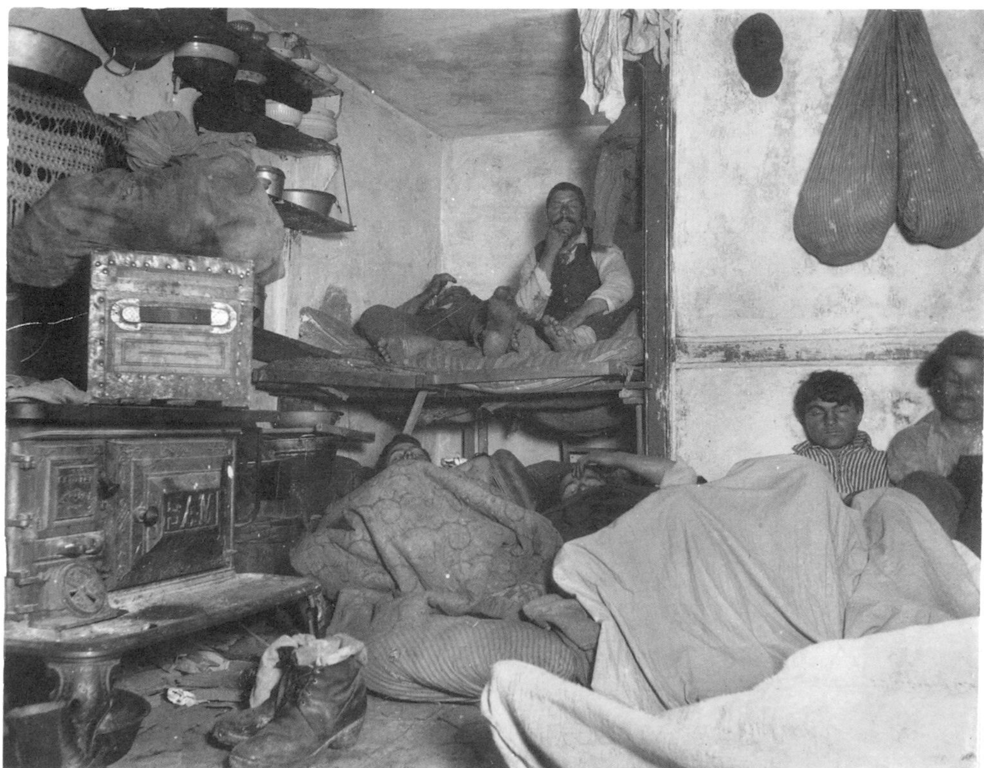

Figure 4.14. Jacob August Riis, Lodgers in Bayard Street Tenement, Five Cents a Spot, 1889. Gelatin silver print, Museum of Modern Art, New York. Object number 338.1964; Gift of the Museum of the City of New York, Museum of Modern Art. Digital image copyright the Museum of Modern Art. Licensed by SCALA/Art Resource NY.

(Figures 4.18 and 4.19). These photographs either depict town squares or are bordered by an arched courtyard entry, and their scenes are enhanced by soft focus and narrow framing. In these images, the location and identification of sites became secondary to the conveyance of "feeling" and "mood."

Susanne Gänshirt-Heinemann, in her comprehensive text about the romanticization of the Krögel, places Dührkoop's photographs between those of classic architectural photographers and other artistic photographers. Dührkoop, she points out, did not work with overemphasized light effects and extensive post-edits, both of which were typical for pictorialists. Like a painter, Dührkoop planned every detail of his images, placed his sitters carefully, and framed them such that the actual location was obscured. He eschewed overviews, which would communicate a clear sense of location, preferring to convey the atmosphere of

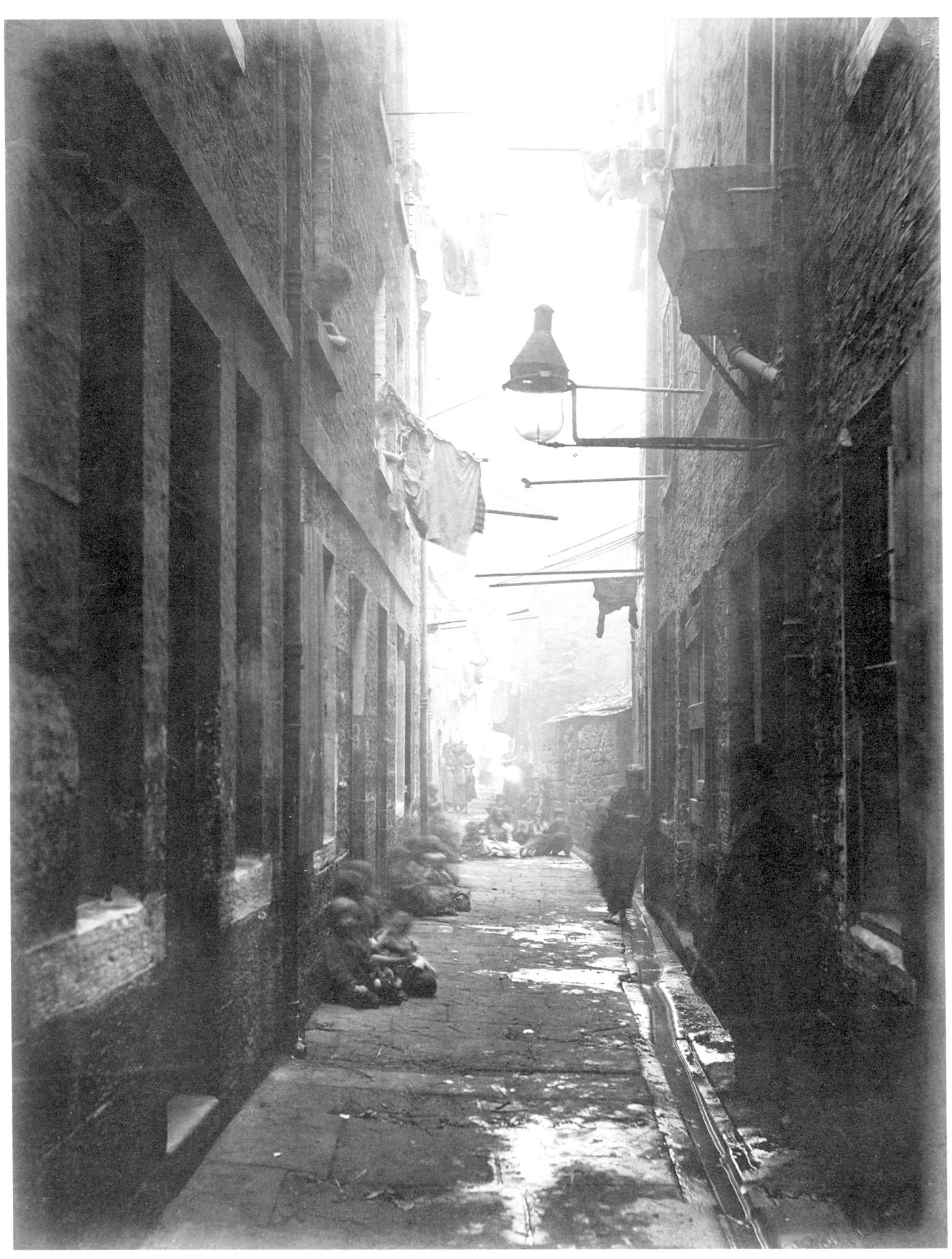

Figure 4.15. Thomas Annan, Glasgow Close No. 80 High Street, 1868 (printed later). Los Angeles County Museum of Art. Accession number M.2008.40.98.11. Wikimedia Commons.

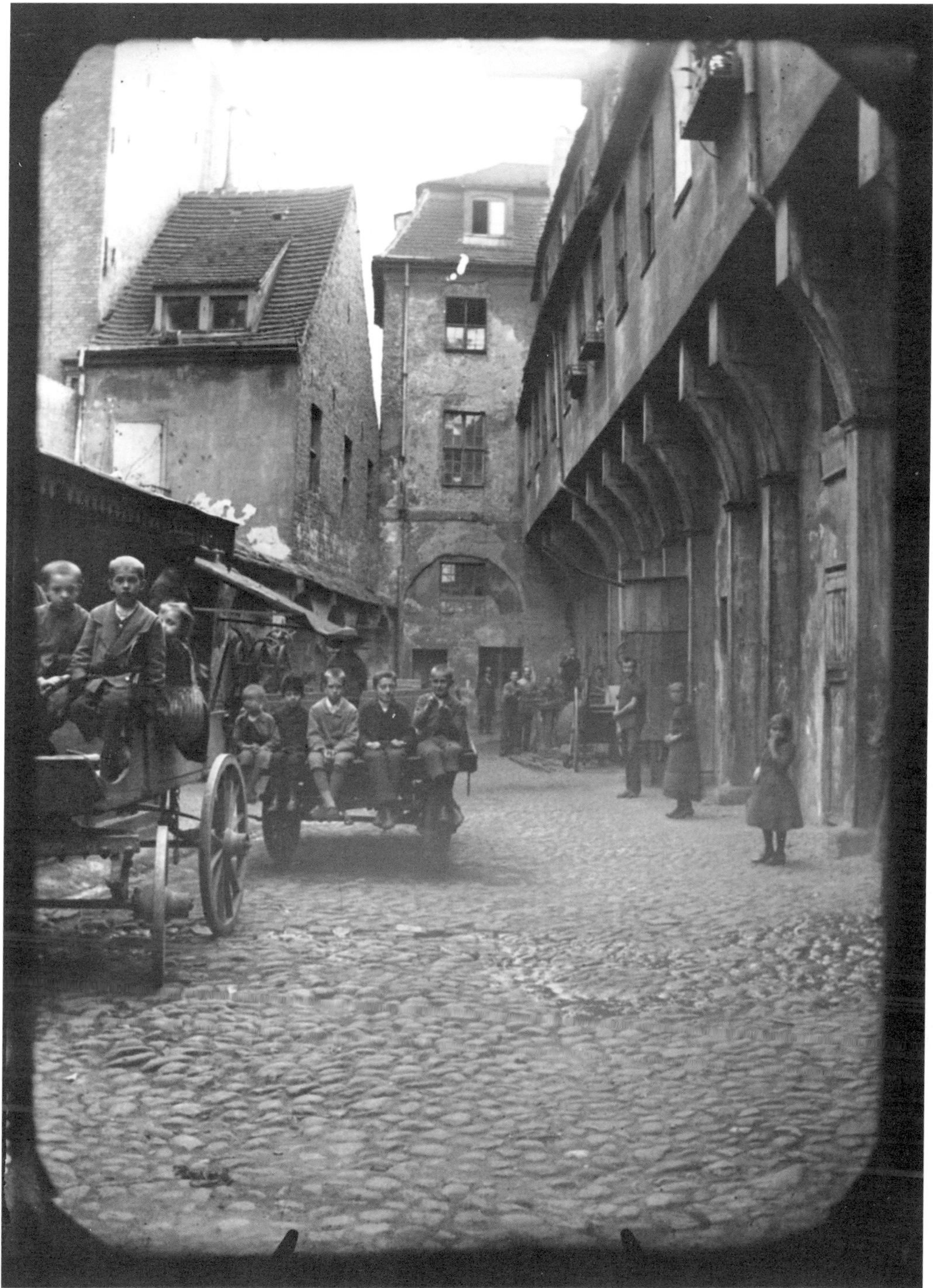

Figure 4.16. Heinrich Zille, first courtyard in Krögel district with children (view from the second courtyard), circa 1896. Inventory number WV32. Photograph provided by Berlinische Galerie, Berlin.

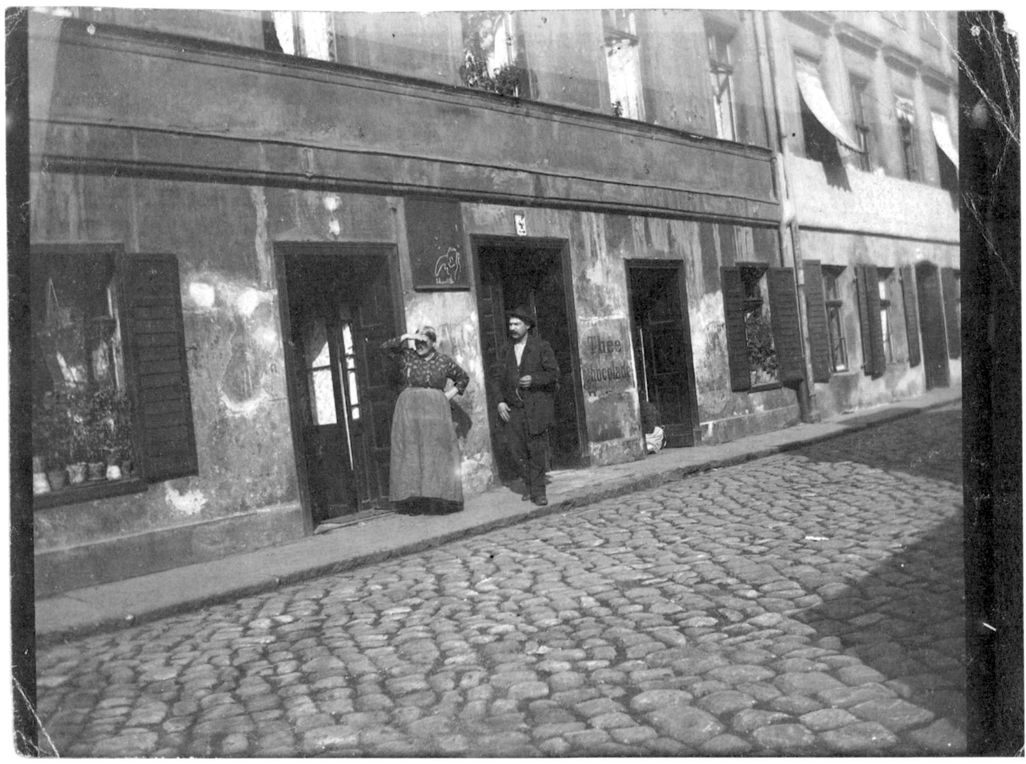

Figure 4.17. Heinrich Zille, street (house number 4) with woman and man (possibly Parochialstr.), 1901. Inventory number WV396. Photograph provided by Berlinische Galerie, Berlin.

a location through physical detail.[53] The art historian Enno Kaufhold confirms that this was typical for pictorialists in whose practice "even city images, which were naturally counted as 'Heimat' images, rarely permitted a clear identifying of a location." It was a central intention of artistic photographers "not to disturb subjective atmosphere by impressions of a tough reality."[54] Paradoxically, such images were in actuality "home-less"; they relied purely on the lyrical emotions of their viewers and did not focus on precise geographical descriptions.

Another image of the first volume taken in this area, titled *Im Krögel*, demonstrates this abstracting strategy.[55] A window and house entry serve as geometric framing devices for the image, and Dührkoop inserts a number of narratives as two women converse while leaning over the window frame. Four children are seated in the house entrance, one telling a story, the others attentively listening. The ends of two laundry lines have been attached to the right doorframe;

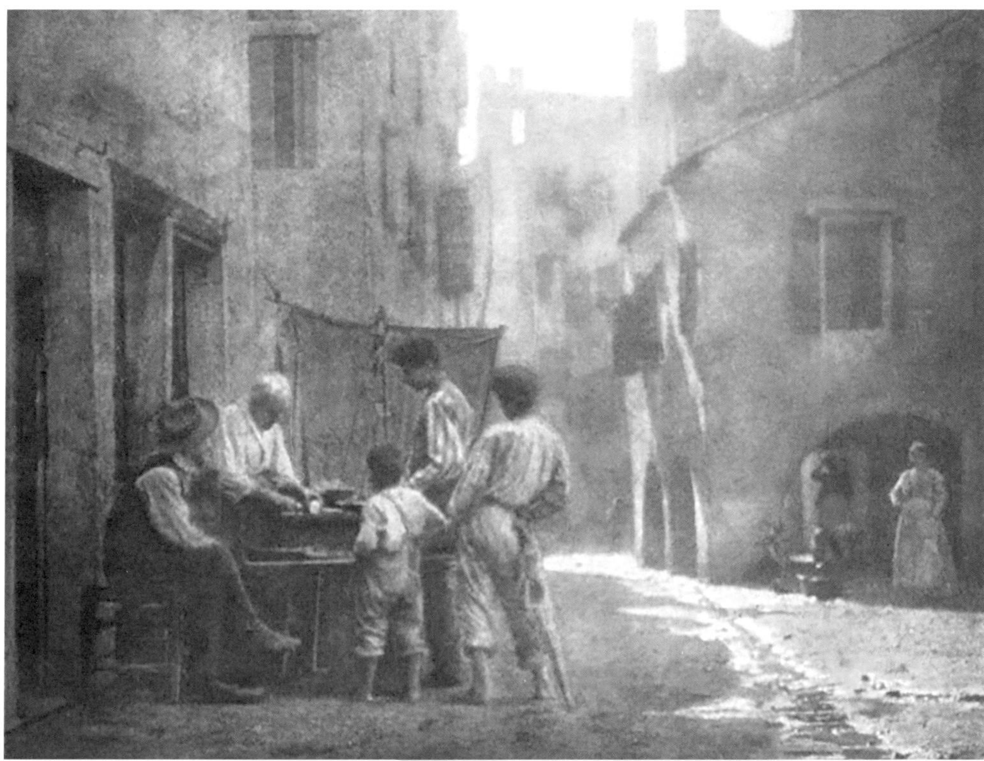

Figure 4.18. Alex Keighley, "Melon-vendor." Photogravure reproduced in *Photographische Mitteilungen* 46 (1909). http://photoseed.com/collection/group/photographische-mitteilungen-1909/. Courtesy PhotoSeed Archive, USA.

drying plain pieces of laundry in the lower right image half correspond with broad white patches of plaster that have been used to haphazardly fix the crumbling façade.

Other images, such as Waldemar Titzenthaler's *Old Houses by Nikolai Churchyard* (Figure 4.20), focus on architecture.[56] This tightly framed image of old, steep rooftops, bare stone walls, and chimneys could be located—if not for a couple of high building walls that cut into this idyll—in a quaint medieval German town. It is the antithesis to the modern city that has erupted around it, which has rendered this part of town almost invisible. The portrait format underlines the static setting and contemplative focus that this and the other two images hoped to create.

These images and their arrangement within the larger context of the three portfolios were obviously not established to create a systematic, historically

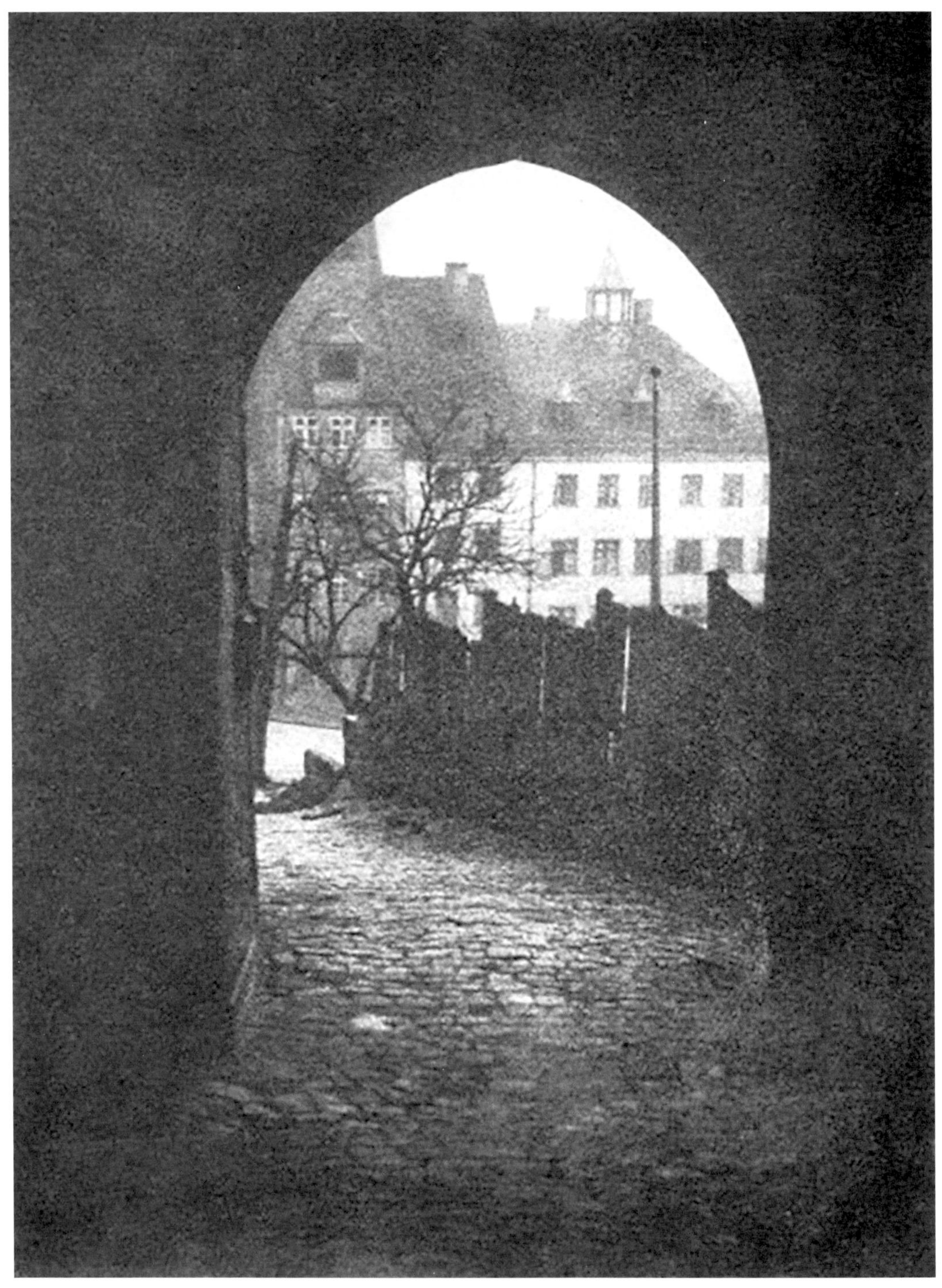

Figure 4.19. Dr. J. Rothberger, "Castle-gate in Nuremberg." Photogravure reproduced in *Photographische Mitteilungen* 46 (1909). http://photoseed.com/collection/group/photographische-mitteilungen-1909/. Courtesy PhotoSeed Archive, USA.

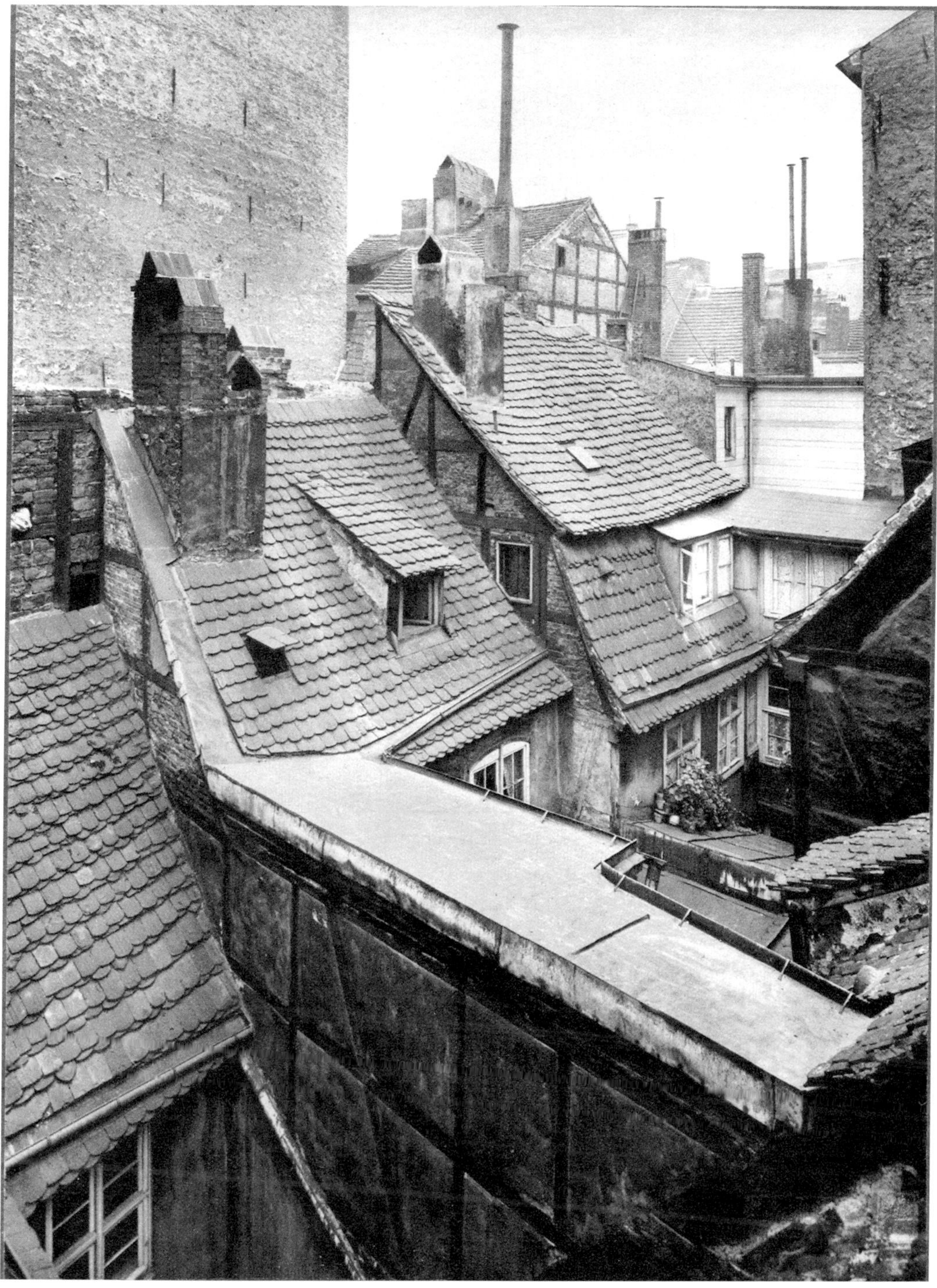

Figure 4.20. Waldemar Titzenthaler, *Alte Häuser am Nikolaikirchhof* (*Old Houses by Nikolai Churchyard*). From the portfolio *Das malerische Berlin: Bilder und Blicke*, vol. 3 (Berlin: Verlag von Julius Bard, 1914), image no. 1. Rotogravure, 36.5 × 28.5 cm. Stiftung Stadtmuseum Berlin.

comprehensive source of reference like *Berlin and Its Buildings* and Borrmann's *Berlin's Architectural and Artistic Monuments*. Their arrangement, in Max Osborn's own words, "neither followed historical nor topographical aspects, but solely the purpose of painterly effect."[57] This way of thinking resonated with Alfred Lichtwark's aspirations in the 1890s to provide an "artistically unspoiled" form of photographic presentation in the service of homeland preservation as they documented "the state of our city and its surroundings in its constant transformation."[58]

Such interlinking of aesthetic concerns with the city's historic roots is palpable in Berlin's deputy mayor Reicke's introduction to the first volume of *Picturesque Berlin*. He described the intentions of the project as striving "to capture in images for the present and the future the beauty that our past has created but nevertheless has to yield under our eyes for the cosmopolitan city." All these efforts, according to Reicke, were eventually meant to "bring their city closer to Berliners and to have them grow more fond of their city."[59] His words in the third volume fuse the era's concern with the disappearance and destruction of historic buildings and districts with the emotional effects of its photographic capture:

> There is an air of fugacity around them [the signs of this time], and, at the same time, a shiver of the past, which evokes the physically decaying matter and wakens it to new life. And as witnesses of an era that has not yet been pulled apart by the unrest of our time, they talk to us in a strangely soothing, almost redemptive language.[60]

Reicke, rhetorically in tune with the turn of the century's understanding of *Einfühlung*, or empathy as an important means of absorbing experiences, defined architecture as telling remnants of the past and implied that their photographic capture eternalized their "soothing, almost redemptive" message. Borrmann and the editors of *Berlin and Its Buildings* originally understood photography as a pragmatic tool of illustration, but Osborn took into account the changing role and use of photography as an explicitly artistic, expressive, and emotive medium. Photography's classically retentive quality, joined by a sense of beauty, rendered it a perfect remedy against the necessary and unstoppable process of time and the sense of alienation that the city inflicted upon its bourgeois citizenry. Reicke's observations and the city's photographic capture also coincided with the emergence of what photography critic Sadakichi Hartmann had described and defined as "straight photography" in his 1904 article "A Plea for Straight Photography." Recognizing photographers such as the American Alfred Stieglitz overcoming photographic pictorialism's extensive manipulation of the negative and print, Hartmann argued for a more immediate approach:

> Rely on your camera, on your eye, on your good taste and your knowledge of composition, consider every fluctuation of color, light, and shade, study lines and values and space division, patiently wait until the scene or object of your pictured vision reveals itself in its supremest moment of beauty. In short, compose the picture which you intend to take so well that the negative will be absolutely perfect and in need of no or but slight manipulation.[61]

This spirit, aided by the topic, the city and its architecture, and the generally more goal-oriented and fact-reliant genre of architectural photography, is detectable in *Picturesque Berlin*. Hartmann points out that he does "not want the photographic worker to cling to prescribed methods and academic standards" or "to be less artistic than he is to-day, on the contrary" he wants "him to be more artistic, but only in legitimate ways." This merging of an understanding of photography as artistic, yet not derivative of a painterly aesthetic, would become the common photographic language of the succeeding decades. Photographers such as Paul Strand and later the California-based f64 group would perfect this "straight" photographic approach. In 1910s Berlin, Reicke's language suggested that the photographic capture of those pockets of the city that were yet uninfected by modernization were a means to hang on, not only to those buildings that would soon have to yield, but also to the entire era, a better past, that was vanishing.

Artist-Surveyors

The photographers of *Picturesque Berlin* who were tasked with making picturesque the city through its last old remnants became "view-makers" in a city that was too fragmented to generate a coherent view or picture. The survey photographer as "recorder and collector of historical data"[62] was replaced by what I call the *artist-surveyor*, who took great liberties to enhance and reinterpret the city's relationship with history. That meant that the entire logic of a survey project shifted. Artistic photographers such as Dührkoop, as Enno Kaufhold observed, "didn't deliver untouched evidence with which to imprint the sign of barbarism onto capitalist excesses, but rather aestheticized counterimages, as they photographed in locations where landscapes and places had been spared modernity's impact."[63] This idea of the counterimage also resonated with what authors of the turn of the century termed "picturesque slum," an image infused with racial and social prejudice and a site of occasional slum tourism.[64] Invoked in conjunction with the discussion of the nineteenth-century city, the picturesque effectively evolved "into the ideological core formula of antimodernism,"[65] which, not coincidentally, was also the essence of the conservative German homeland preservation movement.

The subtitle of this project, "images and views" (*Bilder und Blicke*), gave away the project's true intentions: Instead of documenting buildings and sites of construction or demolition, as Ernst von Brauchitsch's photographs for Ludwig Hoffmann's *New Buildings of the City of Berlin* or the measuring images of the construction site for the Emperor Wilhelm I monument had done, *Picturesque Berlin* was explicitly and unabashedly about creating images that were linked to the subjective, personal, and touristic gaze. The era's articulation of a new conception of city design explicitly as artistic or picturesque in works like Camillo Sitte's 1889 *City Planning According to Artistic Principles*, or Josef Brix's and Felix Genzmer's lectures in Berlin, proved enormously influential for post–World War I city planning and Berlin's understanding of urban design. These lectures, titled "Aufgaben und Ziele des Städtebaus" ("Tasks and Goals of City Planning") by Brix, and "Kunst im Städtebau" ("Artistic City Planning") by Genzmer (published in 1908), summarized the state of knowledge of city planning and design and articulated that city planning was far more than form, but that form was its core.[66] These ideas resonated with the ideologies of preservation and *Heimatschutz* and indicated a changing attitude toward the modern city by the end of the century. Their emphasis on historic city structures and return to forgotten compositional principles created a great sense of urbanity that aimed at fostering public life in enclosed, intimate squares and naturally grown urban sites.

The *Picturesque Berlin* photo portfolios were being assembled just as the collecting policy of the Märkische Museum had changed. From 1912 until 1914, with World War I looming, the budget for photographs was drastically reduced. The museum stopped investing in photographs almost completely and adopted a policy of only accepting gifts. The reduced building activities in and around Berlin just before the war also resulted in a decreased interest in city photography. As photographic aesthetics became a growing concern, photographers, both professional and amateur, were less drawn to architectural documentation. Building projects and processes were simpler and could be documented with less effort and fewer images. The city's architectural history and its heritage had already been documented, and photographers' different motivations and foci had broadened. The need for photo commissions of this kind dissipated after the war,[67] and as a result, the original vision for *Picturesque Berlin* was never realized.

However, the project's claims and effects deserve contextualization and recognition. Today, we recognize that these photographs were far more than witnesses to urban nostalgia; they became active agents of urban perception. The Märkische Museum's collecting activities—including its sophisticated choreography of *Picturesque Berlin*—reflected assumptions of their potential audiences' hope for belonging and relatedness. Berlin, through *Picturesque Berlin*, evolved beyond its signification as marker of an urban state of being and into a unifying generator of a national identity through painterly images and views.

Both this photographic project and its initiation by the Märkische Museum remind us that a museum's raison d'être and the photographic reproduction and interpretation of historical structures in late nineteenth- and early twentieth-century Germany was about more than creating a time capsule. In Germany's climate of recent political and cultural unification, both the photographic depiction of Old Berlin and the museum became affirmative grantors for a city's and a nation's cultural identity. With its historical evidence, city photography not only reflected the existence of the past but was also subject to the projections of national history. "Invented tradition" was put into action by the processes of photographic materialization.

What this project was never able to achieve—due to financial constraints, shifting cultural discourses, and its pronounced concern for Old Berlin—was to build a pictorial bridge between the old and new city. This had been Max Osborn's intention as he embarked on his project for the Märkische Museum in 1910, hoping to reestablish Berlin as an organic whole of old and new.[68]

Becoming, or at least coming across as, such a “logical, organic whole” was never to become a reality for Berlin. Instead, the Old Berlin of *Picturesque Berlin* constituted a kind of antithesis to the New Berlin image of the *Berlin Life* illustrated magazine discussed in chapter 1. While the former hoped to emotionally and aesthetically connect the urbanite to the city, the latter took its strength from keeping distance and deliberate detachment. Old Berlin was supposed to inspire identification, while New Berlin’s panoramas deployed the spectacular comprehensive visual effects aimed at containing the new city’s anxieties and perceived control. Osborn, who spent the 1920s and early 1930s as art critic for Berlin’s *Vossische Zeitung* and as prolific editor and author of a number of critical art-historical works, eventually left Germany as the Nazis burned his books.

CONCLUSION

A Fractured and Transitory Urban Imaginary

> New types are appearing in the nascent society on the other side of the Atlantic. Have these to be ascribed to transitory causes; or, on the other hand, are they the first signs of a future evolution? Europe begins to feel uneasy, and the Old World nations are asking if, after all, they must seek for new models among these barbarians.
>
> —PAUL DE ROUSIERS, *American Life*

Imperial Berlin, as this book has explained, wrestled with forming an identity and image that would firmly place it on par with other European capitals. This assessment of urban status from within a European perspective, however, was less and less capable of addressing the idiosyncrasies of Berlin's urban imaginary. Berlin's struggles in handling its growth and transformation appear in a new light through critics such as Karl Scheffler, Mark Twain, Luc Gersal, Charles Huard, and Madame de Staël, who measured Berlin's image by comparing it to American cities such as New York and Chicago.

Like Twain, the French writer Paul de Rousiers looked at Chicago as an emblematic modern city. In his 1892 publication *American Life*, Rousiers wrote that Chicago was the embodiment of fearless and uncompromising pursuit of progress.[1] Like Berlin, "the large American city, tending to be engrossed with economic expansion and having been faced with a continually unexpected increase of population, has never had much time to consolidate its past gains or leisure to take its attention off the alluring expanding future."[2] Chicago was often labeled a "youthful" and "unfinished" city—characterizations that were frequently uttered by observers of Berlin. However, while these were positive qualifications for an American metropolis, they suggested inferiority when applied to a European city. Being a colonial or frontier city rang very differently depending on whether it belonged to a Prussian or Midwestern American narrative.

Karl Scheffler, in a vehement critique in his 1910 book *Berlin: Ein Stadtschicksal* (*Berlin: The Fate of a City*), claimed that Berlin was historically predisposed to being "Americanized" as the first among metropolises in Europe. According to Scheffler, because of its own history as a colonial city in Europe's uncultured east, it became an eager and emphatic agent for a "new concept of life" (*Lebensidee*), a "promoter of new industrial culture."[3] The "cultural barrenness" of the New World, as cultural sociologist Anselm Strauss wrote in *Images of the American City*,

> is excused in terms of the city's symbolic age. Given sufficient time, some say, the city will grow up, develop a rich cultural life, and take its place among some cities a tithe of its size. The residents of Chicago sometimes use this strategy to console themselves or to ward off attack, and it is probably commonly used in other cities.[4]

This sentiment was reflected in Max Osborn's observations about how Berlin's critics decried it as devoid of culture. It also resonated with critical assessments of Berlin's photographic culture of the 1890s. Critics observed an eager, technocratic, and science-focused pursuit of photography in the city, while photographers in other European metropolises, like Vienna, supposedly approached photographic practice with greater ease and artistic sensibility. Berliners, the critics pointed out, seemed to never have spare time for a more leisurely way to photograph. The writer and photo critic of the late nineteenth century Max Allihn (1841–1910) argued that

> there are people in Berlin who do have time indeed, but they don't engage with photography and it is questionable whether they would achieve something with it anyway. Connected to this is the fact that Berlin's actual strength is in the field of scientific photography, not of artistic photography since these are professional works.[5]

These commentators did not mean to praise such professionalism and scientific focus among Berlin's photographers; instead, they found that the city lacked culture and aesthetic sensibilities. Competition among North American cities was defined by quite different terms. Instead of levels of "culturedness" and artistic creativity, their concern was about which one among them would continue to grow, survive competition with others, and eventually become the most economically powerful in its region.[6] Such questions were raised to determine the best potential places for investments, where to steer one's career, and the best place "to settle down and prosper with the community."[7] The city booster became a familiar figure in the North American West as cities tried to attract settlers and investments. Such boosterism was the origin of grand-style photography as a promotional tool. In Berlin, as discussed in chapter 1, city promotion was aimed both at Berliners and at tourists. When employed in the United States, this type of photography was unapologetically used to attract business; when generated in Berlin, it sometimes turned into an awkward form of self-affirmation.

The conflicting sentiments that were lying beneath Berlin's grand-style photography and its booster spirit is palpable in the city's 1896 trade exhibition, which made claims to being a world's exposition of sorts. The expo was a demonstration of both the city's growing self-esteem and its fascination with its historic roots and the association of historicity with beauty. A typical display included the latest technologies and industrial and artistic developments, which were juxtaposed with the very popular "Old Berlin" section that sold almost eight million tickets,[8] making it the exposition's most visited and profitable exhibit. This emphasis on "Old Berlin" reveals the contradictions of modernism at the time. The clashing narratives of this small, supposedly late-middle-age city,[9] and its "historical likeness" exposed the city's underlying preoccupations. Experiencing Old Berlin, in the words of its creators, would permit the visitor to "leave behind completely the sobering Now" and feel "transported into a different world and long-past times."[10]

This conflicting relationship between old and new was unconceivable in North America and Chicago, where the spectacular World's Columbian Exposition had boosted the city's recognition among great cities in the industrialized world three years earlier. The successful collaboration between photographers such as William Henry Jackson, who documented the exposition, and the administrative circles of the exposition marked a clear departure from conventional architectural photography and resonated with Berlin's "City Image Building" effort by Ludwig Hoffmann and Ernst von Brauchitsch.[11] Brauchitsch's and

Hoffmann's highly choreographed, staged, and carefully framed city image both developed its own celebratory photographic vocabulary and presaged the significance of architectural photography for the modernist project. Modernist tendencies in architecture, which Philip Johnson and Henry-Russell Hitchcock labeled *international style* in their famous 1932 exhibition of the same name, were beginning to unfold as the photographer and the architect set the stage for a new articulation of collaboration between these two professions. The next generation of architects understood photography's intrinsic power to contribute and form an image of the city and of architectural space (and not only to serve as its impartial documentary tool). Indeed, European modernist architects such as Erich Mendelsohn and Walter Gropius embraced North American architectural culture as they discovered North America's industrial architecture of grain silos and elevators as important inspirations for architectural innovations. Instead of engaging a photographer for their documentation, both operated the camera themselves to capture these structures and demonstrate their relevance.[12]

Topics picked up by literary city imaginaries in the early twentieth century were also indicative of the formation of universal urban narratives that were not limited by national and geographic borders. The literary scholar Arnold Weinstein points out that "city writing seems virtually hardwired to notions of bristling change, even of looming crisis," and Georg Simmel's new urbanite, described in *The Metropolis and Mental Life* (1903), appeared to figure centrally as protagonist in that modern city.[13] This urbanite, "an unmoored figure, protectively blasé in his manner, geared to the de-individualizing money calculus, enmeshed in a neural web, at once lost and free,"[14] could be imagined in Berlin, just as it could be in hubs of money, freedom, and anonymity like New York and Chicago. Two seminal works of literature that belong to this genre are John Dos Passos's *Manhattan Transfer* (1925) and Alfred Döblin's *Berlin Alexanderplatz* (1929), which are both determined by a "frenetic pace and disjointed medley of voices and discourses."[15]

By the 1910s, new forms of artistic representation and mediation such as montage and avant-garde cinematography responded to such new urban experiences and became part of the photographic vocabulary on both sides of the Atlantic. In Berlin, it was embedded in the sequential and reportage-like work of the Photogrammetric Institute and rubble photographers. From such projects emerged the photographic reportage story and became the powerful language of photographic narrative in illustrated journals such as *Berliner Illustrirte Zeitung* and *Arbeiter Illustrierte Zeitung*. It was adapted and further developed during the 1930s in the work of the photographers of the Great Depression and *Life* magazine in North America.

City movies of that era, whether about Berlin or New York City, convey the experience of modern architecture and urban life.[16] The "city symphony" became the modern city's transatlantic cinematic form, most famously in Walter Ruttmann's 1927 film *Berlin, Symphonie der Großstadt* (*Berlin, Symphony of a Great City*), in the Russian filmmaker Dziga Vertov's *Man with a Movie Camera* of 1929, and in the American Charles Sheeler and Paul Strand's collaborative film *Manhatta* of 1921.[17]

Today, the question of whether Berlin is a German, European, or American city has become secondary. Cities today are measured not in terms of their age or their ways of handling change and growth. They employ branding agencies to form a unified city imaginary. In Berlin, former mayor Klaus Wowereit's declaration of Berlin as "poor but sexy" was soon used by the city's advertisers to promote that image. Urban critics today discuss the impact of Berlin's neoliberal transformation on quality of life, affordability of housing, degrees of gentrification, and potentials for preservation and renewal. Contemporary urban photographic practices evolve around similar questions that were posed by photographers more than one hundred years ago. They are still tracing change, documenting historic buildings, or depicting the city from a panoramic perspective. Contemporary Berlin is distinguished from its nineteenth-century predecessor by the fundamental redefinition of photographic practice and its ubiquitous distribution. The photograph of the city has morphed into photographs in the city in the form of digital snapshots that are posted online, on social media outlets, via both traditional views and selfies. This city, in the past twenty-five years, has been recolonized by new citizens from around the world. It has physically filled the void of the wall, but its struggle to determine its urban identity persists despite, or perhaps because of, the pervasive nature of its images' dissemination. Berlin continues to consolidate historic narratives, contemporaneous stories, and future projections. The construction of its urban imagery does not give us any reason to believe that the city ceases to continue its fate of eternally becoming and never being.

ACKNOWLEDGMENTS

This book has many sources and has accompanied me in different configurations, in German and then in English, over the incredible period of now almost twenty years. It started as a dissertation project in the aftermath of Berlin's reunification in an academic environment that was otherwise not accustomed to studies that explored photography and interdisciplinary subject matter as part of art history. Pieter Martin at the University of Minnesota Press believed in this book, and I thank him emphatically for supporting it.

I thank my dissertation advisors Wilhelm Schlink and the late Peter B. Hales for making this long journey to publication possible. Without their steady support, openness, and willingness to engage, I would most likely have given up a long time ago.

Researching, writing, and publishing this book would be unthinkable without the generous support of the Evangelische Studienwerk Villigst e.V., which funded three crucial years of my dissertation work. I owe heartfelt thanks to the Graham Foundation and the Julian Park Fund at the University at Buffalo, which together enabled this carefully edited publication of high-quality illustrations. Special thanks go to Michael Needham for his thorough editorial work and for our stimulating conversations during the manuscript's development and to Rachel Van Heart and Deborah Oosterhouse for their excellent editorial work. I thank Lindsey Wikstrom for her powerful imagination; Ana Bichanich for her great diligence and patience during the final production process; and Douglas Easton for his index. I thank the Humanities Institute at the University at Buffalo, and particularly Erik Seeman and Libby Otto, for their tireless support and enthusiasm. Working on this book as a Humanities Institute faculty fellow was one of the highlights and certainly the determining moment that helped to conclude this project. I also thank my directors at the Arts Management program, Ruth Bereson, Roy Roussel, and Franck Bauchard, for their understanding and support during the years of this project's conclusion.

My great gratitude goes to those who instilled in me curiosity for both Berlin and my own identity: my father, Volkmar Paeslack, and my aunt Gundula Tietsch. Through his vividly shared childhood memories and through her tireless enthusiasm walking around old Berlin (or what was left of it in the 1980s), I learned a sense of what it means to belong to a place. I am saddened that neither of them is able to see this book's publication.

The history of photography, now a well-established field of inquiry across the humanities and social sciences, was emerging when I began this project. This book owes much to the late Peter B. Hales, whose book on urban photography in the United States, *Silver Cities,* showed me in convincing and inspiring ways how the project of urban photography and modernity can be tackled. I feel great gratitude toward my teachers of photography and photo history, most of all to Laura Katzman, Ulrich Keller, and the late Diethart Kerbs. My work for Sarah Greenough's Stieglitz Project at the National Gallery in Washington gave me the opportunity and mandate to explore European photo journals for Alfred Stieglitz's publications and let me discover transcontinental relationships in the photo world of the late nineteenth century. Each of them fostered my craving to learn and understand this fascinating medium. Their dedication to photo history has nourished me along the way. My gratitude goes to the Urban Photography, Film and Video Work Group at the European Architecture History Network with which I had the opportunity to discuss parts of this project during its workshop in Turin in 2014.

Once I began archival research I was fortunate to encounter historians, art historians, archivists, and librarians who helped me dig up and understand nineteenth- and early twentieth-century photography in its full complexity: Hela Zettler, Ulrike Griebner, and Ines Hahn particularly were steady and incredibly knowledgeable partners in doing full justice to the amazing photographic collection of the City Museum Foundation of Berlin (Stiftung Stadtmuseum). Here I was pointed to Barbara-Karin Rudolphy, who provided valuable biographical information about the little-known urban photographer Hugo Rudolphy. I am deeply grateful to the Brauchitsch family for making available letters from

Ernst von Brauchitsch's estate that provided a rare insight into his prospects and considerations as a professional photographer. Christine Kühn at the Art Library of the Prussian Heritage Foundation was invaluable; I am particularly indebted to her and Ludger Derenthal as well as to Ines Hahn for their ongoing support as I began publishing parts of the material now united in this book. Beyond the photographic collections, my research and this book would not be possible without the support of the Stiftung Stadtmuseum's Dominik Bartmann, senior curator; Annette Bossmann, collections of painting; Iris Schewe, library; Cornelia Gentzen, archive; and Ines Pannek and Robert Wein, Fotothek.

I am indebted to so many colleagues, friends, and family members for conversations, inspiration, and suggestions over the years that I ask forgiveness if I forget to mention anyone by name. I feel great gratitude to all of you. Irini Fotiadou helped systematically structure the earliest version of this manuscript, as did Eva Vollmer, Kathrin Meyer, Werner and Marika Schade, Andreas Krase, Carolin Förster, and Martin Assig. Sophia Paeslack, Mark Rackles, Johannes v. Gwinner, and Florian Köhl gave me valuable technical support. Astrid Reuter, Albrecht Conrad, and Julia Pasqual edited individual chapters, and Miriam Yegane-Arani was an important sounding board for methodological questions. Gesine Reinecke and Sebastian Conrad contributed important historical and contextual information about the Wilhelmine Era. Libby Otto, Claire Zimmermann, Despina Stratigakos, Harald Stühlinger, and Elisabeth Edwards read and commented on individual chapters of the English manuscript. Conversations and exchanges with Hadas Steiner, Kenny Cupers, Jordan Carver, and Jess Ngan as well as with Ewa Manikowska, Olga Linkiewicz, Dietrich Neumann, and Mary R. Woods, were crucial in contextualizing Berlin's photographic history within architectural, historical, and ethnographic discourses. Johanna Diehl, Elisabeth Neudörfl, and Bettina Lockemann were significant resources as practicing urban photographers in Berlin today.

I thank Cordula Klaffs and Marian Kolenda, Susan Strasser, Christiane Zastrow, Magdalena and Eberhard Häfner, and Gundula and Anselm Tietsch for conversations about Berlin and its relevance in each of their lives and in mine; and my friends and colleagues in Buffalo, New York, Omar Khan, Laura Garofalo Khan, Hadas Steiner, Dalia Muller, Camilo Trumper, and Lucie Muller, for stimulating conversations about the book in its final stage.

A very special thanks goes to my mother, Anneliese, who has heard me talk about this project for the past twenty years and who has instilled in me her curiosity for the world. My sister Sophia has been my companion exploring the city and photography, as well as in conceptualizing the design of the book's cover. Her steady eye, clear aesthetic vision, and technological know-how have been essential for this book. Finally, my husband, Jordan, was first friends with and then married to this project. His strong encouragement and support made the completion of this work possible. To him and to my father Volkmar I dedicate this book.

NOTES

Introduction

1. Saskia Sassen, "Die Reichen möchten in der Stadt nicht belästigt warden," *Süddeutsche Zeitung*, June 5, 2016: "Die Stadt ist ein vielschichtiges, aber unvollständiges System." (All translations provided by the author unless otherwise noted.)

2. Mark Twain, "The Chicago of Europe," *Chicago Daily Tribune*, April 3, 1892, 33; republished in Andreas Austilat, *A Tramp in Berlin: New Mark Twain Stories and an Account of Twain's Berlin Adventures* (Berlin: Berlininca Publishing, 2013), 132–45.

3. Michael Baxandall, *Patterns of Intention: On the Historical Explanation of Pictures* (New Haven: Yale University Press, 1985), 10–11.

4. Karl Scheffler, *Berlin: Ein Stadtschicksal* (Berlin: Erich Reiss Verlag, 1910), 267: "Berlin dazu verdammt: immerfort zu werden und niemals zu sein."

5. Max Osborn, "Ein Berliner Bilderarchiv von Max Osborn," *Der Tag*, July 13, 1910, no pagination: "Man erkennt, daß vor unseren Augen aus dem allzu schnell gewachsenen Gemeinwesen, dem das Parvenutum und die Großmannssucht aus allen Poren schwitzten, eine wirkliche Weltstadt, aus dem Wirrwarr ein modernes Leben von Charakter, aus der Ratlosigkeit nach und nach ein Organismus entsteht. . . . Doch schon heute hat man das erquickliche Gefühl, daß die Stadt allmählich wieder eine Einheit wird, wieder ein Gesicht und eine Seele bekommt. Und nun ist mit einem Male auch zwischen unseren Beziehungen zum Alten und zum Gegenwärtigen eine Brücke geschlagen. Unser modernes Empfinden—das endlich festen Boden gefunden hat, in dem es sich verankern kann, verbindet sich mit dem romantischen. So stand es von jeher um Alt- und Neu-Paris, dessen Nebeneinander nie einen Gegensatz bedeutete, sondern immer zwei eng verknüpfte Teile einer großen logischen, organischen Einheit. So kann es, dürfen wir endlich hoffen, auch mit Alt- und Neu-Berlin einmal werden."

6. Gerhard Masur, *Imperial Berlin* (London: Routledge and Kegan Paul, 1971).

7. Dorothy Rowe, "Georg Simmel and the Berlin Trade Exhibition of 1896," *Urban History* 22, no. 2 (August 1995): 220.

8. Rowe, "Georg Simmel and the Berlin Trade Exhibition of 1896," 220–22; Kathrin Dördelmann, "Die Darstellung Berlins in der populären Zeitschriftenpresse, 1870–1933," in *Metropolis Berlin: Berlin als deutsche Hauptstadt im Vergleich europäischer Hauptstädte, 1871–1939*, ed. Gerhard Brunn and Jürgen Reulecke (Bonn: Bouvier, 1992), 127–50; and Peter Fritzsche, *Reading Berlin 1900* (Cambridge, Mass.: Harvard University Press, 1996).

9. Hermann Jansen, "Wettbewerb Groß-Berlin 1910," Technische Universität Berlin Architekturmusuem, http://architekturmuseum.ub.tu-berlin.de/index.php?set=1&p=79&Daten=147911.

10. Monika Padberg, *Großstadtbild und Großstadtmetaphorik in der deutschen Malerei: Vorstufen und Entfaltung, 1870–1918*, Bonner Studien zur Kunstgeschichte 10 (Münster: Lit Verlag, 1995); Ben Highmore, *Cityscapes: Cultural Readings in the Material and Symbolic City* (London: Palgrave, 2005); Anthony Vidler, "Agoraphobia: Spatial Estrangement in Georg Simmel and Siegfried Kracauer," in special issue on Siegfried Kracauer, *New German Critique* 54 (Autumn 1991): 31–45.

11. Andreas Huyssen, *Other Cities, Other Worlds: Urban Imaginaries in a Globalizing Age* (Durham, N.C.: Duke University Press, 2008), 3.

12. Alan Marcus, "Visualising the City," *Journal of Architecture* 11, no. 5 (November 2006): 521–22; Mitchell Schwarzer, *Zoomscape: Architecture in Motion and Media* (New York: Princeton Architectural Press, 2004); Andrew Webber and Emma Wilson, *Cities in Transition: The Moving Image and the Modern Metropolis* (New York: Wallflower Press, 2008); Huyssen, *Other Cities, Other Worlds*; Miriam Paeslack, ed., "Urban Image Now: Photographic and Filmic Manifestations of a Subjective City Experience," special issue, *Visual Resources: An International Journal on Images and Their Uses* 26, no. 1 (2010): 3–11.

13. Harvey Molotch, "The Space of Lefebvre" [review of *The Production of Space*, by Henri Lefebvre], *Theory and Society* 22, no. 6 (December 1993): 888.

14. Blake Stimson, *The Cinematic* (Cambridge, Mass.: MIT Press, 2007), 96.

15. Charles Baudelaire, *The Painter of Modern Life and Other Essays*, ed. and trans. Jonathan Mayne (London: Phaidon Press, 1964), 13.

16. T. J. Clark, *The Painting of Modern Life: Paris in the Art of Manet and His Followers*, rev. ed. (Princeton, N.J.: Princeton University Press, 1999); Elizabeth Anne McCauley, *Industrial Madness: Commercial Photography in Paris, 1848–1871* (New Haven: Yale University Press, 1994); Shelley Rice, *Parisian Views* (Cambridge, Mass.: MIT Press, 1997); Vanessa R. Schwartz, *Spectacular Realities: Early Mass Culture in Fin-de-siècle Paris* (Berkeley: University of California Press, 1999); David Harvey, *Paris, Capital of Modernity* (London: Routledge, 2003).

17. "mit dem Bewusstsein . . . dass er hier wieder die Luft der rauhen Wirklichkeit atme, wie es heisst": Siegfried Kracauer, *Schriften*, vol. 5.2, *Aufsätze, 1927–1931*, ed. Inka Mulder Bach (Frankfurt am Main: Suhrkamp, 1990), 26. Huyssen's translation in the text; see Andreas Huyssen, "Modernist Miniatures: Literary Snapshots of Urban Spaces," *PMLA* 122, no. 1 (January 2007): 40.

18. Walter Benjamin, *Berliner Kindheit um Neunzehnhundert: Fassung letzter Hand* (Frankfurt: Suhrkamp, 1987) and Walter Benjamin, *Einbahnstrasse* (Berlin: Rowohlt, 1928).

19. Walter Benjamin, "Paris, Capital of the Nineteenth Century," in *Reflections* (New York: Harcourt, 1978), 146–62. First published in German as "Paris, die Hauptstadt des XIX. Jahrhunderts," in *Illuminationen* (Frankfurt: Suhrkamp, 1955).

20. Huyssen, "Modernist Miniatures," 39, quotes Siegfried Kracauer, "Schreie auf der Strasse," in *Schriften*, 5.2:207; and Kracauer, "Strasse ohne Erinnerung," *Schriften*, vol. 5.3, *Aufsatze, 1932–1965*, ed. Inka Mulder Bach (Frankfurt am Main: Suhrkamp, 1990), 170–74.

21. Huyssen, "Modernist Miniatures," 39.

22. Andrew J. Webber, *Berlin in the Twentieth Century: A Cultural Topography* (Cambridge: Cambridge University Press, 2008).

23. See, for example, the registry of Berlin's prominent photo club, the Free Photographical Alliance, in Franz Goerke, ed., *Denkschrift anlässlich des zwanzigjährigen Bestehens der Freien Photographischen Vereinigung zu Berlin* (Halle: Wilhelm Knapp, 1910). A notable exception was the educator, editor, and photographer Marie Goslich (1859–1938): *Marie Goslich: Photographin und Journalistin*, last modified August 5, 2018, http://www.marie-goslich.de.

24. See Anton Holzer, "Einführung in die Fotogeschichte: Recherche, Methoden, Theorie," special issue, *Fotogeschichte* 124 (Summer 2012).

25. Victor Burgin, "Art, Common Sense and Photography," in *Visual Culture: The Reader*, ed. Jessica Evans and Stuart Hall (London: Sage Publications, 1999), 41.

26. Peter B. Hales, *Silver Cities: Photographing American Urbanization, 1839–1939* (Albuquerque: University of New Mexico Press, 2006), 2.

27. Hales, *Silver Cities*, 2.

28. Osborn, "Ein Berliner Bilderarchiv"; Osborn speaks of Berlin as "Amerikanische Europäerstadt."

29. Baudelaire, *The Painter of Modern Life and Other Essays*, 12.

30. Vidler, "Agoraphobia," 32.

31. Scheffler, *Berlin*, 16–17: "Sie sind geworden wie sie sind, . . . weil sie das Herz der Länder waren, zu dem alle Kräfte hinstreben, um gleich auch wieder befruchtet zurückzukehren."

32. Scheffler, *Berlin*, 17.

1. Crafting the Metropolis

1. Hales, *Silver Cities*, 217–18.

2. Friedrich Fuchs, "Neu-Berlin," *Berliner Leben* 4 (1901): 135–36, http://nbn-resolving.de/urn:nbn:de:kobv:109-1-5303823.

3. Fuchs, "Neu-Berlin," 136.

4. Lynn Hollen Lees and Andrew Lees, *Cities and the Making of Modern Europe, 1750–1914* (Cambridge: Cambridge University Press, 2007), 137.

5. Charles Huard, *Berlin comme je l'ai vu* (Paris: Eugene Rey, 1907), 11–13. Quoted after Charles W. Haxthausen, "Eine neue Schönheit: Ernst Ludwig Kirchners Berlinbilder," in *In der grossen Stadt: Die Metropole als kulturtheoretische Kategorie*, ed. Thomas Steinfeld and Heidrun Suhr (Frankfurt am Main: Hain, 1990), 72.

6. Luc Gersal, "Berlin vom Rathausturm betrachtet 1892," in *Berlin in alten und neuen Reisebeschreibungen*, ed. Georg Holmsten (Düsseldorf: Droste, 1989), 193–95. This text originates in Gersal's 1892 publication, *L'Athènes de la Sprée par un Béotien: Croquis berlinois* (Paris: A Savine, 1892).

7. Anne Germaine de Staël-Holstein, *Deutschland*, vol. 1.1 (Reutlingen: J.J. Mäcken'sche Buchhandlung, 1815), 127. Translated from the French. "Ich für meinen Theil, würde mir in America neue Städte und neue Gesetze wünschen; dort sprechen Natur und Freiheit laut genug zur Seele, um die Erinnerungen entbehrlich zu machen; aber auf unserem alten europäischen Boden müssen wir auf Spuren der Vergangeheit stoßen. Berlin, diese ganz moderne Stadt, so schön sie immer seyn mag, bringt keine feierliche, ernste Wirkung hervor, sie trägt das Gepräge weder der Geschichte des Landes noch des Characters der Einwohner."

8. Wolfgang Ribbe and Jürgen Schmädecke, *Kleine Berlin-Geschichte*, ed. Landeszentrale für politische Bildungsarbeit Berlin in Verbindung mit der historischen Kommission zu Berlin, 3rd ed. (Berlin: Stapp, 1994), 106. Additional statistical information in Harald Bodenschatz, *Platz frei für das Neue Berlin! Geschichte der Stadterneuerung in der "größten Mietskasernenstadt der Welt" seit 1871 (Studien zur Neueren Planungsgeschichte)*, vol. 1 (Berlin: Transit Buchverlag, 1987), 53–55. Jochen Boberg, Tilman Fichter, and Eckhart Gillen, eds., *Exerzierfeld der Moderne: Industriekultur in Berlin im 19. Jahrhundert* (Munich: Beck, 1984), 90–232.

9. Boberg, Fichter, and Gillen, *Exerzierfeld der Moderne*, 102.

10. Boberg, Fichter, and Gillen, *Exerzierfeld der Moderne*, 102.

11. Eberhard Siedel, "Immigration to Berlin," *Berlin.de*, https://www.berlin.de/imperia/md/content/lb-integration-migration/fremdsprachig/immigration_to_berlin.pdf?start&ts=1433500348&file=immigration_to_berlin.pdf.

12. Ribbe and Schmädecke, *Kleine Berlin-Geschichte*, 107–9; Bodenschatz, *Platz frei für das Neue Berlin!*, 58; Boberg, Fichter, and Gillen, *Exerzierfeld der Moderne*, 96–98, 182–91.

13. Stephan Oettermann, *The Panorama: History of a Mass Medium*, trans. Deborah Lucas Schneider (New York: Zone Books, 1997), 6.

14. See Oettermann, *Panorama*, 5.

15. Oettermann, *Panorama*, 7.

16. "Eduard Gaertner," National Gallery of Art, http://www.nga.gov/content/ngaweb/Collection/artist-info.1328.html.

17. On the development and establishment of guidebooks for cities such as Paris and the panorama, see Ronzo Dubbini, *Geography of the Gaze: Urban and Rural Vision in Early Modern Europe*, trans. Lydia G. Cochrane (Chicago: University of Chicago Press, 2002). Chapter 7, "Gazing at the Metropolis," is especially relevant.

18. Karl Baedeker, *Berlin und Umgebung: Handbuch für Reisende von K. Baedeker*, 13th ed. (Leipzig: Verlag von Karl Baedeker, 1904), 46: "Die Umgebung des Schlosses ist in Anlehnung an die Barockformen des Schlosses neu gestaltet worden. Es bildet sich jetzt in Wirklichkeit aus Lustgarten, Opernplatz, Linden eine Monumentalstraße ersten Ranges, wie sie ähnlich in Wien erreicht ist, Paris und London aber fehlt. In der Straße Unter den Linden, die ihrem alten Rufe nicht mehr entsprach, machen die alten Häuser mehr und mehr Prachtbauten für Gasthöfe und Geschäften Platz: die Baumreihen und Wege sind neu geordnet."

19. Harald Bodenschatz and Benedikt Goebel, "Berlin—Stadt ohne Altstadt," in *Berlins vergessene Mitte, Stadtkern 1840–2010* (Berlin: Stiftun Stadtmuseum, 2010), 17–36; and Celina Kress and Georg Wagner-Kyora, "Der Streitfall Alt-Berlin im Städtebau und die Mentalität der Metropole seit 1840," in *Berlins vergessene Mitte*, 49–72.

20. Baedeker, *Berlin und Umgebung*, 131: "Vom Turme beste Rundsicht über Berlin." In an introductory section to the city (p. 34), the guidebook specifies the opening seasons and hours (April 1–October 1, daily 10–3) and charge (20 pfennigs). By "city hall," Baedeker was referring to the older of the two city halls in town, which is also called "red" city hall (*rotes rathaus*) after its red brick color. The newer city hall was the one Ludwig Hoffmann finished in 1911.

21. Bernard Comment, *The Panorama* (London: Reaktion Books, 1999), 70.

22. Valentin Kockel, "Das Rom-Panorama von Josef Bühlmann im Kontext des 19. Jahrhunderts," in *Das antike Rom und sein Bild*, ed. Hans Ulrich Cain, Anette Haug, and Yadegar Assisi (Berlin: de Gruyter, 2011), 35–36.

23. Oettermann, *Panorama*, 22.

24. This city hall (*rotes rathaus*) was built between 1861 and 1869 after plans by Hermann Friedrich Waesemann (1813–79).

25. The original prints were most likely albumen prints. Today, only Meydenbauer's glass negatives survive. Jean-François Lejeune, "Schinkel and Lenné in Berlin—from the Biedermeier flâneur to Beuth's Industriegroßstadt," in *Karl Friedrich Schinkel: Aspects of his Work/Aspekte seines Werkes*, ed. Susan M. Peik (Stuttgart: Edition Axel Menges, 2001), 82.

26. The Pantoskop was a wide-angle lens covering 100 degrees and equipped with a 22f-stop. According to the author of the technical article "On Modern Types of Lenses and Their Application" in the photographic journal *Das Atelier des Photographen* 11, no. 5 (1904): 76, it was well suited for "architecture, panorama and photogrammetric images." On Busch's biography, see Karl Albrecht, "Busch, Friedrich Emil," in *Neue Deutsche Biographie* (Berlin: Duncker & Humblot, 1957), 3:61; online access: http://www.deutsche-biographie.de/pnd137229240.html.

27. Hales, *Silver Cities*, 218.

28. Hales, *Silver Cities*, 217–18.

29. Eve Blau, "Patterns of Fact: Photography and the Transformation of the Early Industrial City," in *Architecture and Its Image: Four Centuries of Architectural Representation. Works from the Collection of the Canadian Centre for Architecture*, ed. Eve Blau and Edward Kaufman (Montreal: Canadian Centre for Architecture, 1989), 43.

30. Fritzsche, *Reading Berlin 1900*.

31. Lees and Lees, *Cities and the Making of Modern Europe*, 229.

32. Blau, "Patterns of Fact," 43.

33. Bernd Weise, "Reproduktionstechnik und Medienwechsel in der Presse," in *Fotografie gedruckt* (Münster: Waxmann Verlag, 2015), 6–7. See also Frank Heidtmann, *Wie das Photo ins Buch kam* (Berlin: Berlin-Verlag Spitz, 1984), 668–89.

34. See Boberg, Fichter, and Gillen, *Exerzierfeld der Moderne*, 376, and Fritzsche, *Reading Berlin 1900*.

35. *Berliner Leben* 1 (1898): 204: "Dies herrliche 'Berliner Leben' wurde in diesen Blättern, die seinen Namen tragen, in Bild und Wort festgehalten. Alles, was es *Schönes, Anregendes, Eigenartiges und Bedeutendes* bietet, sei es in *Hof und Gesellschaft, Wissenschaft, Kunst und Litteratur*, dies Alles und noch viel mehr, hat der soeben vollendete 1. Jahrgang von 'Berliner Leben' Zeitschrift für Schönheit und Kunst in vollendeter künstlerischer Weise verzeichnet. . . . Wir werden . . . darauf bedacht sein, ihn [den Freundeskreis] zu vergrössern und das '*Berliner Leben*' zu einem treuen immer willkommenen Hausfreund in Stadt und Land, in Palast und Bürgerhaus zu machen."

36. "Geld und Kaufkraft ab 1871," *GenWiki*, last modified May 22, 2011, http://wiki-de.genealogy.net/Geld_und_Kaufkraft_ab_1871. On Berlin's bourgeoisie, see Rüdiger vom Bruch and Hans-Christoph Liess, *Bürgerlichkeit: Staat und Kultur im Deutschen Kaiserreich* (Stuttgart: Franz Steiner Verlag, 2005). About Berlin's societal and cultural fabric, see Heinz Reif, "Hauptstadtentwicklung und Elitebildung: 'Tout Berlin' 1871 bis 1918," in *Geschichte und Emanzipation: Festschrift für Reinhard Rürup* (Frankfurt/Main: Campus Verlag, 1999), 679–99.

37. Others were Conrad Hünrich, F. Kullrich, Ed Scherner, Franz Kühn, Georg August Busse, Max Ziesler, Hermann Boll, Ottomar Anschütz, the Haeckel brothers, and Fotostudio Zander & Labisch.

38. Georg Busse pioneered large photomontages and published a number of them in *Berlin Life* between 1900 and 1904. They were set in market halls, major squares, and thoroughfares. Others adopted his style, such as Waldemar Titzenthaler and Hermann Boll, as well as Gordan & Delius. Max Missmann also created two-page panorama images of Berlin squares for *Berliner Leben*.

39. Oskar Bätschmann, *Entfernung von der Natur: Landschaftsmalerei 1750–1920* (Cologne: DuMont, 1989), 93. See also Oettermann, *Panorama*.

40. Robert Jütte, *Geschichte der Sinne: Von der Antike bis zum Cyberspace* (Munich: Beck, 2000), 210–12. The English version of the book was published in 2005 as *A History of the Senses: From Antiquity to Cyberspace*, trans. J. Lynn (Oxford: Polity Press).

41. While panoramic cameras had been developed as early as the 1840s (Friedrich Martens constructed one in 1845), they became accessible for a broader audience in the 1890s. One major obstacle was the use of glass-plate negatives, which was resolved with the invention of roll film in the 1880s. The first mass-produced American panoramic camera, the Al-Vista, was introduced in 1898. The following year, Eastman Kodak introduced the #4 Kodak Panoram panoramic camera that proved popular with amateur photographers. In 1907, the German Ernemann company announced the development of a "panorama-in-the-round camera" (Panorama-Rundkamera) with a 360-degree viewing angle.

42. Halensee was founded as an affluent neighborhood in Berlin's southwest only in 1880. It attracted civil servants, members of the military, literary figures, and retirees who lived there in spacious rental apartments or single-family residences.

43. *Berliner Leben* 4 (1901): 169. "C. Schütte," the name at the bottom right corner of the photograph, was either the author or the reproduction technician of this image.

44. The Darmstädter Bank für Handel und Industrie was located at Schinkelplatz 1–4, east of the Kommandantur Unter den Linden. See also the reference for a photograph of the church and Old Museum by Max Missmann (1905), which reveals a similar balustrade. Stiftung Stadtmuseum Berlin, ed., *Unter den Linden: Historische Photographien; Mit Texten von Dieter Hildebrandt, Hans-Werner Klünner, Jost Hansen* (Berlin: Argon Verlag, 1991), 19, 21.

45. *Berliner Leben* 4 (1901): 142.

46. Jochen Boberg, Tilman Fichter, and Eckhart Gillen, eds., *Die Metropole: Industriekultur in Berlin im 20. Jahrhundert* (Munich: Beck, 1986), 133.

47. Baedeker, *Berlin und Umgebung*, 39.

48. Dismar Dägen, *Friedrichstadt mit Rondell und Halleschem Tor in Berlin*, Berlin Märkische Museum (today: Stiftung Stadtmuseum), lost; reproduced in *Stadtbilder: Berlin in der Malerei vom 17. Jahrhundert bis zur Gegenwart*, exhibition catalog (Berlin: Berlin-Museum, 1987), 23. Information about this site and the context of this

painting in Thomas Wellmann, "Das Auge schweift über das Weichbild der Stadt," in *Stadtbilder*, 19.

49. Haxthausen, "Eine neue Schönheit," 75. Besides Belle-Alliance Plaza, Kirchner also painted Strack's Halle Gate buildings and Bülow Square in a painting titled *Hallesches Tor*, oil on canvas, 70 × 78 cm, 1913, private collection.

50. Boberg, Fichter, and Gillen, *Die Metropole*, 133.

51. William Sharpe and Leonard Wallock, "From 'Great Town' to 'Nonplace Urban Realm': Reading the Modern City," in *Visions of the Modern City: Essays in History, Art, and Literature*, ed. William Sharpe and Leonard Wallock (Baltimore: Johns Hopkins University Press, 1987), 16–17. The authors talk more specifically about balloons and airships.

52. "unruhige, aber doch kraftvoll lebendige Wesen": Willi Warstat, "Die Schönheit der großen Stadt als künstlerisches Problem für den Photographen," in *Die Photographische Kunst im Jahre 1909: Ein Jahrbuch für künstlerische Photographie*, ed. F. Matthies-Masuren (Halle/Saale: Wilhelm Knapp, 1909), 14. I invoke the term "ornament" deliberately to reference Siegfried Kracauer's unique approach to culture by addressing an epoch based on its everyday rituals, specific details, and banal ornamentations in his 1927 publication *Ornament der Masse* (*The Mass Ornament*).

53. Sharpe and Wallock, "From 'Great Town' to 'Nonplace Urban Realm,'" 16ff.

54. See a comparative discussion of this question in Sharpe and Wallock, "From 'Great Town' to 'Nonplace Urban Realm,'" 17–18.

55. Boberg, Fichter, and Gillen, *Die Metropole*, 33.

56. See Wolfgang Schivelbusch, *The Railway Journey: The Industrialization of Time and Space in the Nineteenth Century* (Berkeley: University of California Press, 1979), 33–44.

57. "Nie die Residenzstadt sah und doch sie gern möcht sehen, dem liegt jetzt die Erfüllung nah, er braucht nicht hinzugehen; gar prächtig und mit Künstlerhand, naturgetreu in Bildern ein hochmodernes Blatt erstand Berlin so recht zu schildern. Von allem zeigt euch die Copie, macht Herz und Geister heben; durch Wahrheit, ohne Phantasie: das ist 'Berliner Leben,' durch Wahrheit ohne Phantasie: das ist 'Berliner Leben'": Gustav Wanda, "Berliner Leben," *Berliner Leben* 4 (1901): 164–65.

58. Bätschmann, *Entfernung von der Natur*, 96.

2. Framing Progress

1. Dörte Döhl, *Ludwig Hoffmann: Bauen für Berlin 1896–1924* (Tübingen: Wasmuth, 2004), 66.

2. See Döhl, *Ludwig Hoffmann*, 186–99, specifically 194 quoting Paul Westheim.

3. Döhl, *Ludwig Hoffmann*, 65. See also the 2001 online publication (which is the basis for Döhl's assumptions), Miriam Paeslack, *Fotografie Berlin 1871–1914: Eine*

Untersuchung zum Darstellungswandel, den Medieneigenschaften, den Akteuren und Rezipienten von Stadtfotografie im Prozess der Grosstadtbildung, 2001, https://www.freidok.uni-freiburg.de/data/1493.

4. See also Paeslack, *Fotografie Berlin 1871–1914* and Döhl, *Ludwig Hoffmann*, 65.

5. Johann Christoph Müller and Georg Gottfried Küster, *Altes und Neues Berlin*, vol. 1 (Berlin: Johann Peter Schmid, 1737); Johann Christoph Müller and Georg Gottfried Küster, *Fortgesetztes Altes und Neues Berlin*, vol. 2 (Berlin: Haude- und Spenerische Buchhandlung, 1752); Georg Gottfried Küster, *Des Alten und Neuen Berlin dritte Abtheilung* (Berlin: Hallischer Buchladen, 1756); Georg Gottfried Küster, *Des Alten und Neuen Berlin vierte Abtheilung* (Berlin, 1769); Georg Gottfried Küster, *Des Alten und Neuen Berlin fünfte Abtheilung* (Berlin, 1769); Friedrich Nicolai, *Beschreibung der Königlichen Residenzstädte Berlin und Potsdam, aller daselbst befindlicher Merkwürdigkeiten, und der umliegenden Gegend*, 3rd rev. ed. (Berlin: Friedrich Nicolai Publisher, 1786).

6. Barry Bergdoll, "A Matter of Time: Architects and Photographers in Second Empire France," in Malcolm R. Daniel, *The Photographs of Édouard Baldus* (New York: Metropolitan Museum of Art; Montreal: Canadian Centre for Architecture, 1994), 111. See also a similar argument in James S. Ackerman, "On the Origins of Architectural Photography" (lecture, Canadian Centre of Architecture, Montreal, December 4, 2001), 11; the document was obtained from the CCA website: https://www.cca.qc.ca/cca.media/files/1481/1382/Mellon02-JA.pdf. Ackerman points out that architect patronage became more common "as it became evident that photographic portfolios could serve as a way of spreading awareness of their works and attracting clients."

7. Sigrid Schulze, *Leopold Ahrendts (1825–1870) and the Early Days of Photography in Berlin*, trans. Jill Denton (Berlin: Galerie Berinson, 2011); Lothar de Maizière and Antonius Jammers, *Bevor Berlin zur Weltstadt wurde: Die Residenz in Fotografien von Leopold Ahrendts* (Berlin: Braun, 2001); Sigrid Schulze, "Sent by the Princess Frederick William: A Portfolio of Photographs of Berlin by Leopold Ahrendts," *History of Photography* 26, no. 4 (Winter 2002): 324–40.

8. Hermann Wilhelm Vogel, "Theil 3: Die Kunst der Photographie, Einleitung," in *Lehrbuch der Photographie: Drei Theile in einem Bande enthaltend die photographische Chemie, Praxis und Aesthetik*, 3rd rev. and enlarged ed. (Berlin: Verlag von Robert Oppenheim, 1878), 467.

9. The courthouse was designed in an Italian neo-Renaissance style in collaboration with Peter Dybward (1859–1921).

10. Dieter Hoffmann-Axthelm, "Stadtbild-Baumeister," in Boberg, Fichter, and Gillen, *Die Metropole*, 66–80.

11. Döhl, *Ludwig Hoffmann*, 12–13.

12. Döhl, *Ludwig Hoffmann*, 30.

13. Döhl, *Ludwig Hoffmann*, 62–63. See also Ludwig Hoffmann, introduction to *Neubauten der Stadt Berlin*, vol. 1 (Berlin: Hessling, 1902).

14. Hoffmann-Axthelm, "Stadtbild-Baumeister," 66.

15. Hoffmann-Axthelm, "Stadtbild-Baumeister," 66.

16. From Hoffmann's introductory text to volume 1 of *Neubauten der Stadt Berlin*. These images included both images of the "original drawings of the façades, of interiors supplied with measurements" as well as "images of nature," and Brauchitsch's photographs. The first volume came out in 1902, and a new volume was published each year, except 1906, until the publication of the last, volume 11, in 1912; two volumes (5 and 6) were published in 1907.

17. Review of *Neubauten der Stadt Berlin*, by Ludwig Hoffmann, *Schweizerische Bauzeitung* 49, no. 23 (June 8, 1907): 278.

18. This description of the rank of the portfolios is a summary of Döhl, *Ludwig Hoffmann*, 66.

19. Döhl, *Ludwig Hoffmann*, 65.

20. This letter was discovered and described by Döhl, *Ludwig Hoffmann*, 66. It is archived at Landesarchiv Berlin, *Rep. 010-01-01*, vol. 2, no. 10989.

21. Quoted in Döhl, *Ludwig Hoffmann*, 66, from the Wasmuth letter.

22. This notion of "renderings after nature" was very common to the time, especially in scientific photography. See Peter Gallison and Lorraine Daston, *Objectivity* (New York: Zone Books, 2007).

23. See Döhl, *Ludwig Hoffmann*, chap. 8; Wolfgang Schäche, ed., *Ludwig Hoffmann, Stadtbaurat von Berlin, 1896–1924: Lebenserinnerungen eines Architekten* (Berlin: Gebr. Mann, 1983), 135–36, 202–3. In Buch, Hoffmann created a sanatorium for lung ailments, a home for the elderly, an insane asylum, and a cemetery. See Döhl, *Ludwig Hoffmann*, chap. 9; Schäche, *Ludwig Hoffmann*, 145–47, 173–74.

24. This paragraph is a free translation from Diego Caltana, "Psychiatrische Krankenanstalten in der Provinz der Monarchie: Görz und Triest: Die Architektur der psychiatrischen Krankenanstalten von Triest und Görz," SpringerMedizin.at, last modified November 13, 2008, http://www.springermedizin.at/artikel/1412–psychiatrische–krankenanstalten–in–der–provinz–der–monarchie–goerz–und–triest.

25. See Döhl, *Ludwig Hoffmann*, 134.

26. Julius Posener, "Ludwig Hoffmann," in "Vorlesungen zur Geschichte der Neuen Architektur II: Die Architektur der Reform (1900–1924)," special issue, *Arch+* 53 (1980): 14.

27. See Hoffmann's description in the Buch volume, Ludwig Hoffmann, *Neubauten der Stadt Berlin*, vol. 7, *Irrenanstalt Buch* (Berlin: Wasmuth, 1908), p. i.

28. Posener, "Ludwig Hoffmann," 14: "Die Schönheit seiner Schulen, Bäder, Krankenhäuser war Teil der sozialen Reform."

29. See, for example, the image of the back side of Buch's administration building (Hoffmann, *Neubauten der Stadt Berlin*, vol. 7, Verwaltungsgebäude, Rückseite, F14), the main building at Virchow (Ludwig Hoffmann, *Neubauten der Stadt Berlin*, vol. 6,

Rudolf Virchow–Krankenhaus [Berlin: Wasmuth, 1907], Hauptgebäude, E9), and both chapels in Buch and Virchow (vol. 6, Kapelle, Virchow, E45, and vol. 7, Kapelle, Buch, F49).

30. Hoffmann, *Neubauten der Stadt Berlin*, vol. 7, III. Irrenanstalt in Buch, Verwaltungsgebäude, F15; Hauptgebäude, E10; vol. 6, Virchow, Pathologisch–Anatomisches Institut und Kapelle, E48; vol. 7, III. Irrenanstalt in Buch, Kapelle, F50.

31. Hoffmann, *Neubauten der Stadt Berlin*, vol. 6, Virchow, "Pförtnerhaus am Haupteingang zur Anstalt," E4; see also vol. 7, Buch, Zugang zur Anstalt, F9, p. iii: "Hat man das Tor beim Pförtnerhäuschen passiert, so erblickt man am Ende der Allee das größere Pförtnerhaus, durch welches die innere, durch Mauern abgeschlossene Krankenanstalt betreten wird und dahinter den einzigen dreistöckgen Bau der Anstalt, das Verwaltungsgebäude (Tafel 9)," and in the text for Ludwig Hoffmann, *Neubauten der Stadt Berlin*, vol. 10, *Neues Stadthaus* (Berlin: Wasmuth, 1911), J13, "Virchow, Abb.5, Hauptgebäude. Durchfahrt"; "Fassade an der Stralauer Strasse. Untere Geschosse."

32. See Posener, "Ludwig Hoffmann," 13.

33. The building's design was based on the plans of its original architects, Martin Gropius and Heino Schmieden.

34. The majority of Schwartz's Berlin photographs are housed today in the photographic collection of the Stiftung Stadtmuseum (City Museum Foundation) and the Landesarchiv (Archive of the State of Berlin and Brandenburg) in Berlin.

35. See Dorothy Rowe, "Seeing Imperial Berlin: Lesser Ury, the Painter as Stranger," in *The City and the Senses: Urban Culture Since 1500*, ed. Alexander Cowan and Jull Steward (London: Ashgate, 2007), 205. See also Angelika Wesenberg, ed., *Impressionismus/Expressionismus: Kunstwende*, exhibition catalog (Munich: Hirmer Verlag, 2015).

36. The photographs for this project were taken between the mid-1910s and the 1940s. A first selection was published in 1929 titled *Antlitz der Zeit: Sechzig Aufnahmen deutscher Menschen des 20. Jahrhunderts* (Munich: Kurt Wolff Verlag/Transmare Verlag); a more comprehensive publication was August Sander and Heinrich Lützeler, *Deutschenspiegel: Menschen des 20. Jahrhunderts* (Gütersloh: Sigbert Mohn Verlag, 1962).

37. Cervin Robinson and Joel Herschman, *Architecture Transformed: A History of the Photography of Buildings from 1839 to the Present* (Cambridge, Mass.: MIT Press with the Architectural League of New York, 1987), 76.

38. Robinson and Herschman, *Architecture Transformed*, 76.

39. Robinson and Herschman, *Architecture Transformed*, 76.

40. By sculptor Ignatius Taschner.

41. Schäche, *Ludwig Hoffmann*, 202–9.

42. Hoffmann, *Neubauten der Stadt Berlin*, 10:iv.

43. Robinson and Herschman, *Architecture Transformed*, 72–73.

44. Robinson and Herschman, *Architecture Transformed*, 81.
45. Robinson and Herschman, *Architecture Transformed*, 58.
46. Robinson and Herschman, *Architecture Transformed*, 58.
47. Robinson and Herschman, *Architecture Transformed*, 78.
48. Robinson and Herschman, *Architecture Transformed*, 78.
49. "Als die leitende Arbeitsstätte einer Stadt mit über zwei Millionen Einwohnern mußte das Stadthaus bei aller Lebhaftigkeit im einzelnen in seiner Gesamtwirkung Kraft und Ruhe zum Ausdruck bringen. So ging gas Bestreben bei der architektonischen Gestalung und Durchbildung des Bauwrks dahin, bei einer lebhaften Behandlung im einzelnen, im ganzen eine energische, ruhige, und dabei nicht unfreundliche Stimmung zu erziehlen." Hoffmann, *Neubauten der Stadt Berlin*, 10:iii.
50. Robinson and Herschman, *Architecture Transformed*, 83.
51. See Claire Zimmerman, *Photographic Architecture in the Twentieth Century* (Minneapolis: University of Minnesota Press, 2014), 55.
52. Döhl, *Ludwig Hoffmann*, 192. Döhl quotes Erdmann Graeser, "Das neue Stadthaus in Alt-Berlin. Gulliver in Liliputland," *Berliner Allgemeine Zeitung*, October 28, 1911: "Fremdling, der sich wie Gulliver im Liliputland über die kleinen Häuser der Umgebung erhebe."
53. Döhl, *Ludwig Hoffmann*, 192.
54. Boberg, Fichter, and Gillen, *Die Metropole*, 69. Kress and Wagner-Kyora, "Der Streitfall," 66.
55. Kenneth Frampton, *Modern Architecture: A Critical History*, 3rd rev. and enlarged ed. (London: Thames and Hudson, 1992), 122.
56. Döhl, *Ludwig Hoffmann*, 195–96.
57. Yi-Fu Tuan, "Place: An Experiential Perspective," *Geographical Review* 65, no. 2 (April 1975): 152.
58. Hoffmann-Axthelm, "Stadtbild-Baumeister," 66.
59. Posener concludes that the image that Hoffmann crafted through *Neubauten* did not demonstrate participation in modern developments. While Hoffmann's buildings were modern initially, their style reflected stagnation once the twentieth century progressed. Posener, "Ludwig Hoffmann," 14–15: "Hoffmanns Bauten wirkten, als er antrat außerordentlich modern, 1912 waren sie immer noch modern, aber sie hatten . . . an der Entwicklung, die in diesen Jarhen stattfanden nicht teilgenommen. Nach dem Kriege mußten sie anachronistisch wirken . . . Hoffmann's Generation machte einen Schritt und blieb stehen."
60. Wolfgang Ribbe and Wolfgang Schäche, eds., *Baumeister, Architekten, Stadtplaner: Biographien zur baulichen Entwicklung Berlins* (Berlin: Stapp Verlag mit Historische Kommission zu Berlin, 1987), 283. Julius Posener characterizes Hoffmann's architecture similarly as "corresponding to the Wilhelmine Era's intentions: Impressionist, progressive, appeasing, yet authoritarian." Posener, "Ludwig Hoffmann," 15.

61. Kevin Lynch, *The Image of the City* (Cambridge, Mass.: MIT Press and Harvard University Press, 1960), 6.

62. See Zimmerman, *Photographic Architecture in the Twentieth Century*.

3. Tracing Transformation

1. Bergdoll, "A Matter of Time," 101.

2. Cuthbert M. Bede, "Photographic Pleasures 1855, an excerpt," in *Photography in Print*, ed. Vicky Goldberg (Albuquerque: University of New Mexico Press, 1981), 84; Laszlo Moholy-Nagy, "From Pigment to Light" [1936], in Goldberg, *Photography in Print*, 348.

3. Georg Simmel, "The Metropolis of Modern Life," in *Simmel: On Individuality and Social Forms*, ed. Donald Levine (Chicago: Chicago University Press, 1971), 324.

4. Bergdoll, "A Matter of Time," 108–9.

5. Bergdoll, "A Matter of Time," 108.

6. See Bodenschatz and Goebel, "Berlin—Stadt ohne Altstadt"; Kress and Wagner-Kyora, "Der Streitfall."

7. Bodenschatz and Goebel, "Berlin—Stadt ohne Altstadt," 23. The authors point out the largest of such projects: the opening of Kaiser-Wilhelm-Straße (today Karl-Liebknecht-Straße), the broadening of Mühlendamm, and the erection of the city rail system along the former track of the city fortification.

8. Bergdoll, "A Matter of Time," 108.

9. Karen Rosenberg, "A Last Look at Old Paris, before Demolition: 'Charles Marville: Photographer of Paris' Debuts at the Met," *New York Times*, January 30, 2014.

10. Julius Rodenberg, *Bilder aus dem Berliner Leben*, 3 vols. (Berlin: Verlag von Gebrüder Paetel, 1885–87).

11. Quoted from the *Imperial Review* (October 1883): "Da ist keine Lücke zwischen der todten Vergangenheit und der lebendigen Gegenwart, wie in Rom und Paris. Das Leben der jugendlichen Stadt ist ein ununterbrochenes gewesen. Es ist die Hauptstadt eines kommenden, nicht eines scheidenden Volkes." Rodenberg, *Bilder aus dem Berliner Leben*, 1:186.

12. See a summary of Berlin's urban transformation after the removal of the city walls during the 1860s and through speculation in the 1870s in Masur, *Imperial Berlin*, 65–67.

13. Eberhard Roters, "Emporgekommen," in *Berlin um 1900*, exhibition catalog (Berlin: Berlinische Galerie, 1984), 45–53, 46–47. Furthermore, about Wilhelm II's use of media, see Martin Kohlrausch, *Der Monarch im Skandal: Die Logik der Massenmedien und die Transformation der wilhelminischen Monarchie* (Berlin: Akademie-Verlag, 2005).

14. Simultaneous to the inner-city developments was the expansion of the city into either northern and eastern working-class districts and then, later, the suburban developments in the south and west.

15. Landesdenkmalamt Berlin, ed., *Denkmale in Berlin, Bezirk Mitte, Ortsteil Mitte* (Petersberg: Michael Imhof Verlag, 2003), 85.

16. Hela Zettler and Jost Hansen, *Berlin zwischen Residenz und Metropole: Photographien von Hermann Rückwardt 1871–1916* (Berlin: Nicolaische Verlagsbuchhandlung, 1994), 31.

17. "Geschichte des Messbildarchivs," Brandenburgisches Landesamt für Denkmalpflege und Archäologisches Landesmuseum, http://www.bldam-brandenburg.de/messbildarchiv/236-geschichte-des-messbildarchivs.

18. Measuring image of Berlin's Französische Dom, 1882. Courtesy of Prof. Albertz, Technical University of Berlin.

19. Robinson and Herschman, *Architecture Transformed*, 69.

20. Between 1885 and 1920, the institute created circa 20,000 images of approximately 2,600 buildings. In Berlin alone, they took 2,000 images. Since 1991, the institute's archive has been administered by the Historic Preservation Office of the State of Brandenburg. See Richard Schneider, *Berlin um 1900* (Berlin: Nicolai Verlag, 2004).

21. "Meßbildfotografie in London," *Photographisches Wochenblatt* 7 (1881): 154.

22. "Die Schlossfreiheit," *Berliner Verkehrsseiten: Online-Magazin zur Berliner Verkehrsgeschichte*, August, 2005, http://www.berliner-verkehrsseiten.de/schloss/Sfreiheit/sfreiheit.html.

23. Robinson and Herschman, *Architecture Transformed*, 72.

24. Files of the Ministerium der öffentlichen Arbeit Nr. 2373–2375, Geheimes Staatsarchiv Preußischer Kulturbesitz, I. HA Rep. 93 B. For a detailed analysis of the political quarrels around the monument, and Wilhelm II's domineering role in the decision process about the site, aesthetic, and symbolic meaning of the monument, see Michael B. Klein, *Zwischen Reich und Region: Identitaetsstrukturen im Deutschen Kaiserreich (1871–1918)* (Stuttgart: Franz Steiner Verlag, 2005), 214–15.

25. "Besonders lustig scheint das neue Jahr siebenundneunzig nicht zu werden. Wenigstens der Anfang wirkt so. Das deutsche Volk, insbesondere das berlinische, schreitet zwar mit geschwellter Brust der nationalen Feier entgegen, welche die Enthüllung des Monarchendenkmals mit der weggelassenen Wahlurne an der Schlossfreiheit bringt; auch haben studentische Vereine schon jetzt begonnen, sich zu Ehren dieses Festes in gemeinsamer Sitzung, Kommers genannt, rechtzeitig zu bezechen. Aber die Stimmung, die allgemein im Innern herrscht, ist flau." Günther Rühle, ed., *Alfred Kerr, Wo liegt Berlin? Briefe aus der Reichshauptstadt*, 3rd ed. (Berlin: Siedler, 1997), 232–233, 253–55.

26. Schäche, *Ludwig Hoffmann*, 134.

27. Schäche, *Ludwig Hoffmann*, 134.

28. Max Osborn, *Berlin: Berühmte Kunststätten*, vol. 43 (Leipzig: E.A. Seemann Verlag, 1909), 256–58.

29. Emperor Wilhelm II, "Die wahre Kunst," in *Die Berliner Moderne, 1885–1914*, ed. Jürgen Schutte and Peter Sprengel (Stuttgart: Reclam, 1987), 571.

30. See the official files about the motivation and the decision-making process in Eger, "Die Gründungsarbeiten zum Bau des Nationaldenkmals für Kaiser Wilhelm I an der Schloßfreiheit in Berlin," *Centralblatt der Bauverwaltung* 16, no. 34 (1896): 373–75, 386–89, http://digital.zlb.de/viewer/image/14688302_1896_059/1/LOG_0003/.

31. Oliver Wendell Holmes, "The Stereoscope and the Stereograph," *Atlantic Monthly*, June 1859, 3.

32. Only by looking at these two images from a certain distance and with both of our eyes open does our brain perceive three-dimensional space.

33. Henri Le Secq (1818–82) was one of a number of photographers who worked for the Historic Monuments Commission (Commission des monuments historiques) and its photo-documentary project, the "heliographic mission" (Mission Héliographique).

34. Rudolf Meyer, ed., *Albrecht Meydenbauer: Baukunst in historischen Photographien* (Leipzig: VEB Fotokinoverlag, 1985), 28–29. On photogrammetry and Albrecht Meydenbauer, see photographic journals such as *Photographisches Wochenblatt* 7 (1881): 42–43, 123–24, 133–34, 141–42, 149–50, 158–59, 166–67; 8 (1882): 171 (Photographischer Verein zu Berlin), 282, 289, 297; 10 (1884): 276–78, 304; 11 (1885): 36, 83ff., 137ff., 170ff., 203, 204, 248, 297ff., 393ff.; and *Photographische Mittheilungen* 26 (1889/90): 143–44, 157–58; and 33 (1896/97): 262.

35. As quoted in Herta Wolf, "Das Denkmäler-Archiv Photographie," *Camera Austria* 51/52 (1995): 135.

36. See Meyer, *Albrecht Meydenbauer*, 28–29.

37. Jütte, *Geschichte der Sinne*, 212–13. Jütte addresses the nineteenth-century ambivalence at the daguerreotype's uncanny precision and detail of representation as well as Holmes's commentary.

38. Jonathan Crary, *Suspension of Perception: Attention, Spectacle, and Modern Culture* (Cambridge, Mass.: MIT Press, 1999), 344.

39. The German original reads: "Die Ruine schafft die gegenwärtige Form eines vergangenen Lebens, nicht nach seinen Inhalten oder Resten, sondern nach seiner Vergangenheit als solcher." First published as Georg Simmel, "Die Ruine," *Der Tag*, no. 96 (February 22, 1907), http://socio.ch/sim/verschiedenes/1907/ruine.htm.

40. Fuchs, "Neu-Berlin," 135–36.

41. Robert R. Shandley, *Rubble Films: German Cinema in the Shadow of the Third Reich* (Philadelphia: Temple University Press, 2001), 2.

42. Eric Rentschler, "The Place of Rubble in the *Trümmerfilm*," *New German Critique* 110 (Summer 2010): 9–30. Shandley, *Rubble Films*, 1. Martina Moeller, *Rubble,*

Ruins, and Romanticism: Visual Style, Narration, and Identity in German Post-War Cinema (Bielefeld: Transcript, 2013).

43. Brian Dillon, "Decline and Fall," *Frieze Magazine*, no. 130 (April 2010): http://frieze.com/article/decline-and-fall. Dillon quotes from Rose Macaulay, *Pleasure of Ruins* (London: Thames & Hudson, 1984), 454–55.

44. See Jeff Byles, *Rubble: Unearthing the History of Demolition* (New York: Three Rivers Press, 2005) and Brian Dillon, "Fragments from a History of Ruin," *Cabinet*, no. 20 (Winter 2005–6): http://www.cabinetmagazine.org/issues/20/dillon.php. For the significance of the ruin in eighteenth- and nineteenth-century painting, see Werner Hofmann, *Das Irdische Paradies: Kunst im neunzehnten Jahrhundert* (Munich: Prestel, 1974), 41–43.

45. Dillon, "Fragments from a History of Ruin"; see section header 1.

46. Dillon, "Fragments from a History of Ruin." Sigmund Freud picked up on this notion when he compared Rome's palimpsest-like map to human memory in the introduction to his 1929 text *Civilization and Its Discontents*. See also a reference to Freud and Rome in Jan Assmann, *Religion and Cultural Memory* (Palo Alto, CA: Stanford University Press, 2006), 25.

47. Dillon, "Fragments from a History of Ruin."

48. Dillon, "Fragments from a History of Ruin."

49. F. Albert Schwartz and Georg Bartels were presumably the Märkische Museum's most active suppliers of demolition photographs. Starting in 1905, Hugo Rudolphy was also documenting for the museum. After 1909, and Bartels's death, he was the sole demolition photographer.

50. Jagow Street is located in Berlin's semi-industrial Moabit district and was developed, if we consider historic maps of Berlin, only during the late 1880s.

51. Georg Bartels documented here a measure to widen Rosenstraße. This made it necessary to demolish an entire block of thirty-one buildings between Neuer Friedrichstraße, Klosterstraße, and Rosenstraße.

52. This image is part of Menzel's "Kinderalbum," an album of forty-four gouaches he created between 1860 and 1863 and in 1883 for his sister's two children. Irmgard Wirth, *Mit Adolph Menzel in Berlin* (Munich: Prestel, 1965), 30, 39, ill. 11.

53. Carl Abt, "Gebäudeaufnahmen in verkehrsreichen Straßen," *Photographische Mitteilungen* 48 (1911): 142–43.

54. Hofmann, *Das Irdische Paradies*, 178. This now lost painting was based on a 1815 drawing that showed the intact Jacobi Church in Greifswald as a ruin.

55. Hofmann, *Das Irdische Paradies*, 178.

56. Charles Baudelaire, "The Salon of 1859," in *Art in Paris*, trans. J. Mayne (London: Phaidon, 1965), 149–55.

57. Felling, who worked in 1940s New York, listened to police radio constantly to hear about and quickly race to crime scenes.

58. Walter Benjamin, "A Short History of Photography," *Screen* 13, no. 1 (Spring 1972): 25; originally published in three installments in *Die Literarische Welt*: September 18, 1931; September 25, 1931; and October 2, 1931.

59. The image and term of the "murdered city" refers to the title of a 1964 book by Wolf Jobst Siedler and Elisabeth Niggemeyer, who bemoaned the transformation of German cities during the post–World War II era: *Die gemordete Stadt: Abgesang auf Putte und Straße, Platz und Baum* (1964; repr., Berlin: Siedler, 1993).

4. Inventing Tradition

1. Dr. Reicke, unpaginated introduction to *Das malerische Berlin: Bilder und Blicke*, vol. 1 (Berlin: Märkische Museum, 1911): "[Diese Veröffentlichungen] . . . werden bestrebt sein, für Gegenwart und Zukunft im Bilde festzuhalten . . . was als Zeuge einer zu Unrecht halb vergessenen Kultur sich bis in unsere Tage hinübergerettet hat und mit unserer Liebe dauernde Erhaltung verdient; was, allen wohlbekannt, durch neuen Blickpunkt eigenartige Reize zu enthüllen vermag; bisweilen auch, was von den meisten Augen unbeachtet, da oder dort noch mitten in der Weltstadt sein stilles malerisches Dasein führt—alles letzten Endes dazu bestimmt, den Berlinern ihre Stadt näher zu bringen und lieber zu machen."

2. Friedrich Fuchs, "Das malerische Berlin," special issue, *Berliner Leben* 5 (1902): 205–8.

3. Fuchs, "Das malerische Berlin," 208.

4. Kress and Wagner-Kyora, "Der Streitfall."

5. On Endell's theorizing and translating into design of the concept of emotion into design, see Zeynep Çelik Alexander, "Metrics of Experience: August Endell's Phenomenology of Architecture," *Grey Room* 40 (Summer 2010): 50–83.

6. August Endell, *Die Schönheit der großen Stadt* (Stuttgart: Verlag von Strecker & Schröder, 1908), 48.

7. Warstat, "Die Schönheit der großen Stadt als künstlerisches Problem für den Photographen," 14. See also Warstat's publication about artistic photography: Willi Warstat, *Die künstlerische Photographie: Ihre Entwicklung, ihre Probleme, ihre Bedeutung*, Aus Natur und Geisteswelt 410 (Leipzig: B.G. Teubner, 1919).

8. Warstat, *Die künstlerische Photographie*, 12.

9. Anton Mayer, "Bilder des Großstadtlebens," *Photographische Mitteilungen* 46 (1909): 235–37 and 249–52. Mayer also authored a book about the single-lens reflex camera: Anton Mayer, *Die Spiegelreflexkamera: Ihr Wesen und ihre Konstruktion; nebst Ratschlägen für die Auswahl und praktische Verwendung, sowie tabellarische Übersicht und Liste der Patente und Gebrauchsmuster* (Halle: W. Knapp, 1910).

10. Mayer, "Bilder des Großstadtlebens," 236, 250–51.

11. He might have thought of photographers such as Edward Steichen, Frederick H. Evans, and, in Germany, Rudolf Dührkoop.

12. Mayer, "Bilder des Großstadtlebens," 237, 251.

13. Sharpe and Wallock, "From 'Great Town' to 'Nonplace Urban Realm,'" 7–8.

14. Sharpe and Wallock, "From 'Great Town' to 'Nonplace Urban Realm,'" 35–36.

15. Georg Dehio, *Denkmalschutz und Denkmalpflege im Neunzehnten Jahrhundert: Rede zur Feier des Geburtstages Sr. Majestät des Kaisers gehalten in der Aula der Kaiser-Wilhelms-Universität am 27. Jan. 1905* (Strasbourg: J. H. Ed. Heitz [Heitz & Mündel], 1905), 10: "Ihr [der Sammelmotivation] letzter Beweggrund ist die Achtung vor der historischen Existenz als solcher."

16. John Ruskin, *The Seven Lamps of Architecture* (New York: John Wiley, 1849), 146–65; Eugène-Emmanuel Viollet-le-Duc, *The Foundations of Architecture: Selections from the Dictionnaire raisonné* [1854], trans. Kenneth D. Whitehead (New York: George Braziller, 1990), 195.

17. Dehio, *Denkmalschutz und Denkmalpflege im Neunzehnten Jahrhundert*, 5–27.

18. Dehio, *Denkmalschutz und Denkmalpflege im Neunzehnten Jahrhundert*, 18: "In alle Schichten muß das Gefühl eindringen, daß das Volk, das viele und alte Denkmäler besitzt, ein vornehmes Volk ist."

19. Dehio, *Denkmalschutz und Denkmalpflege im Neunzehnten Jahrhundert*, 18: "Ohne Sentimentalität, ohne Pedanterie, ohne romantische Willkür wollen wir Denkmalpflege üben als eine selbstverständliche und natürliche Äußerung der Selbstachtung, als Anerkennung des Rechtes der Toten zum besten der Lebendigen."

20. Fritz Kempe, ed., *Photographie zwischen Daguerreotypie und Kunstphotographie: Bilderhefte des Museums für Kunst und Gewerbe Hamburg*, vol. 14 (Hamburg: Museum für Kunst und Gewerbe Hamburg, 1987), 22–24.

21. Gabriele Betancourt Nuñez, "Juhl, Ernst," in *Hamburgische Biografie*, vol. 3 (Göttingen: Wallstein, 2006), 186–88; Rüdiger Joppien and Claudia Gabriele Philipp, eds., *Kunstphotographie um 1900* (Hamburg: Museum für Kunst und Gewerbe Hamburg, 1989); Margret Kruse, ed., *Kunstphotographie um 1900: Die Sammlung Ernst Juhl*, Dokumente der Photographie 3 (Hamburg: Museums für Kunst und Gewerbe Hamburg, 1989).

22. Dehio, *Denkmalschutz und Denkmalpflege im Neunzehnten Jahrhundert*, 17: "Unsere ruhelose Zeit hat nichts nötiger als daß der Jugend ein örtliches Heimatgefühl in klaren, unvergesßlichen Bildern ins Leben, das sich zumal für die höhreren Stände als ein ewiger Ortswechsel gestaltet, mitgegeben werde. Ich denke endlich an Erziehung zur Denkmalsfreundschaft mit allen jenen Mitteln von Wort Schrift und Bilddruck, die uns heute in so mannigfaltiger Anwendbarkeit zur Verfügung stehen."

23. Alfred Lichtwark, "Dilettantismus und Volkskunst," in *Vom Arbeitsfeld des Dilettantismus* (Berlin: Bruno Cassirer, 1902), 15, 24, 34.

24. Andreas Huyssen, "Escape From Amnesia: The Museum as Mass Medium," in *Twilight Memories: Marking Time in a Culture of Amnesia* (New York: Routledge, 1995), 19.

25. Hermann Fillitz, ed., *Der Traum vom Glück: Die Kunst des Historismus in Europa*, vol. 1 (Vienna: C. Brandstätter, 1996), 20.

26. Eric Hobsbawm and Terence Ranger, eds., *The Invention of Tradition* (Cambridge: Cambridge University Press, 1983). Andreas Huyssen, *Present Pasts: Urban Palimpsests and the Politics of Memory* (Stanford, Calif.: Stanford University Press, 2003), 37. See also a comprehensive study about Germany's memory and monument culture in Rudy Koshar, *From Monuments to Traces: Artifacts of German Memory, 1870–1990* (Berkeley: University of California Press, 2000).

27. See Enno Kaufhold's comprehensive overview of the *Heimatschutz* movement's establishment and its impact on photography in Enno Kaufhold, *Bilder des Übergangs: Zur Mediengeschichte von Fotografie und Malerei in Deutschland um 1900* (Marburg: Jonas Verlag, 1986), 50–58.

28. See §1 Charter of the Bund Heimatschutz of 1904, in Klaus Bergmann, *Agrarromantik und Großstadtfeindschaft*, Marburger Abhandlungen zur Politischen Wissenschaft 20 (Meisenheim am Glan: Hain, 1970), 122. Kaufhold, *Bilder des Übergangs*; Joppien and Philipp, *Kunstphotographie um 1900*; Christian Joschke, *Les Yeux de la nation: Photographie amateur et société dans l'Allemagne de Guillaume II, 1888–1914*, Œuvres en sociétés (Dijon: Les Presses du réel, 2013); Silke Göttsch-Elten, "Die schwere Kunst des Sehens: Zur Diskussion über Amateurfotografie in Volkskunde und Heimatschutzbewegung um 1900," in *Medien populärer Kultur: Erzählung, Bild und Objekt in der volkskundlichen Forschung, Rolf Wilhelm Brednich zum 60. Geburtstag*, ed. Carola Lipp (Frankfurt/Main: Campus Verlag, 1995), 395–405.

29. (Lord Mayor of Berlin) Robert Zelle, unpaginated preface to *Die Bau- und Kunstdenkmäler von Berlin*, ed. Richard Borrmann (Berlin: Julius Springer Verlag, 1893).

30. Magistrate meeting, January 1, 1886, Landesarchiv Berlin, *Rep.10-02*, no. 16 355.

31. To give a point of comparison, an ordinary worker earned approximately 60 marks per month in 1900.

32. *Online Etymology Dictionary*, http://www.etymonline.com/index.php?term=survey: "survey (v.) c.1400, 'to consider, contemplate,' from Anglo-French surveier, Old French sorveoir 'look (down) at, look upon, notice; guard, watch,' from Medieval Latin supervidere 'oversee' (see supervise)," plural surveys.

33. Summary of archival materials on photo acquisitions generated by Cornelia Gentzen, director of visitor services, internal archive at Stiftung Stadtmuseum Berlin.

34. Pniower continues to explain that "these photographs are not exhibited but stored in portfolios. They are located in drawers of the vitrines in room 43 [December

9, 1909]." Stiftung Stadtmuseum, Archival memo "MPM Schriftverkehr 1874 – 1925," no. 26.

35. January 1, 1886, Landesarchiv Berlin, *Rep.10-02*, no. 16 355.

36. Zelle, "Preface," not paginated.

37. *Berlin und seine Bauten*, ed. Architekten-Verein zu Berlin, 2 vols. (Berlin: Ernst und Korn, 1877). *Berlin und seine Bauten*, vol. 1, *Einleitendes—Ingenieurwesen*; vol. 2, *Hochbau*, pt. 1; and vol. 3, *Hochbau*, pt. 2, ed. Architekten-Verein zu Berlin und der Vereinigung Berliner Architekten (Berlin: Wilhelm Ernst & Sohn, 1896).

38. See a partial biography of Krajewski at "Die Fotografen Lilienthals—Jeder Selbst ein Pionier," Otto Lilienthal Museum, http://www.lilienthal-museum.de/olma/bagraf.htm. Ernst Wasmuth founded an architectural bookstore and, soon after that, a publishing house. Between 1905 and 1928, Wasmuth published Dehio's architectural handbook of German monuments and Berlin-related publications such as *Architektur Berlins* and *Architektur der Gegenwart.* The publishing house still exists today, and its extensive collection of architectural photographs is part of the collection of the Kunstbibliothek of the Prussian Heritage Foundation.

39. See the foreword by the editorial committee, A. Wiebe, Borrmann, Eger, Fritsch, Gottheiner, Hofsfeld, Housselle, Muthesius, of *Berlin und seine Bauten* (1896), not paginated.

40. Borrmann, *Die Bau- und Kunstdenkmäler von Berlin.* The heliogravures and the photographs they were based upon were taken by Hermann Rückwardt. The publication also included zinc etchings (Riffarth Co.) and pen drawings.

41. Richard Borrmann, *Die Bau- und Kunstdenkmäler von Berlin* (Berlin: Springer, 1893), vi.

42. Gesine Asmus, ed., *Hinterhof, Keller und Mansarde: Einblicke in Berliner Wohnungselend, 1901–1920* (Reinbeck: Rowohlt, 1982); Werner Michael Schwarz, Margarethe Szeless, and Lisa Wögenstein, eds., *Ganz unten: Die Enteckung des Elends: Wien, Berlin, London, Paris, New York* (Vienna: Christian Brandstätter Verlag, 2007).

43. Kurt Winkler, ed., *Gefühlte Geschichte—100 Jahre Märkisches Museum* (Berlin: Verlag M, 2008), 17.

44. Max Osborn, "Ein Berliner Bilderarchiv von Max Osborn," *Der Tag*, July 13, 1910, no pagination: "Langsam und ganz heimlich ist eine neue Liebe zu Berlin herangereift. Jahrelang war es Mode, die Hauptstadt mit ästhetischer Nichtachtung zu strafen; mehr als sie es je verdiente. Dann kam die große historische Welle, und man begann sich zu erinnern, daß auch diese 'amerikanische' Europäerstadt eine sehr reizvolle künstlerische Geschichte hat. . . . 'Alt Berlin' wurde Trumpf, und es erwachte eine vordem ungeahnte Zärtlichkeit für die spärlichen Zeugen und Denkmäler verklungener Zeiten."

45. Georg Reicke (1863–1923) was the mayor of Berlin, from 1902 to 1920.

46. Märkische Museum, *Das malerische Berlin: Bilder und Blicke*, 3 vols. (Berlin: Märkische Museum, 1911–14).

47. Osborn, *Berlin*.

48. Thank you notes from recipients of the volumes are kept in the archive of the Stiftung Stadtmuseum in Berlin-Spandau, of which the former Märkische Museum is a part.

49. By 1914 the rotogravure was abandoned as a printing process for picture postcards with the reasoning that it had "not fulfilled expectations." *Photographisches Wochenblatt* 40 (1914): 105.

50. Wolfgang Gottschalk, ed., *Alt-Berlin: Historische Photographien von Max Missmann* (Leipzig: Kiepenheuer, 1987), 13. Susanne Gänshirt-Heinemann, *Die Entdeckung der Ästhetisierung der Altstadt Berlins: Der Krögel in Fotografien 1887–1938* (Berlin: Berliner Wissenschafts Verlag, 2003).

51. Winfried Ranke, *Heinrich Zille Photographien Berlin, 1890–1910* (Munich: Schirmer Mosel Verlag, 1975), 143.

52. Enno Kaufhold, *Heinrich Zille: Photograph der Moderne* (Munich: Schirmer Mosel Verlag, 1998), 26–27.

53. Gänshirt-Heinemann, *Die Entdeckung der Ästhetisierung der Altstadt Berlins*, 46.

54. Kaufhold, *Bilder des Übergangs*, 54.

55. Rudolf Dührkoop, *Im Krögel*, Berlin, 1911, from the portfolio *Das malerische Berlin*, vol.1, image no. 11, rotogravure (Kupfertiefdruck), 37.0 × 29.2 cm. © Stiftung Stadtmuseum Berlin.

56. See also a detailed annotation by Max Osborn on the creation of this photograph and the history of this site in *Das malerische Berlin*, vol. 3, no pagination.

57. Osborn, Annotations in *Das malerische Berlin*, vol. 3, no pagination: "Die Anordnung der Bildtafeln dieses Heftes folgt weder historischen noch topographischen Gesichtspunkten, sondern lediglich den Zwecken malerischer Wirkung, denen unsere Sammlung überhaupt dienen will."

58. After 1900, *Heimatschutz* and artistic photography (pictorialism) joined ranks, which further complicated the range of messages and interpretations of history through landscapes and cityscapes generated in images. Kaufhold, *Bilder des Übergangs*, 51.

59. Märkische Museum, *Das malerische Berlin*, vol. 1: "Sie [die Veröffentlichungen] werden bestrebt sein, für Gegenwart und Zukunft im Bilde festzuhalten, was unsere Vergangenheit Schönes schuf und was dennoch unter unsern Blicken der Weltstadt weichen muß"; "den Berlinern ihre Stadt näher zu bringen und lieber zu machen."

60. Märkische Museum, *Das malerische Berlin*, vol. 3: "Ein Hauch von Vergänglichkeit ist es, der sie [die Inseln historischer Bauten] umwittert, aber zugleich weht ein Schauer der Vergangenheit um sie, der das körperlich Verfallende im Geiste zu

neuem Leben heraufbeschwört. Und als Zeugen einer von der ständigen Unrast unserer Tage noch nicht zerpflückten Zeit reden sie zu uns eine seltsam beruhigende, fast erlösende Sprache."

61. Sadakichi Hartmann, "A Plea for Straight Photography," Photography Criticism CyberArchive, last modified 2003, http://www.nearbycafe.com/photocriticism/members/archivetexts/photocriticism/hartmann/pf/hartmannstraightpf.html; originally published in *American Amateur Photographer*, no. 16 (March 1904), 101–9.

62. Blau, "Patterns of Fact," 44.

63. Kaufhold, *Bilder des Übergangs*, 57. See Kurt Winkler's insightful analysis of this tension in his contribution to the publication *Gefühlte Geschichte*, especially 20–21.

64. J. D. Fitzgerald, writing in the September 2, 1907, edition of the monthly Australian magazine *The Lone Hand*, points out that "the slum is often the most picturesque quarter of a city—at a distance. . . . The slum, however picturesque from a distance, is on close scrutiny, hideous, pestilential." J. D. Fitzgerald, "Sydney Slums: Picturesque and Pestilential," *The Lone Hand* 1 (May–October 1907): 562–63.

65. Winkler, *Gefühlte Geschichte*, 20–21.

66. Felix Genzmer, "Kunst im Städtebau," in *Städtebauliche Vorträge aus dem Seminar für Städtebau an der königlich technischen Hochschule zu Berlin*, vol. 1.1 (Berlin: W. Ernst & Sohn, 1908), 21–32.

67. See Stiftung Stadtmuseum Berlin, *Unter den Linden: Historische Photographien*.

68. Osborn, "Ein Berliner Bilderarchiv."

Conclusion

1. "It is here, indeed, that the American 'go ahead,' the idea of always going forward without useless regrets and recriminations, with an eye to the future, fearless and calm . . . attains its maximum intensity." Paul de Rousiers, *American Life*, trans. A. J. Herbertson (Paris: Firmin-Didot, 1892), 73.

2. Anselm L. Strauss, *Images of the American City* (New Brunswick, NJ: Transaction Books, 1976), 204–5.

3. Scheffler, *Berlin*, 140–41.

4. Strauss, *Images of the American City*, 117–18.

5. Max Allihn, quoted in *Berliner Nachrichten* reporting on the international Amateur-Ausstellung in Berlin, in *Photographische Correspondenz* 33, no. 435 (1896): 610. Arguing similarly, see Fritz Hansen, *Photographisches Centralblatt* 4, no. 2 (1898): 43–44; and Konrad Biesalski, "Die Ausstellung für Künstlerische Photographie, Berlin 1899," *Photographische Mitteilungen* 36 (1899): 77–81, 99–103, 109–16.

6. Strauss, *Images of the American City*, 155.

7. Strauss, *Images of the American City*, 155.

8. The "Old Berlin" section, according to Alexander C. T. Geppert, functioned as a direct contrast to the two other "exotic" sections, one of which was "Kairo." See Alexander C. T. Geppert, "Weltstadt für einen Sommer: Die Berliner Gewerbeausstellung 1896 im eurpäischen Kontext," *Die Geschichte Berlins: Verein für die Geschichte Berlins e. V., gegr. 1865*, last modified 2016, http://www.diegeschichteberlins.de/geschichteberlins/berlinabc/stichworteag/550-gewerbeausstellung.html. About the culture of amateur photography and "Old Berlin" specifically, see Katherine Zelljadt, "History as Past-time: Amateurs and Old Berlin, 1870–1914" (PhD diss., Harvard University, 2005).

9. It was designed after plans by Karl Hoffacker (1856–1919).

10. Quoted after Geppert, "Weltstadt für einen Sommer."

11. Hales, *Silver Cities* and Peter Bacon Hales, "Photography and the World's Columbian Exposition: A Case Study," *Journal of Urban History* 15, no. 3 (May 1, 1989): 247–73.

12. Erich Mendelsohn, *Amerika: Bilderbuch eines Architekten* (Berlin: Rudolf Mosse Buchverlag, 1926).

13. Arnold Weinstein, "Fragment and Form in the City of Modernism," in *The Cambridge Companion to the City in Literature*, ed. Kevin R. McNamara (Cambridge: Cambridge University Press, 2014), 138.

14. Weinstein, "Fragment and Form," 138.

15. Weinstein, "Fragment and Form," 138.

16. Weinstein, "Fragment and Form," 147.

17. The city symphony film is a poetic, experimental documentary that presents a portrait of daily life within a city while attempting to capture something of the city's spirit. It depicts the life of a city, mainly through visual impressions in a semidocumentary style, without the narrative content of conventional films. The sequencing and chronology of events may imply a kind of loose theme or impression of the city's daily life.

INDEX

Page numbers in italics refer to illustrations.

MIRIAM PAESLACK is associate professor of modern and contemporary visual culture and arts management at the University at Buffalo (SUNY). She is author of *Berlin im 19.Jahrhundert: Frühe Photographien 1850–1914* and editor of *Ineffably Urban: Imaging Buffalo.*